Gideon's Book flows gentl[illegible] life moved at a slower pace and a modern family that walks to a different beat in its decade, yet this poignant story explores some of the most difficult subjects we face. Finding love, fighting cancer, building families, unplanned babies, medical ethics, having faith, and overcoming the unthinkable are interwoven with the lightest, most honest touch through a narrative peopled with men and women we recognize as our neighbors and ourselves. Lose yourself in a story that dares to ask the big questions we won't speak aloud—a story that, at its heart, dares to expose the greater joys we know when God writes our every chapter.

— LORI ROELEVELD, AUTHOR AND SPEAKER

In her debut novel, North Carolina author Maureen Miller offers a finely crafted story rich in character development and resounding with biblical truth. Told with great heart and gentle humor, Miller has skillfully layered her dual-timeline tale with thoughtful examinations of universal themes: racial reconciliation, adoption, and the value of all human life. This beautiful novel will help readers grapple with the truth of their own stories. Highly recommended.

— MAGGIE WALLEM ROWE, SPEAKER AND AUTHOR OF *THIS LIFE WE SHARE: 52 REFLECTIONS ON JOURNEYING WELL WITH GOD AND OTHERS*

Every person searches for love and significance. What we're really looking for, though, is redemption. In *Gideon's Book*, readers walk alongside Cassie, Ava, and Gideon as they journey through health issues, shattered relationships, and broken dreams toward a future and a hope they never expected. Maureen Miller engages both heart and mind as she weaves together the lives of three people who wrestle with sensitive issues such as abortion, cancer, and racism. Through all the pain, they realize that God's sovereignty and love can heal every wound and bring blessings they never imagined. Their story will renew your hope and strengthen your faith in Jehovah-Rapha, the Lord who heals.

— DENISE K. LOOCK, AUTHOR, *OPEN YOUR HYMNAL: DEVOTIONS THAT HARMONIZE SCRIPTURE WITH SONG*

In her debut novel, *Gideon's Book*, author Maureen Miller offers an engaging story of God working in different times and in different generations through one providentially placed Gideon Bible. She doesn't shy away from gritty topics but confronts them head-on with grace and sensitivity. Her characters are endearing, and her message is life-affirming and uplifting. You'll come away glad you read this book.

— ANN TATLOCK, NOVELIST

Maureen Miller's novel *Gideon's Book* will be a read to give you all the feels. It's heartfelt and relatable in so many ways. With her knowledge and life experiences, she's the perfect writer for penning this story. From tears to smiles, Maureen's book is one not to miss.

— TAMMY KARASEK, SPEAKER AND AUTHOR OF *LAUNCH THAT BOOK*

Endearing—this hits the nail on the head for author Maureen Miller's debut novel, *Gideon's Book.* A story that is memorable, touching, and heartfelt with characters that stay with you once the read is done. Beautifully and tenderly written, Miller brings it home in this timeless tale.

— CINDY K. SPROLES, BEST-SELLING, AWARD-WINNING AUTHOR OF *THIS IS WHERE IT ENDS* AND *COAL BLACK LIES*; DIRECTOR OF ASHVILLE CHRISTIAN WRITER'S CONFERENCE.

Sometimes a book comes along that's more than just a story. *Gideon's Book* is one of these rare gems that tugs your heartstrings, makes you think, and challenges the "accepted" views of our culture.

— LORI HATCHER, AUTHOR/SPEAKER

Gideon's Book is a tender, soul-stirring reminder that our stories—no matter how complicated, broken, or unexpected—are never beyond God's reach. It takes readers on a courageous, redemptive journey that doesn't shy away from the complexity of race, faith, grief, and healing, exploring the choices we make, the pain we carry, and the grace that meets us in the middle.

— CHRISTINA CUSTODIO, SPEAKER / AUTHOR OF *WHEN GOD CHANGED HIS MIND*

GIDEON'S BOOK

To Wendy,
Because of love—

GIDEON'S BOOK

a novel

MAUREEN MILLER

Published by Redemption Press, 1602 Cole Street, Enumclaw, WA 98022, (360) 226-3488.

Redemption Press is honored to present this title in partnership with the author. The views expressed or implied in this work are those of the author. Redemption Press provides our imprint seal representing design excellence, creative content, and high-quality production.

All Scripture quotations in this publication are taken from the Holy Bible, King James Version, 1972.

George Matheson, "O Love that Wilt Not Let Me Go," 1882, Hymns of the Christian Faith, Christian Publications, 1978. Public domain.

James Rowe, "Love Lifted Me," 1912, Hymns of the Christian Faith, Christian Publications, 1978. Public domain.

Mary Lundie Duncan, "Jesus, Tender Shepherd, Hear Me," 1839, Women of Christianity, March 29, 2018, https://womenofchristianity.com/jesus-tender-shepherd-hear-me-by-mary-lundie-duncan/. Public domain.

Edward Mote, "My Hope Is Built," 1834, Hymns of the Christian Faith, Christian Publications, 1978. Public domain.

ISBN 13: 978-1-64645-904-9 (paperback)

ISBN: 978-1-64645-905-6 (ebook)

Library of Congress Catalog Card Number: 2025902869

To Cindy, Michelle, and Jenna—because you chose.
To Dorian, Jacob, and Allie—because they did.

O Love, that wilt not let me go,
I rest my weary soul in Thee;
I give Thee back the life I owe,
That in Thine ocean's depth its flow
May richer, fuller be.

—George Matheson
"O Love That Wilt Not Let Me Go"

PROLOGUE

WITH A TREMBLING HAND, she wrote:

9:00 PM

Standing before the mirror in what, two hours earlier, had seemed like a sterile bathroom, I examined my face. With one hand pressed firmly on the sink, I steadied myself before brushing a shaky finger across the abrasion above my right eye. I winced and the room spun, then went black.

Moments later, I came to, then stripped off my clothes, and left them in a bloody heap on the tile floor. After turning on hot water, I stepped in and filled the tub. The heat burned my skin, especially the places where debris remained, but I scrubbed just the same. To wash away dirt. To wash away my filth.

And now, here I am, and I can't help but ask, "Where were you, God?"

No. Where are you?

But again, my questions go unanswered. The only sound? Crashing waves—that which is and forever will be a reminder of this night when, once more, you were silent.

~

11:58 PM

Earlier, I fumbled with the tiny buttons remaining on my cotton dress ...

CHAPTER 1

CASSANDRA BILLINGS— APRIL 2016

"When will I ... know something?" Cassie wrung her hands. The strain of worry pulsed at her temples, the voice of condemnation loud. *You're not enough.*

Dr. Spencer's hesitation—her impregnable silence—told Cassie what was coming. Finally, the doctor spoke. "The results should be back in a few days. You'll receive a call. But Cathy—"

"Cassie." Her response was abrupt, rude. In the awkward beat of silence, she forced her eyes to meet her physician's. "I'm, yes ... I'm sorry. You were saying?"

"Cassie, you should ... you need to prepare yourself. Looking here—" Turning the computer screen so Cassie could see it, Dr. Spencer pointed to the x-ray. "There's definitely reason to be concerned. The lump is of significant size, and see this haze? It indicates possible spreading. When we have a conclusive diagnosis, we'll meet again, discuss treatment options—most likely surgery, then radiation and chemotherapy." She cleared her throat. "Until then, take these brochures, and do some research. Of course, discuss this with your family."

Family? That might prove problematic. While Grant would

have something to say—Momma and Daddy also—the people she needed to hear from, for medical purposes, were .... "Yes, I will. Thank you, Dr. Spencer."

Concern was etched across the gynecologist's forehead, though she didn't say the specific diagnostic word. Nor did Cassie. But after the doctor exited, pulling the door closed behind her—gently, as if attempting to soften the blow—Cassie ripped off the pink paper gown in an attempt to also destroy the unspoken word's reality.

Not yet dressed, she stared at her reflection. It had only been a few days since she'd discovered the lump. Right away, Cassie had phoned her mom, then dialed Greensboro's Orchard View Obstetrics and Gynecology, only to learn her physician was booked solid for weeks. She'd had to settle for a new one. A stranger. Not like Dr. Morris, who'd delivered Cassie's two biological children and knew her inside and out.

The morning she'd made the call, she'd pressed the phone to her ear and heard the receptionist's clicking on the computer keyboard. It conjured the image of long, painted acrylics, unlike Cassie's own short and brittle nails. It would be a week before the new doctor could see her. Checking her desk calendar, Cassie had realized—she'd have to cancel a lunch date with Jane.

Crossing off her colleague's name—seeing the bright-red ink on her calendar—made reality hit home. Was it true? She'd been so diligent—especially given her fair, freckled complexion. Every year, she made her annual trip to the dermatologist. Of course, her skin was a concern, but this?

Voices outside the examining room brought her back to the present. Cassie's right hand pressed the soft tissue just outside her left arm pit, willing the lump gone. But no. Not bigger than a tiny house-finch egg, tender to the touch, it was still there—that interruption, which took the beauty of a brilliant spring day and wadded it up like the paper gown she'd trashed.

In the span of days since her discovery, there had been moments when she'd forget, caught up in a writing project or tending the kids. Worse, some mornings Cassie awoke with the joy of a new day, only to sense that creeping shadow, the reality of the lump, not to mention the other unknowns. Yes, worry—a thief, stealing her peace.

But facing the very thing she hated most—that which had taken too many loved ones over the last half-dozen years—she knew it might be worse than she'd first feared. The possibility gripped her stomach, clenching it, twisting her insides.

Cassie fumbled to dress, then checked out—the receptionist mentioning they'd call for a follow-up, if necessary. Her emphasis on *if* rang of mockery.

Outside, Cassie gasped for fresh air. With one hand clasping her throat, she detected it, that rhythmic tempo a reminder.

She was still alive.

In the sunshine, her breathing slowed, and she paused, the day's warmth easing her heightened anxiety. Lifting her face, she closed her eyes to inhale, breathing in the fragrance of, what was it?

Cherry blossoms.

But even their sweet aroma, usually a favorite, brought no pleasure. It unnerved her. A sign?

Oh, please, please help me. I'm so scared. I know we don't live forever, and impermanence is part of life. But so soon? I'm not even forty-seven, and my family needs me. I beg you—please, make this not so.

As she prayed, birds sang. Clueless creatures. Threat of illness, death even, didn't deter them. Lyrics from a *Les Mis* song played in her mind, and Éponine's lament echoed, stirring the question.

Would the world go on without her?

Her purse vibrated, and she rummaged to locate her phone.

"Hey, hon."

"So? What'd they say, Cass?" Grant cleared his throat.

"Won't know anything for several days. Dr. Spencer ..." She swallowed the words.

"Cassandra?" Grant's voice registered his fear.

"She ... she said to prepare myself. Once there's a diagnosis, I'll have another appointment, hear my options. Then we'll need to discuss them. With Mom and Dad too."

"What about with—"

"Maybe. Not yet. I need to think about it."

A silence hung between husband and wife. Finally, Grant took a deep breath, then exhaled slowly, through his mouth. She could tell, just like she'd witnessed too many times to count. When her husband of nearly a quarter of a century worked to gather his senses, calm his temper, prepare to say something important, there it was. A deflating balloon, speaking his weariness, the depth of his worry. More, it spoke hopelessness, though Grant's words—their meaning—contradicted.

"We'll get through this, Cass. I promise." He cleared his throat once more before continuing. "And next time, I promise to be with you."

At home, Grant met her at the door. Collapsing in his arms before her feet crossed the threshold, she wept, her face pressed against his broad chest.

He stroked her hair. "I should've been there."

She was silent. After all, she'd wanted him with her. To say otherwise was a lie. But she understood. It was too soon—the angst he would have experienced had he joined her. Less than a year since Grant had left the medical practice he'd served for more than a decade, the majority of the other Orchard View doctors and PAs were still angry with him for leaving. Had she not been in dire straits, she'd have made an appointment with another medical practice, but given that Orchard View was where she'd been a patient for so long and because she needed to be seen quickly, she'd succumbed.

Cassie, understanding his hesitation, had tried to reassure him. "It's ... it's all right. I'll be fine going alone."

But as she'd driven herself to the appointment less than three hours earlier, that familiar mockery had hissed, *You're not enough.* With a flip of a switch, the radio had blasted. Heat had risen on Cassie's cheeks with the irony of the Contours' 1962 lyrics, making her ask aloud, though her husband couldn't answer, "Do you love me?"

Now, Grant's hand pressed firm against the back of her head, and she swallowed rising resentment, a bitterness that threatened. But Cassie knew. They needed one another now, more than ever, and she echoed her words from days ago.

"It's all right."

"Momma! Momma!" Charlotte ran for Cassie, flinging her bright Dora backpack on the tiled kitchen floor, then wrapping her arms about her mother's legs.

Chester followed close behind, little shoulders slumped, brown forehead crinkled.

Cassie kissed Charlotte. "What's the matter, son? Hard day in kindergarten?"

With a humph, Chester plopped in a chair. "Mason's mad at me, again."

"Do you know why?" She smooched his head too, his tight brown curls tickling her lips.

"Says I tried to copy his coloring. But I didn't. Promise." Her six-year-old's crossed arms plunked on the wooden tabletop, followed by his chin, dimpled from frowning. A slight quiver forecasted coming tears.

"It's all right, son. He won't stay angry." She stroked the top of his head. "Maybe next time, tell him, 'You're super good at art, so it's not copying—just admiration.'"

"You think I copied too." Chester buried his face in his arms, attempting to conceal tears.

"I didn't say that. Not at all." Her gaze met Charlotte's. "You guys want a snack?"

The diversion sufficient, she poured two glasses of milk and placed a handful of gingersnaps on a plate. Charlotte pulled her chair close to her twin's.

"Char, what did you learn today?"

Brushing crumbs from her lips, her daughter offered a toothless grin.

"You lost the other one! Did Ms. Atkinson let you keep it?"

Charlotte dug in her jeans pocket to reveal a wadded tissue. After placing it on the table, she unfolded it with care. "Here!"

Cassie smiled, forgetting for a moment the day's difficult news, until—

Oh, how I wish it weren't so. Please make it not so.

"That's wonderful, dear. You'll need to put it under your pillow for the tooth fairy."

"What's this about a fairy?" Lannie joined her younger siblings at the table. "Who lost a tooth?" Her eyes darted back and forth from brother to sister several times before she added, "Let me guess. Char?"

"How'd you know, Thith?"

Lannie smiled. "I'm just that good."

At eleven, Grant and Cassie's oldest child had many skills, though they doubted ESP was one. However, they had recognized, despite her age, a discerning sensitivity.

"Good guess, sweetheart. Would your precision have anything

to do with the fact that last night Char couldn't eat her corn on the cob?"

Lannie laughed, then dropped her book bag on the floor and gave her mom a bear hug. Pulling back, she shoved a bouquet of white and buttery yellow blossoms toward Cassie. "For you. Just because."

Cassie's fingers wrapped around the nosegay her daughter held out. White clover and several green sprigs with bright-yellow petals popped, thrown in for good measure. "How perfect. Clover and cinquefoil. But how did you know?"

"Know what?" Lannie was already filling a small vase with water.

"This bouquet represents 'think of me'—clover—and 'beloved daughter'—cinquefoil. Nice touch, by the way—the cinquefoil." Standing beside her oldest child at the sink, she kissed her auburn head, then arranged the tiny posies. "There. Perfection!"

"So, how was your day, Momma?"

How like Landry Hazel to think of her, but what should she say?

Before Cassie could respond, however, Ben joined their quartet. Turning his ball cap backward, a prior-to-eating habit, he wasted no time and grabbed the last cookie.

"What's everyone talking about?" His words were garbled. After grabbing Chester's glass, he washed down the gingersnap.

"Bennett Billings, please don't talk with your mouth full." Cassie thumped the fabric bill of her oldest son's Yankees cap.

"Hey, that's my milk," Chester complained.

Sliding his younger brother's glass back across the table, Ben swiped a white mustache from his upper lip and asked again. "What y'all talking about?"

"Just Char's lost tooth and a visit from you-know-who." Lannie winked at her little sister.

"Who?" Chester drank the last of the milk.

"Tooth fairy, ooth airy. Not if I scare that ol' wives' tale away." Ben gulped air, then burped for emphasis. "Like that."

"Ew. Gross." Lannie slugged her brother on the arm. "You wouldn't dare. Hey, Momma, may I have some milk too, please?"

Walking to the fridge, Cassie noticed a pile of mail on the counter. As she thumbed through the envelopes, her attention was piqued by one in particular. Her name, written in bold black, was central on the envelope. It was from a woman she knew, a friend—Fiona Davis.

Cassie slipped a single sheet of paper from the envelope and read as Lannie crossed the kitchen to retrieve two glasses, then poured milk for herself and her brother.

And as children laughed and talked around the dining table, their voices dissipated with Fiona Davis's words. The letter was a request, commissioned work of a very unique nature.

And the memory of the day's earlier events vanished.

CHAPTER 2

CASSIE—MAY 2016

SHE EXPERIENCES SNEEZING FITS every morning. Is that normal?" Cassie struggled to keep the phone next to her ear as Millie Kate squirmed on her lap, trying to free herself. "I know. I know. Just a minute, love."

"Mrs. Billings, remind me of your daughter's full name and date of birth."

"Mildred Kathleen Billings. February third, 2014."

The receptionist typed, her staccato clicking coming through the phone. No doubt, the fingernails of the woman on the other end were long, painted to perfection.

"Off you go, lovie." Released from Cassie's grasp, Millie toddled in the direction of her toy box, stopping once to pick up her stuffed rabbit. With her hands now free, Cassie stretched out her fingers to inspect her nails. Brittle, short, unpainted.

How long had it been since she'd taken time to—?

"Says here in the files from your daughter's previous pediatrician that, due to her addiction to methadone at birth, she suffered from occasional diarrhea, irritability, and frequent sneezing." More typing. "Does she still have those other symptoms?"

"No, not typically. Just the sneezing."

Millie sneezed, punctuating Cassie's answer.

"Hear that?"

"Poor thing. If you're concerned, we can schedule her for a visit."

The week ahead was full. Her biopsy had led to a mastectomy, and now she had an oncology appointment as well as the other kids' activities. Was a ped visit necessary?

"I'll call back if I decide to bring her in. She doesn't have any fever or anything. Thank you."

She laid her cell phone on the kitchen counter. Had she made the right decision? Another sneeze came from the living room. Cassie followed the sound, then sat on the braided rug beside her daughter, soothing back Millie's dark, soft curls. "Whatcha got there?"

"Bun." The child held out her plush toy. "Hugs?"

Cassie hugged the rabbit, then kissed its velvet nose, the cloth worn thin from affection. "Thank you, love."

How Cassie cherished these mornings with her youngest, with the others at school. On rare occasions, Grant lingered too, sipping that second cup of coffee. Then they'd take turns holding Millie, playing with her. After all, there was so much time to make up for, Millie having only joined their family six short months earlier, right after Thanksgiving.

"Wanna read a book?" Cassie smiled at her toddler.

Millie rose and lifted the toy-box lid, then pulled out a well-worn copy of *Goodnight Moon*. She held it up. "Night-night."

"Come here." Cassie plopped onto the sofa, then patted its worn cushion. Millie toddled over, and Cassie carefully hoisted her daughter before sitting her on the couch and enfolding her in a colorful afghan crocheted by Grandma Patricia. The child's tiny brown toes poked through the blanket's weave. "Piggies!" And Cassie kissed them, one by one.

If only Millie could tell her more about those 650-plus days she'd lived—survived—prior to becoming a Billings.

Cassie leaned in close. Her lips touched the edges of her daughter's ear, and she whispered, "What can you tell me, dear? What was it like living in those two foster homes, with different families?"

But of course, the toddler couldn't tell her. And with the passing of time, even when she could articulate, there'd likely be less Millie would recall.

A grace.

Cassie kissed her daughter's curly head, then, pulling her closer, opened *Goodnight Moon*. Millie shoved her thumb in her mouth, the soft sucking a comfort. A small scar on the back of her hand reminded Cassie. Although only two, her daughter had lived a difficult life.

But more than the physical wounds were the emotional ones. Even then, though they couldn't know for certain what demons haunted their child's dreams, she'd wake up in fits—lathered in sweat, crying. Perhaps it was best they didn't know, though they prayed God would heal Millie's wounded heart and mind.

And for anything bad she doesn't remember, *thank you!*

"Bun-Bun's brush. Mush." Millie pointed to a bowl on the bedside table in the picture book. "Num, num." She smacked her lips, pearly teeth showing behind perfect rosebud lips.

"Good thinking. Let's get breakfast."

While Millie napped, Cassie sat at her antique oak desk tucked in a sunny spot in the corner of the kitchen. She'd placed a fresh bouquet from Lannie there earlier, and she smiled at her daughter's thoughtfulness. A ray of sunshine landed on the flowers, creating a silver hue on the clover, highlighting the gold petals of the cinquefoil.

Beloved daughter. But ... was Cassie beloved?

The angst the question stirred unsettled her, drawing to the surface the decades-old insecurity, shedding light again on the reality of what she faced—what seemed the most horrendous antagonist in her story. In anyone's story.

As Cassie fingered a green leaf poking up from the lip of the vase, a whisper—

Daughter, your faith has healed you. Go in peace.

She shook her head at the words, their timeliness, the confirmation giving her the gumption to do .... What was it her favorite writer, Elisabeth Elliot, had encouraged? Do the next thing.

The next thing. Still wedged between a pottery vase holding a bouquet of pens and pencils, the letter from Fiona Davis vied for an answer, and Cassie slipped it from its spot.

She removed the single sheet of letter-size stationery and unfolded it to read again what Fi had penned on Friday, April 15, 2016.

Friday, April 15, 2016

Dear Cassie,

Happy Tax Day! Ha! I hope this finds you well—your family also. We were overjoyed to hear about the adoption of Millie Kate. What a sweet name and for an even sweeter little one, I'm sure. Loved the family photo you shared in your announcement, which, of course, I showed to Brent and the kids. Everyone oohed and aahed. Bethany Lila found a magnet, so we could stick it on the fridge. And that's where it remains! Anyway, we love it and hope to meet Millie in person one day.

As you may recall, Mom and Dad will be celebrating their fiftieth wedding anniversary in September 2019. While perhaps that seems a long way off, what I'm going to ask you, what I feel I'm supposed to ask you, will 1) take some time to ponder and then, should you decide yes, 2) take some time to accomplish. So, here goes.

You're a gifted writer. I need a gifted writer. I understand it will require much from you, may even be painstakingly tough at times, but you're the one I think of each time I pray, "Lord, who should write this?"

It will mean the world to them, their love story being so unique. And we both know they're not getting any younger, as is true for your own parents. (Isn't it hard to see them age?)

For their 50th anniversary, we would love to have their memoir written. Yes, their love story. Honestly, I can't think of anyone better equipped to do this, though it won't be easy. Will take some intentionality.

I figure—between what I share with you, perhaps some emails back and forth as well as some phone calls and texts (Yes, Mom and Dad text, which is a hoot!)—maybe even a face-to-face visit or two—you can gather the information you'll need.

Oh, Cassie—it will mean so much! And not just for our family but for a broader audience too, I hope. Their story is powerful, pointing to a redemptive God.

So, won't you prayerfully consider this? Please.

If you could let me know in the coming weeks, even if you decline, then we can move ahead—with you or, if it's not meant to be, with someone else.

"Thank you" hardly expresses my gratitude. I'm grateful you're even considering this request. Again, I know how difficult this may prove to be—with your workload at the paper, your personal blog, and, most importantly, your family ... yes, your

growing family! For all the reasons. Anyway, bless you, dear friend.

Much love,
Fi

Cassie smoothed the paper on the worn surface of her desk, as if the very movement might somehow squeeze out an answer.

Could she do this? Should she do this?

Fi was right. Saying yes would be a sacrifice—of her time, her emotions. And now, this other thing.

With medical appointments added to an already full schedule and the possibility of feeling puny, downright sick sometimes, in the coming weeks and months, could she manage?

Was she meant to take this on, especially now, with—

Should I say yes, God? Are you saying, "Go in peace" as an answer to this very question?

What Cassie knew of Fiona's parents, Gideon and Ava Stallings, was intriguing, no doubt. After all, theirs was a special love story. Beautiful, yet marked with pain, spanning many years. In truth, Cassie longed to know more, even believed knowing more would—

A cry rang out from Millie's room. Another bad dream. Her daughter's timing? An answer itself.

Demons. They haunt everyone.

CHAPTER 3

CASSIE—JUNE 2016

JOINING HER FRIEND JANE Freemont at the dining table, Cassie said, "It's only nine o'clock, and I'm pooped. Man, this post-surgery stuff's kill ..."

Her unfinished sentence hung between them. The irony of what Cassie had almost said struck her, and she was glad she had stopped short of saying it. She and Grant had decided on the life-saving measure they'd determined was best.

"Let me rephrase. Post-surgery, I've just been so tired." Cassie fingered the soft white petals of the Madonna lilies Jane had brought her, arranged in a tall, pink vase. "These are beautiful." She bent, taking in their fragrance. "You know what they symbolize? Healing. Promise. Perhaps a sign?"

Though Jane wasn't what Cassie considered an empath, her gaze was tender. "Really? I had no idea." She took another swig of coffee. "I hope you don't mind me asking but ..." Jane hesitated. "What sort of treatment will you be doing? Perhaps you already are." Her brown, deep-set eyes reflected concern.

Jane had first been an acquaintance, then a friend for ... what? Five, six years? Ever since Cassie had accepted a job with the

Greensboro News and Record. Jane wrote for the paper too, though her articles were more raw journalism, unlike Cassie's occasional columns with personal touches reflecting her unique faith-based style.

"Hey, this is me, Jane. You can ask anything. I know you and your inquiring mind." Cassie chuckled. "After the mastectomy in late April, they discovered some metastasis, which I'd feared. Because it was already in the lymph nodes, they staged it at IIIB, and I've already undergone a couple chemo treatments."

Although Cassie rarely talked about her treatment to anyone outside her family, it was comfortable sharing with a friend. "And another thing. Grant and I decided to invest in a new, quite experimental treatment. It's costly, since insurance won't cover it, but my oncologist told us about a cold cap procedure, something I do at my chemo appointments. He said it should help me keep a lot of my hair. Google it."

As she spoke, Cassie instinctively reached up and ran fingers through her long auburn tresses. How much would she lose?

Jane's mouth hung open for a moment. "I've never heard of that, but I imagine it could help boost the spirits. We both know how much maintaining a positive attitude helps with one's overall health and healing." She shook her head. "Losing hair, especially for women, would feel, I don't know. Demoralizing?" Jane shook her head and picked up her cell phone. "Siri, remind me to Google 'cold caps' at three o'clock today." Her gaze met Cassie's again. "Thanks. Who knows? Maybe I'll even write an article about it."

Cassie chortled. "You should. Like I said, it's not widely known and still very expensive. Maybe, over time and with the right attention, insurance will cover it." She blew on her coffee. "Anyway, all things considered, I'm lucky. Dr. Spencer says we caught it fairly early, so my chances of beating this bas ..." She stopped, holding back the curse word. "Let's just say, the likelihood I'll be around to pester you for years to come is pretty doggone good."

Jane sighed. "Phew. That's the best news I've been given in a long time." Her hand bypassed her mug to grasp Cassie's arm. "But I am sorry, Cassie. Truly."

Without thinking, Cassie moved her hand to the place her left breast had been, the place that still ached, even after a little more than a month. Earlier that day, dripping wet in the shower, she'd traced the red, mottled skin where a scar was beginning to form. Grant had knocked, then opened the bathroom door, asking if he could say goodbye. When he pulled back the shower curtain, there she stood. Naked. Vulnerable. She'd wanted to hide, but when he placed his hand on the vacant place, right there, over her heart, she relaxed at his touch.

"No shame, my love." That was what Grant had said.

Jane interrupted Cassie's reflection. "Look on the bright side. Gives you some good writing material too." Jane squeezed Cassie's arm once more and winked. She picked up her mug.

"Always looking for stories, said like a true journalist." Cassie dabbed her mouth with a napkin.

"Speaking of which, did you see the article the other day? Protestors protesting the protestors at Planned Parenthood?" Jane's lips pursed, and she puffed air five times, emphasizing the string of p-words.

"Protestors protesting the protestors. Ha, now, that's a mouthful." Cassie sipped her coffee. "Yeah, I read about it. Interesting, to say the least."

"The anti-abortion folks were demonstrating. Rioting, more like it." Again, Jane's eyes spun like marbles on a roulette wheel. "Thankfully, several in the pro-choice camp confronted them. Didn't it say three people walked away with injuries?"

"At least, and one was a child." Cassie lifted her index finger, then pointed at her friend. "Really? A child."

"But just a flesh wound." Jane spoke with an English accent, then snickered at her Monty Python pun. "To be expected."

"Expected?" Heat rose on Cassie's cheeks. "Violence, toward peaceful demonstrators? Whose side are you on anyway?"

Jane stared into her coffee cup. After a moment's lull, her gaze met Cassie's. "I think you know. I'm pro-choice, but I do believe, at least in most cases, the best choice is life."

Cassie considered her friend's words, wondering what exceptions she might make. In the case of a woman's health? Conception due to incest? Rape?

"I suppose I knew where you stood on the abortion issue. Still, I don't think violence is right, no matter the circumstances. One person hurt is one too many."

The irony of her words.

Jane nodded. "I agree. It's such a heated topic right now, that's all. I'm sorry for bringing it up."

The awkward moment between friends passed. Cassie had poured each of them a second mug of coffee when, "Mo-mma." It was Millie Kate calling from her room. "Excuse me." Cassie set the mugs on the table. "Be right back."

A minute later, she returned with a sleepy-eyed Millie. "Say hello to Ms. Jane."

"Hewo." Millie rubbed her eyes with one hand. The other clutched a pastel animal-printed blanket. "Juice?"

"Can Ms. Jane hold you?" Cassie sat her daughter on Jane's lap, then filled a sippy cup with apple juice and handed it to Millie.

As her youngest daughter snuggled close to Jane, Cassie shared Millie Kate's story. How her birth mom was only sixteen, her bio dad eighteen. How she came into the world addicted to methadone and had to undergo a "scheduled withdrawal." How her birth mom, despite a crisis pregnancy and being abandoned by the father, had done the honorable, courageous thing.

"And she chose life." Cassie set her mug down with a thud. "In my opinion, Millie's birth mom is a hero." Her gaze flicked from Jane to her daughter. "Any birth mom is, isn't that right, Millie

Kate?" She chuckled. "But Momma sure can be long-winded, huh?"

As if to prove Cassie's point, Millie wiggled on Jane's lap.

"Guess you want down now, eh?" Jane released her grasp around Millie Kate's middle.

In a moment, the toddler disappeared around the corner, and the tinny melody from a battery-operated toy floated to the kitchen.

"You are my sunshine, my only sunshine—"

"I miss those days." Jane took a swig. "Has it been hard—you know, adding a fifth to your already full brood?"

Cassie considered her answer. "I think adding Char and Chester was harder. I mean, they did come, just like in the days of Noah, two by two." She chuckled. "Not to mention, Grant's mom had just passed, and things in his practice were heating up."

Jane offered an understanding nod. "I recall that being a difficult season. If you don't mind me asking, does Grant keep up with any of his former colleagues?"

The honest answer was yes, but Cassie hesitated. This fact wasn't widely known. Could Jane be trusted? Cassie had never known her to betray a confidence. Still—

The kitchen clock chimed the hour, and Jane glanced at her wristwatch. "Unbelievable. Ten o'clock already. Time sure flies with you, Cassie!"

"It's because I'm so much fun."

Jane's question was forgotten for the time being, and Cassie silently said a prayer of thanks.

The truth that Dr. Grant Billings was still in contact with one of the newer Orchard View PAs wouldn't remain a secret forever. But for now, it was best.

The inquiring mind of Jane Freemont, *Greensboro News and Record* reporter, would have to wait. Truth would reveal itself in time.

CHAPTER 4
CASSIE—JUNE 2016

Hello, Fiona.

I'm sorry this is belated, but after much consideration and prayer, Grant and I both feel this is something I can do. That I'm supposed to do. Even as I type, I'm laughing at God's sense of humor. But he must know, despite the plethora of reasons why I could decline, I'm the one for this job. And honestly, I'm honored —truly.

This will take a lot of diligence on my part, as you wrote in your letter, intentionality. But, with today's modes of communication, I'm sure I can gather all I need to write your parents' story. (Like you, it still cracks me up when I receive a text from my own mom or dad! Who would have ever imagined?)

I'm sure you don't know, but I was diagnosed with breast c-#^$-r (I still won't say/write the word!) back in mid-April. Thankfully, it was caught early, and I'm already undergoing chemotherapy, which, while an inconvenience, hasn't been bad ... yet. Just some nausea, hair loss, and (worse!) fatigue. It's* *difficult for me to believe I ever ran a half marathon and, even more, that I'll ever do so again. All that to say, any prayers you might muster are greatly appreciated.*

I remember you telling me your momma had the same some years ago, so perhaps this will enable me to ask her some questions about it as well. (Isn't life funny?)

Anyway, let me know when we can meet. It's simply been too long. I can work out childcare for the kids if it's after school ends for summer, and it's a bit easier since Lannie's almost twelve. She's very helpful!

I'll look forward to hearing from you. And again, despite my own frailty—all the reasons to perhaps say no—I'm banking on his strength to be made perfect in my weakness.

Blessings, Cassie.

HER RESPONSE FINALLY WRITTEN, she hit *Send*, then breathed a prayer. Okay, God. I'm banking on you to show up.

Cassie sat at her dining table and scanned through her iPhone apps, looking for Notes.

After opening it, she spoke to her phone, adding thoughts to the journal she'd begun since her diagnosis.

June 14, 2016—Today, I'm tired. So, so tired. I try to keep how I'm feeling from the kids, but the two older ones can tell. Lannie especially. She's helpful, and I'm grateful. Grant recognizes how weary I am too. This chemo's pretty icky, and this particular go-around left me punier than other times.

Thankfully, however, the cold cap's working, and I haven't lost much of my hair, so that's a plus. Grateful to know about it and that we can afford it. What's that Bible verse? The one about hair being a woman's crown of glory, or something like that. Anyway, just sent my letter to Fi. Even though I feel certain this is for me, that God even confirmed as much, I'm nervous. To write another's love story—well, I'm gonna need his help. And maybe, just maybe, writing this will finally silence the ugly voice of condemnation, which too often mocks, making me question—Am I enough? More, am I loved?

~

"How's this, Lannie?" Cassie, mustering as much height as her petite five-foot-two frame possibly could, stood erect in front of her full-length bedroom mirror, inspecting the completed ensemble. Not too casual. Not too formal.

Still in pajamas, Lannie perched at the end of her mother's bed, legs crisscrossed, head slightly tilted. "Yep. Looks good to me."

Jumping to her feet, then taking several strides to stand alongside her mother, Lannie giggled at her own disheveled appearance before breathing into her cupped hand. "Good thing I'm not going with you. Look at that bedhead! And talk about morning breath—gross."

Lannie raked her fingers through her own auburn mop, then, face close to the glass, mouth ajar, she removed gritty sleepers from both her green eyes. "Phew, that's better." She shifted her gaze back to her mother's reflection, eyeing her up and down. "Now, most important—what shoes are you wearing?"

"Good question." Cassie opened her closet door and ran her finger along several canvas shoe cubbies, then stopped three down from the top. "How about these? They'll offer a splash of red."

Lannie laughed at the idea of her mom wearing Chuck Taylor high-top sneakers. "Ha, ha! Funny, Mom. Try those, two down from the Chucks."

Cassie slipped the black canvas Toms from their holder. "Yeah, I suppose they're a bit more appropriate."

"Plus, they'll bring out the dark script in your T-shirt."

Once more, Cassie considered her attire. The blue cotton tee was not only comfortable—a must since her recent surgery—but it was appropriate, with its floral border, a centered typewriter with a single sheet of paper and "Life is good but best when writing" in bold black. Just a touch of professionalism. And the khaki skirt? The perfect, smart-casual finish.

"Good thinking. Now, socks or no?"

"How about those little liner ones? That way your shoes don't get stinky." Lannie opened the top dresser drawer and removed a pair of white footies and handed them to her mother. "Think about it, Mom. You're gonna be nervous. And when you're nervous ... you know." Lannie's face crinkled.

"Really, Lannie, that bad? But hey, that reminds me. Probably should take my deodorant, huh? Just in case."

Lannie was right. Already butterflies danced in her stomach, the slice of toast and coffee having done little to calm them. Not to mention, the routine nausea brought on by chemo added to her queasiness. Her prescribed treatment wasn't for the faint of heart, nor stomach, and Cassie wondered if she'd ever grow accustomed to it.

But this was Fiona. Like Cassie—wife, mother, homemaker. Though it had been quite some time since they'd visited face-to-face, they'd corresponded over the years.

As if discerning her mother's thoughts, Lannie offered encouragement. "Don't forget, Momma, she asked you. Said you were perfect for the job." Lannie squeezed her mother's middle. "You've got this!"

How did her adolescent daughter know just what to say to quell her insecurities?

"Thanks, Lan. And you? Feel good about helping Daddy today, especially with Millie Kate?"

"Yep. All good. We're gonna take the kids to get lunch and have a picnic at the park. By the time you're home, everyone will be fed, bathed, and sound asleep."

Cassie loved how Lannie referred to her siblings as kids, as if she were so much older, more mature. Cassie kissed Lannie's messy mop. "What did I ever do to deserve you?"

On the road, Cassie sang along, classic '70s and '80s hits from her favorite radio station filling her Camry, floating out the open windows. When Fleetwood Mac's "Landslide" began, the song's solo guitar stirred memories of her college coffeehouse days, singing on weekends with Grant accompanying her—when her medical-resident boyfriend wasn't on call.

Had it been love at first sight when she'd laid eyes on the tall, blue-eyed, brown-haired acoustic guitar player?

Stevie Nicks crooned, "What is love?" and Cassie smiled.

Yes, it had been, at least for her, but did that mean love was easy? It hadn't been, in their experience. In fact, not long after they'd married, they'd talked of separating, wondering if they'd made a mistake. And there'd been several other times too. Marriage was hard, downright grueling at times, but they'd worked through the difficult days, pressing on to better ones.

Their silver anniversary. It was just around the corner. Still undecided regarding a gift for Grant, Cassie considered a trip in the months ahead. Just the two of them. Italy perhaps? Or Ireland?

Journey's "Don't Stop Believing" began, jolting Cassie back to the present and to the day ahead. Her GPS informed her there were fewer than twenty miles to go.

The drive from the Billingses' home on the outskirts of Greensboro to Fiona Davis's in Eden was under forty-five minutes, and the bright summer morning was unseasonably cool for central North Carolina. Cassie's earlier queasiness was gone, her excitement regarding the day bringing a different sort of flutter.

The ensuing visit had been planned several weeks prior. When she'd written, Cassie was certain, but now? Not to mention, she'd planned to spend the majority of the drive pondering additional questions to ask Fiona, going over the list she'd made. But with little traffic on US 29-N that Saturday morning, she was surprised when she passed the *Welcome to Eden* sign.

Turning onto a tree-lined street, Cassie again sensed stirring flutters. The houses, though in an older part of town, were each unique with manicured lawns and flowerbeds. Children played on the sidewalk or rode bikes and scooters.

And her GPS told her she'd arrived at 342 Wren Way.

Cassie's insides flip-flopped, and she laid a trembling hand on her waist. Hadn't she been sure? Why was she questioning, her shakiness indicating ... what? Insecurity? Fear?

Please be with me and Fiona as we visit today. Give us clarity, and help me gather the information I need to get started on what has to be something you planned. I'm trusting you, believing you created me for this good work.

That morning, having read those very words during her quiet time, Cassie sensed once more that something—someone—bigger than her was at work. Hadn't she and Grant believed as much after weeks of praying?

Unbuckling, she checked to be certain her notebook and computer were in her canvas tote, then slung it over her shoulder and grabbed her purse.

Cassie unfolded from the vehicle, then smoothed the wrinkles from her khaki skirt and tucked in her T-shirt. Was she underdressed? So confident earlier, why was she suddenly uncertain?

She took another deep breath, then squared her shoulders, standing tall. Confidence. That was what she needed to show, telling Fi she was up for the task. One more deep inhale, and she closed her eyes. A familiar fragrance filled her nostrils, and she knew.

Cassie scanned the Davises' yard and landscape, searching for what her nose told her was there, somewhere. Locating the bushy plant, she smiled. Lush and green, the rosemary spilled over the edges of its terra cotta pot just to the right of Fi's front porch.

Cassie climbed the steps, then reached to run her fingers over the plant's spindly leaves, squeezing a little to release its scent before rubbing her fingers and thumb together. Hand to her nostrils, she inhaled deeply.

Fitting. After all, that was what this day was about.

Remembering.

~

"Coffee? Juice ... I mean, tea?"

Fiona was nervous too. Cassie sensed it in her voice, as if the purpose of their visit was sacred yet fragile. Something to be handled with great care.

"Been filling too many kids' juice glasses this morning, I reckon."

"How I understand that." Cassie chuckled. "Yes, coffee, please. With cream."

Cassie's and Fiona's relationship was decades old, though their actual face-to-face encounters had been few and far between. Besides the occasional phone conversation and get-together, they'd mostly stayed connected through social media. Still, Cassie considered Fi a dear friend, a sister.

Settled on the well-worn leather couch, Cassie tugged at a loose thread on the hem of her skirt, then smoothed its pleats. When she opened her computer, it came alive, the screen erupting with a colorful photograph of her five children, a recent one Grant had taken. Millie Kate was laughing in Lannie's arms, with Chester and Charlotte sitting in the grass, Ben making bunny ears behind his younger brother's head.

Handing her a steaming mug, Fiona plopped down beside Cassie. "Phew. What a morning." She nodded toward the photo. "Such a beautiful family. When was that? Recently, I'm guessing."

"Yep. Very. Memorial Day weekend, camping trip to Lake Norman."

"Look at Millie. Such a happy girl."

"Most of the time. She has her moments." Cassie blew on her coffee before sipping, then took a deep swallow. "Sometimes we wish she could tell us more. You know, about life before us. Other times, we know it's for the best. Still, I wonder what she remembers."

Fi clicked her tongue. "Yeah, I'm sure some of it's not so good, though I do hope, for the most part, it's okay."

"Her medical files and those from the social worker say otherwise." Cassie traced an imaginary circle around her youngest daughter. "She's certainly a gift to us. Such a special girl."

"And the others? How did they respond to her coming?"

Cassie pondered her answer. "Lannie's very easygoing. She's a great help. Ben, he's quiet, so we don't always know what's going on in that nine-year-old head of his. Overall, he's adjusted well. He's all baseball and Legos, making our biggest problem being sure he picks up the pieces so Millie won't choke."

"I haven't forgotten those days." Fi sipped her coffee. "And the twins?"

"They sort of have each other, you know? Since their adoption was finalized in 2012, they've grown even closer. Almost like they have a sixth sense between them. It's weird." Cassie paused, considering her words. "They weren't yet three when their adoptions were final, and we'd fostered them prior, so Grant and I are pretty much all they've ever known, with the exception of a few months right after they were born."

"And their personalities?"

"Chester, he's introverted. Easily hurt, carries a chip on his shoulder. Loves to draw. Charlotte? She's quick-witted. Loves friends, and—"

"Loves her twin?" Fiona's gaze met Cassie's. "Sorry for interrupting, but that's what I'm guessing."

"Yes. Fiercely. And very protective." Cassie paused. "Being dark-skinned in an almost all-white school ... that can be hard. But even though Chester's more sensitive—you know, desiring to be accepted, worrying at times he's not—Char's more comfortable in her skin. She's got attitude, that one, and she's good for Chester in that regard. Does that make—"

With the doorbell's chime, Fi patted Cassie's leg. "Yes. Yes, it does." She rose from the couch. "And now for a little surprise."

Cassie wondered what it might be and raised an eyebrow.

"My parents. I invited them too. Hope that's okay."

Mr. and Mrs. Stallings? Here? Now?

Cassie's stomach flip-flopped, and she twisted her hands together, managing a one-word response. "Sure."

"It'll be fine." Fiona, having rounded the corner, disappearing from Cassie's sight, spoke, though her words sounded far away. "Just like them to be early."

The front door opened, and the sounds of happy voices muffled by what Cassie imagined were hugs came from beyond. She fought the urge to escape to the bathroom to regain her composure. Instead, she tucked a strand of hair behind her ear, then, running her hand down her neck, felt her quickened pulse as butterflies raged.

An aching throb where her left breast had been reminded her. If Fiona's parents were here, her mother having also gone through something similar, this was her opportunity to ask. Some things were better spoken about in person rather than in text messages or email. This was one of them, the perfect time to—

"If it isn't Cassandra." An elderly woman with a pile of white hair pinned atop her head held out her arms. The man beside her, tall and broad, his hair wavy and dark, with the exception of some gray at his temples, smiled with his eyes.

Cassie stood, then took several steps toward the newcomers. Her face flushed, and she extended her arms.

Fiona's mother enveloped her, and Cassie breathed in Avon's Spring Song. Closing her eyes, she fought tears. Lily of the Valley, a favorite.

And at that moment, the incriminating whisper came once more. A last-ditch effort to thwart what she'd been sure was for her, part of a bigger plan. Was she up for the task—to journey with this aging couple, returning with Ava and Gideon Stallings to their joy, much of which had been birthed from deep sorrow?

Could she write their beautiful love story? Do it the justice it so deserved?

But in her ear came an answer. "Cassandra, dear, we're ever so thankful you said yes. There's no one we'd want more. No one in all the world."

CHAPTER 5

CASSIE—JUNE 2016

"So wonderful to see you." Cassie's heart rate slowed, enveloped in the elderly woman's embrace.

"Please tell me, dear—how have you been?" Ava Stallings squeezed Cassie's hand gently before letting it go with a pat. "My, my. It's been far too long."

Initial welcomes and hugs over, the quartet arranged themselves in Fiona's living room. Cassie, erect on the soft leather sofa, noticed her hands trembling as she tapped the computer keyboard. As she awakened it, the photograph of her family shone again as she set her laptop before her on the cherry coffee table.

"What a beautiful family." Perched beside her, Ava smiled at the photograph filling the computer screen. "Just precious."

"Thank you." Cassie paused, then shared with Ava much of what she's shared with Fi before the Stallingses's arrival. Concluding, she shook her head. "Honestly, sometimes I pinch myself and ask God how I got so lucky."

Ava sighed. "My, my. They sure are a beautiful bunch. You're blessed indeed, Cassandra."

A beat of silence fell, then Fiona broke the quiet. "I almost forgot. Excuse me."

Less than a minute later, she returned, carrying a polished silver tray with a carafe, several mugs, creamer, pitcher, and sugar bowl, as well as a plate piled high with pastries. "Can't get distracted by grumbling stomachs." She laughed, setting everything on the table. "Now, who wants coffee? And Cassie, a warm-up perhaps?"

"I would love some." Gideon's voice, rich and deep, resonated in the quiet room, stirring a question.

"Remind me." Cassie's face warmed. "Did you ever work in broadcasting, either television or radio? I mean, you've such a nice speaking voice."

Gideon chuckled. "If I had a button. Isn't that right, Ava?" As he reached for the steaming mug from his daughter's outstretched hand, he winked at his wife, then sipped his coffee. "Now, that's a funny story."

Ava patted Cassie's hand. "My Deon. What he means to say is, 'If I had a dime.' He does have a romantical voice, doesn't he?"

Gideon chortled. "I don't know about all that, but she's correct. You're certainly not the first to ask. In all seriousness though, I was never in broadcasting. Teaching, yes. My many years as an architect have opened doors of opportunity to speak at conferences now and then. Just returned from one in Myrtle Beach. What was it, my love?"

"Three weeks ago this Friday." Ava turned once more to Cassie. "We do love our trips to Myrtle." She paused. "And I could listen to my husband read the phone book."

Ava's green eyes, her lashes lush for a woman her age, grew softer at their edges as she spoke, recalling this recent trip.

"Do you always travel together—for conferences, that is?" Again, Cassie's face warmed.

Gideon stretched his long legs, then settled deeper into the plaid-upholstered recliner situated across from Cassie and Ava.

Fixing his gaze on his wife of nearly half a century, he shook his head. "Not always, and honestly, since I retired some time ago, I travel less—even to teach. But when I do, and the conference happens to be in Myrtle Beach, I insist Ava comes along. Isn't that right, my love?"

Ava blushed, and Cassie, too, sensed heat rising once more, as if she were entering not only a significant part of their story but an intimate one as well, like sacred ground. Another lull fell between them. Their smiles conveyed that Gideon and Ava Stallings were remembering, knowing just what the other was thinking, recalling. Something special from their past, that which joined them together, Cassie was certain.

Lifting her computer from its place on the table, Cassie felt her tension ease, and she shifted her position on the couch as she laid the device—a source of security—on her lap. Fingers hovered over the keys as she prepared to type, and something stirred inside, a flutter indicating, at least for Cassie, that a story was about to unfold.

Fi cleared her throat. "Seems we've stepped into a story. How does it go? Once upon a time."

Cassie's fingers fidgeted in anticipation, like little race horses preparing to sprint from the gate.

"Let me see. It was 1969. March, isn't that right? Spring break, that trip I worked so hard to earn." Ava tittered, remembering.

Cassie tapped in perfect tempo with Ava's words, writing what she'd said, stopping only when the storyteller leaned forward to set her mug on the coffee table. Settling back again, Ava clasped her own hands, folding them in her lap.

"Seems like only yesterday." Nodding, she lifted her gaze to meet Gideon's. "More grains than can be counted, except by the one who knows them all." Her head bobbed and several loose strands of silver fell, framing her heart-shaped face.

It was Gideon's turn to speak. "Yes, my love. Known only by him—the one who knows their exact number on the shore."

Ava smiled. "Yes indeed. If a solitary word summed up our story, that's what it would be. Small as it is in the vast expanse of words, it would be etched on the mirror of our lives, read by those searching for a reflection of our past, to bring truth to the present." She paused once more, but only for a moment. Then, with a faraway look, her green eyes glimmering, she continued.

"Sand. That's the word. After all, Cassandra, it's where we began."

AVA JACKSON'S STORY

O Light, that followest all my way,
I yield my flickering torch to Thee;
My heart restores its borrowed ray,
That in Thy sunshine's blaze its day
May brighter, fairer be.

—George Matheson's
"O Love That Wilt Not Let Me Go"

CHAPTER 6

AVA—JANUARY 1969

January 13, 1969

Dear Diary,

Water. How I love the way it ebbs and flows, taking the form of whatever vessel it fills, where it finds its home. And I wonder—am I like water? Ebbing and flowing based on circumstance? Who I'm with? What I'm doing? Because, while I love this natural form, I'm not supposed to be conformed to the ways of the world but, as I've heard it said, to be transformed by the renewing of my mind. And this is where I struggle—desiring things I shouldn't, lacking contentment at times because I can't have what I long for. I even tell myself, justify my thinking, by saying I can say I'm sorry later. How does it go? Better to ask forgiveness than permission. But I believe that's wrong. Still, I fear I'm heading for bad decisions—things that might carry me away on the waves of some vast ocean. And knowing, believing anyway, that there's already a plan—that God already knows—well, that bothers me. Confuses me. Makes me wonder why God can't keep me from sin. Change the way I think, which in turn affects the way I feel. But he's not a puppet master, like Buffalo Bob, and I'm certainly not Howdy Doody (except for auburn hair and freckles). I guess I'm asking for help, and even as I write this, I'm in a battle with my will—not sure I want the help I'm asking for if it means changing my thoughts and desires. Maybe first I need to ask God to make me willing to be ... made willing.

I CLOSED THE FABRIC-COVERED BOOK, then slipped it back inside the Keds shoebox I hid under a stack of sweaters on my closet shelf. A birthday gift from Momma, purchased at DeHart's Five and Dime, she'd inscribed a message on the inside of its front cover before wrapping it and giving it to me.

For my little woman, who loves to write her heart. Happy nineteenth birthday, Ava.
Remember—It's because of love.

She was right. I was a woman. Then why did I feel so young?

Sprawled out on my bed, I clasped my hands behind my head and considered the words I'd just penned. The plans I held in my heart, I'd confirmed with Elaine only the day before.

"They're still plannin' to be gone this Friday. Goin' to supper club with the Halls. Won't be back until well after midnight, I 'spect."

"Where will you"—Elaine's voice lowered—"get it?"

I twirled the cord of my slimline telephone. "I've got my connections, so don't you worry your pretty li'l head, Elaine Marie

McLeod. Just come over—say eight o'clock. And bring your things to stay the night, okay?"

It was settled. Elaine and I would ring in the New Year, belated though we were. We'd planned it months earlier, waiting for the right time.

Who better to drink my first beer with than my best friend? The one who'd been with me when Jake King gave me my first kiss. Who knew when I started my period. Was with me when I purchased my first bra. And I was with her through many coming-of-age experiences too. Through thick and thin, that was what we'd promised.

At first, excitement stirred as I'd considered our scheme—knew just who to ask to purchase the six-pack of Pabst. He'd been more than willing, so long as I forked over the money, plus promised him a copy of my notes prior to our next Statistics exam. A fellow Rockingham student, Scott McMillan was perfect. Not a friend really, so no harm to my reputation. Rather a reliable acquaintance.

But as the weeks passed since our initial conversation, I sensed a nagging in the pit of my stomach, and I questioned our plan. Was it wrong? I was an adult. Still, did that make it right?

The fact that we had to sneak beer answered my question. It wouldn't ever matter how old I was. Momma and Daddy would never approve. Teetotalers, that was what they were.

Not like Elaine's parents. I doubted they'd care one bit. After all, Elaine had confided when we were still in grade school how she'd sipped champagne to ring in the New Year. And her mom and dad knew, encouraged her even.

The trill of an incoming call startled me. After reaching for the phone on my bedside table, I answered. "Hello."

"Guess what, Ava. Guess."

I chuckled. "Now, Elaine, how could I? Tell me already."

"Nope. Not until you guess. Just once."

I considered what could have stirred such excitement. "How

about your mom finally broke down and bought you that dress you've been dreamin' of. You know, the one from Kress?"

"Aw, no. That's not it, though it sure would be nice. Guess again, once more."

"Nope. You said one. Tell me. Tell me now before I come over there and squeeze the answer out of you."

My best friend giggled. "Okay, okay."

The sound of paper rustled. "A letter arrived today. From Bobs."

"My heavens. Really? Bobby wrote? He's not even been out to sea all that long. Mail must travel fast, even from the South Pacific."

"Yep. Wanna hear it?"

Did I? "Of course."

Papers rustled again as she prepared to read, and she cleared her throat. "It's postmarked January eighth. Less than a week ago. Wow—that is fast. Listen."

Dear Sis,

After only a couple days on board, I can tell things are a bit different here on the USS Enterprise, especially compared to Eden. Let me paint you a picture—

Imagine all men (no females, so no frills) and never—never!—silence, no matter the time of day. Last night, in fact, I stood under the Pacific stars, gazed up at the vast expanse, and from somewhere came the whir of a motor, the clanging of metal on metal. No matter it was midnight. No matter I was all alone on that tiny speck of this massive ship. Zero silence. None.

And the smells ... did I mention, we're all men? (I'll leave it there!)

The food's not bad—not good either. But thus far, I've purchased three chocolate bars at the ship's commissary and savored each bite, once on my bunk and the other two with buddies while we played cards.

Which leads me to recreation. There's not a lot, let me tell you (but not a lot of free time either). As I said, we play cards, and though I've yet to see one, I'm told they'll offer the occasional picture show, which I look forward to. (Sure wish I had Sarah Kramer here to hold my hand. Wink! Wink!)

We'll soon be off the coast of Hawaii, near Pearl Harbor, in fact. We'll conduct some battle drills—what I've come to know as Operational Readiness Inspection (ORI)—then on to Vietnam and ... yes, war.

Can you imagine, Sis? Me, a navy Seaman.

Please tell Mom and Pop I love them. And yeah, I love you too ... I reckon. (Again, wink! Wink!)

Yours truly,
Bobs

Elaine sighed. "Gracious, Ava. Can you even imagine? How different life must be for him, so unlike the blah, blah, blah of living here in Eden. But he did a swell job describin' it, don't you think?"

"Good ol' Bobby. Nice of him to write, and so soon too."

"Mom cried when she read it. She misses him somethin' fierce."

That tugged on my heart. After all, I knew from experience, from having lived nearly two decades with Momma.

A mother never stops missing her son.

Two days later, after a torrent of rain the day before, a sudden drop in temperature left Eden covered in ice.

Momma stirred me from sleep. "Ava, there's no classes today. Roads are slick."

Not yet coherent, I rubbed my eyes and yawned. "What? What'cha say?"

"No school today, sweets. You can sleep in a bit."

After she'd closed the door, I rolled onto my side, stretched, and, with a smile, yawned. An entire Tuesday free. Maybe I'd go shopping or perhaps bundle up and go for a leisure walk around—

The telephone rang, and I jolted upright, then reached to answer.

"Hello."

"Ava, did you hear?" Elaine's breathing was heavy.

"Hear what?"

"The terrible news. Happened yesterday, around one o'clock our time. Ava ..." Elaine's voice broke.

"What? What is it? What happened?"

"On the *Enterprise*. An explosion off the coast of Hawaii, near Pearl Harbor. Sailors were killed. Do you think—"

I gasped, trying to think what to say. "Now, Elaine, stop. You mustn't think that, not for a single second."

"But, what if ..." Elaine sobbed into the receiver.

"He's gonna be fine. I promise. I mean, what are the chances Bobby was one of the ones...you know?"

Still, I wondered. The likelihood of Elaine's only sibling, her older brother and their father's namesake—Robert Timothy McLeod—being one of those killed was impossible .... Or was it?

"Please now, try not to worry. Hey, want me to come over?"

Silence on the line.

"Elaine?"

"I'm, I'm here." She sniffed, then blew her nose. "No, but thank you. Mom and Daddy are worried too. They called Father Cunningham. He'll be comin' over shortly. I'll ... I'll keep you posted." Elaine sniffed again. "Please, just pray, Ava."

Pray? Something I'd found more difficult lately, as if a vast expanse separated me from God—like I was drifting out to sea, and him? He seemed farther and farther away.

"I-I will," I promised. What more could I say?

I hung up, then leaned back against my pillow. My head spun, recalling how proud Elaine had been when Bobby had enlisted in the navy less than two years earlier.

"My brother, a sailor." That was what Elaine had shared, followed with a daydreamy sort of sigh. "Can you imagine? Out of Eden, off to find excitement, no doubt."

Elaine had never mentioned concern regarding Bobby, never seemed worried he might be injured. Or worse. Not even when, less than two weeks earlier, Seaman Robert T. McLeod had departed with hundreds of others, the USS *Enterprise* setting sail from California heading south, deployed to Vietnam. Trained as a mechanic, Bobby was to work maintenance on the aircraft carrier. And how excited Elaine had been to share his letter the other day, even though he'd mentioned heading off to Vietnam and ... war? *My* Bobby McLeod. The notion had raised goosebumps on my arms, the hair at the back of my neck standing on end.

And now, this.

I turned from my back to my side. The cool coverlet of my pillow kissed my cheek and stirred a memory.

Though not my first, Bobby McLeod had kissed me too. How I hoped there would be another.

CHAPTER 7

AVA—FEBRUARY 1969

"ANY WORD FROM BOBBY?" My question hung on the line between us, my best friend's silence indicating bad news. "Elaine?"

Finally, she spoke. "Mom and Daddy received a phone call late last night. He's, he's gonna be okay. But Ava, he was injured in the explosion. Pretty bad, I think. Bad enough they're sendin' him home."

My heart leapt. "But isn't that good news? I mean, he's alive." Another moment's pause. "Elaine, what is it?"

"I don't know exactly how he was injured, and my parents haven't said much. They've been secretive, but I stood at their bedroom door last night and listened to them talk after they thought I'd gone to bed. Mom was cryin'. I think Dad was too."

The rustle of tissue told me Elaine was wiping her eyes, and she sniffed. "Ava, I think it's an injury to his spine. Something that's affected his ..." Elaine lowered her voice. "His, his, you know. I'm, I'm not sure. I overheard Mom ask if Daddy thought he'd still be able to ... You know what I'm talkin' about, right? Like maybe he wouldn't and, and then, never be able to have kids."

I understood what she meant.

"I'm sorry, Elaine."

~

By the end of January, Bobby was home—black and blue, his right leg in a cast, his right hand missing fingers. Any other injuries went undisclosed, at least to those outside the McLeod family.

The day of our planned, belated New Year's party had come and gone, and besides a few phone conversations, Elaine hadn't seen each other. I wondered what she knew.

Finally, I dialed her number, then counted the rings. On the fifth, I was about to hang up when—

"Hello."

"It's me. Can you talk?"

"Let me switch phones." Elaine's voice was muffled, though I could still make out her words. "Mom, will you hang this up, please? I'll take the call in my room." A beat of silence fell between us before the familiar click. "Okay, Mom. You can hang up."

Another click as the receiver was returned to its base, and Elaine sighed. "Just a second, Ava." We waited, making certain no one was listening. "Okay, I think we're safe."

"How are things?"

"Everythin' considered, I guess all right. I think Bobs is adjustin' to being home, though he won't talk about what happened. Father Cunningham came over yesterday after dinner. Sat with him a spell."

"That's good, right?"

"Yeah. Before leavin', Father sat with Mom and Daddy in the livin' room, prayed with them."

"Where were you?"

"Around the corner, in the dinin' room." Elaine sighed. "I prayed from there. Seems I've been doin' a lot of prayin' lately."

Perhaps Elaine's increased praying made up for the lack of my own. Although I managed to keep my promise, praying a little for Bobby right after hearing about the explosion, my words only hit the ceiling. In fact, I wondered if God heard them at all.

"Do you know any more about ..." I cleared my throat, pushing down the lump that threatened to steal my voice. "You know, about, his other injury?"

"Mom said time'll tell. There's so much even the doctors don't know right now, like the severity of—"

"I understand. At least he's walkin'. Some spinal cord injuries leave folks paralyzed or worse."

"Yeah, we're lucky to have him home. Not sure for how long. Right now, he says he's never goin' back, but we'll see."

"Any chance we could get together soon? I miss you, Elaine."

"Miss you too. How about tomorrow? I don't work. You?"

"I put in extra hours after classes this week, so Ms. Cole told me to take the weekend off. 'Read some of those books rather than just check them out for others.' Somethin' like that." I twirled the telephone cord around my wrist. "Yeah, tomorrow should work great. And I've been thinkin'. Any plans for spring break?"

"Are you kiddin'? I haven't had a chance to think about anythin' but Bobs for weeks. When's your break?"

"Rockingham's begins after classes on March fourteenth. I return on March twenty-fourth, but I'm not even talking about goin' for the whole week. Maybe a long weekend."

Truth was, I doubted Momma and Daddy would agree to any of it, but I'd been saving money from my library job, not to mention devising a plan to present the idea. I was waiting for the perfect time.

"Anyway, think about it. It's still more than a month away. With everythin' that's happened, it's probably hard to even consider somethin' so trivial. But wouldn't it be fun?"

"A trip to the beach might be exactly what we need, Ava—with bikinis and sunshine and refreshin' drinks with those cute little umbrella do-dads. Anyway, a girl can dream."

After we hung up, having decided to meet for milkshakes at Circle Drive-In the next afternoon, I retrieved my journal from the closet shelf. My heart was full.

February 7, 1969

Dear Diary,

Elaine said Bobby's doing okay, though he won't talk about what happened. Not yet, anyway. The extent of his injuries is unknown, and they're concerned about that, not to mention whether he'll ever return to the navy.

Makes me sad, especially since he was so excited. So proud.

I'm thankful he didn't die, not that my prayers helped any. Did you even hear, God? Did a single word reach your ears?

I hate that I doubt, but I do, and I wonder if praying makes any difference at all.

I mean, think about Momma and Daddy. They prayed real hard for children when they first got married. And they waited and waited. Did they ever wonder if their prayers worked, especially when they suffered their miscarriages?

After John Paul was born, I bet they believed beyond doubt that God had answered their prayers. So why'd he die?

"As North Carolina cherry blossoms were born, like

springtime snow—" That's how Momma describes the season of JP's passing, but with a far-off look.

He only lived those few months, then died on a bright spring morning when all he'd ever known was cold? Didn't even get to see his first daffodil dancing along the road to Eden's First Church's cemetery. And the irony? He's buried there—his death shrouded in mystery, though I sense his presence sometimes—not in any eerie manner. Just the memory of him, I suppose—like a lingering shadow on the wall.

I imagine the pain of losing a child never fully goes away, though I can't possibly understand, and I hope I never do. I'm right thankful Mr. and Mrs. McLeod won't have to feel that heartache either, now that Bobby's safely home.

Perhaps losing JP caused Momma and Daddy to be more protective of me, and—in all honesty—I resent that at times, but then I feel guilty. After all, at least I'm alive and get to experience all the beauty life offers—like the flurry of cherry blossoms. The dancing daffodils.

Maybe soon, I'll plant some daffodils on JP's grave. After all, springtime's on its way—a new beginning for us all.

Goodnight.

There. Funny how pouring out my heart on the page was a way of releasing, yet I received something in return.

I hid my journal, then flopped down on my bed. The springs creaked their familiar sound. Could I ever sleep in a quiet bed, one with a new, tight-spring mattress?

Hands clasped behind my head, I scanned my bedroom. Not much had changed over the dozen years I'd called it my own. Yellow paint on the walls, though chipped and faded in places. Red-and-white gingham curtains with white eyelet trim, pulled back with ribbons on sunny days. Because neither was east-facing, I never requested blinds. The thin cotton coverings were sufficient, though I didn't undress directly in front of them unless the lights were out.

Against the far wall was my oak desk with its cane chair—gifts from Grandma Jean and Grandpa Fred Jackson for my thirteenth birthday. Above the desk, a watercolor painting by Grandpa Dennis, a depiction of his and Grannie Alice Schmidt's farm. Beside the desk, my hand-painted, metal trash can, bright with daisies against its deep red finish. How many wadded-up writing assignments and letters had I tossed in it? Too many to count. It once belonged to Momma, then she gave it to me because, like her, daisies were among my favorite flowers.

I shifted my gaze to my bedside table and recalled a conversation with Elaine years earlier. She'd come for a sleepover, her sleeping bag spread out on the floor beside my bed.

After we'd turned off the lamp, we whispered in the dark. Elaine shared that she doubted I had what her dad had in his bedside table drawer.

Of course, I was curious. All I kept in mine was some tissue, hand lotion, a pad of paper and, a pen.

That was when she spilled the beans, telling me how she'd discovered a dirty magazine in his.

How we giggled, blushing in the dark, grossed out at the thought.

I rolled onto my side and flipped on the lamp, then opened the drawer to rummage through the items. Still, a small notebook and pen, as well as Jergens hand lotion. But there was more. A small jar of Vaseline, Vicks VapoRub, a hairbrush. And, tucked in the back, half a roll of tangerine Life Savers, its inner wax paper and foil folded over to keep the hard candy fresh.

How long had it been there?

I unwrapped it, then popped a piece in my mouth. The sweet, sour flavor tweaked my salivary glands, making me pucker, and I bit down. Time had softened the candy, and it crumbled into pieces, which I spit out in a tissue, then threw away.

Time. The sweet and sour of life. But unlike the timeworn softened sweet, my heart had hardened, soured, over the years.

Are you even there, God?

The notion he wasn't, that God didn't exist, meant John Paul no longer existed. Instead, after his passing, he was simply gone, buried deep beneath the cold ground, with no hope of spring.

CHAPTER 8

AVA—FEBRUARY 1969

February 14, 1969

Dear Diary,

I'm mad—and I'm not supposed to be mad. It's Valentine's Day, but the only red I'm experiencing is the red-hot anger boiling inside me.

I finally worked up the nerve to ask Momma and Daddy about going to the beach for spring break. Not even for the entire week, only a weekend, and not by myself. Elaine too.

We had it all planned out. Last Saturday, when we met at Circle Drive-In, we talked for well over an hour—sort of mapped out a plan. With my savings and Elaine's babysitting money, we have plenty for lodging. Bus tickets aren't that expensive, and Myrtle Beach isn't so far.

Monday, after school, I called Greyhound and asked about the cost of a round-trip ticket—Greensboro to Myrtle. I have enough with plenty left over to pitch in for lodging, not to mention buying a new swimsuit and, perhaps, a new dress.

So Elaine and I made a promise—to ask our parents before week's end. Even pinky swore—we'd not get to Saturday without discussing the subject.

Honestly, I've been nervous about it all week, but tomorrow's Saturday, and I knew I had to just go ahead and do it already.

This morning, Daddy seemed in good spirits, sitting there in the sunny kitchen, reading the paper, sipping his coffee. Momma too—hair coiffed to perfection, all dolled up for a ladies' luncheon. She hummed as she scrambled eggs, and I thought her song choice, "This Girl Is a Woman Now" was a sign.

Sitting down at the breakfast table, I commented on how everyone seemed quite chipper, wishing them a happy Valentine's Day before presenting the card I'd purchased at DeHart's.

After Momma served the eggs, she sat down, and together they opened the card and read it. I'd signed the Valentine and included a PS—I know what you can get me for Valentine's Day.

Daddy's eyebrow rose, and Momma asked me what that might be.

I'd rehearsed what to say. "Spring break's comin' up and ...."

Momma folded her napkin, then laid it beside her plate. Daddy glanced from me to her, then back to me and raised his eyebrow again. (I hate it when he does that!)

I took a deep breath, then told them how Elaine and I had been saving, how we'd like to take a weekend trip to the beach. Take the bus and have a girls' getaway.

Then, without even so much as a moment's consideration, in unison, they said no.

Well, that red-hot anger rose in my face, and, to save pride, I gathered my things and left for school. Only in the safety of the car did I let my frustration out, and I slammed my fist on the dash—so hard, in fact, I think I broke my right index finger, which I discovered in typing class.

Not much of a happy Valentine's Day for me. No boyfriend to buy me chocolate and no spring-break trip either. I don't know how they can breathe with their heads so deep in the sand, but it certainly doesn't seem I'll be burying anything in sand this spring.

Can't they see I'm growing up—like the song, their girl's a woman now? (No, because—as I said—their heads are stuck in S.A.N.D!)

Blast! I did terrible on my typing test, and my finger still hurts.

Hoping tomorrow's better.

I CLOSED MY JOURNAL with a snap. Hot anger still boiled, and my face warmed. I stood before my bureau mirror and smirked at my reflection. "Look at you! You're as red as the Valentine you didn't get."

That wasn't entirely true. I'd received a pretty pink one from my parents, a crisp ten-dollar bill tucked inside, along with a small heart-shaped box of chocolates. Momma and Daddy loved me. Of this, I had no doubt.

I opened the floral journal again and flipped through the entries I'd written in the weeks since receiving it. Right then, I had the urge to fling the book across the room, as if doing so might relieve my frustration. Instead, I breathed deep and returned it to its hiding place.

I flopped down on my bed, and the words spoken more times than I could count, Momma's mantra for as long as I could remember, echoed.

It's because of my love, dear. Only and always love.

Why, then, did I feel as though my wings were fettered and I couldn't fly?

Not to my surprise, the walls offered no answer.

~

February 20, 1969

Dear Diary,

I'm about to bust out of here! I'll give Momma and Daddy one more chance to say yes, or who knows? I may be out of the family come this time next week!

Tomorrow's the day to ask again, but before I do, I've got to run by the bank and get a current statement, not to mention stop by Mr. Barnes's office to pick up the letter he wrote on my behalf. He said he'd write it on *official letterhead, stating he'd scheduled a mock interview and Career Opportunity Day with Smith's Print Shop in North Myrtle Beach for March 21. He'd explain how I was to earn extra credit for my participation, which would help my overall grade, which, by the way, happens to only be 79 percent.*

But even if they say no, I may find a way to bust out and go. I'm just plain tired of being held back. I want to fly!

Wish me luck!

A week having passed, I regained my courage and prepared to ask again. This time, I had a bit of leverage from one of my professors. Because I was a second-year student in Rockingham Community College's secretarial science program—part of a dual-enrollment program with Eden High I began my senior year—I, along with my fellow classmates, was encouraged to research opportunities for work-study. We were told any experience we gleaned prior to graduation would be beneficial for employment down the road.

My secretarial procedures professor, Mr. Barnes, took an entire class period, telling us about potential avenues and explaining the process of applying for these programs. He even mentioned offering extra credit to those who returned to school after spring break having done so. What he said stirred my curiosity, and I met with him one afternoon after class. I figured I had nothing to lose.

"Mr. Barnes, let's say one was to go somewhere over spring break. Myrtle Beach, for example. How might you suggest she do this research, even if it's only over a long weekend?"

"Why, Miss Ava, I happen to have family in Myrtle Beach. My cousin Barbara Smith and her husband, Ed—they run a small printing business." He leaned back in his chair and scratched his chin. "If you happen to visit, I could put you in contact with them.

They hire their own secretaries, often fresh out of school, usually keeping at least two at a time. You know, to manage their books, correspond with clients, and the like. Would you be interested in a mock interview? Never know. It could even lead to the real thing."

I smiled my enthusiasm. "Yes. Yes, I would, Mr. Barnes. Thank you."

But how to convince my parents, make them change their minds? A few days earlier, under my breath at dinner, I had let it be known that Elaine's mom and dad had said yes to spring break. That went unnoticed or ignored. How to go about it this time?

It irked me to no end that I worried so much. Why not come right out and ask them? The trip was more now, not only a time to get away for some fun in the sun with Elaine but an opportunity to further my future career.

The thought of being free for once, even if only for a long weekend, was the motivating factor, of course. I was nineteen. Maybe this research idea would be just the thing to get Momma and Daddy to agree, sending me soaring, and with their blessing.

I admit, I'd even considered going without their blessing. I had the funds, after all, not to mention a willful streak. And it wasn't the first time I'd dreamed of disobeying to do what I wanted.

Though it was still months away, I'd daydreamed of hitchhiking or catching a ride with friends, heading to upstate New York in August for what was rumored to be three days of peace and music. Billboards and fliers advertised these very words in Greensboro, though not in my small town. Eden and Bethel, New York, seemed as far apart as Earth and Mars. Still, news of this outdoor music festival found its way to our small North Carolina community.

I'd first learned of it from Rockingham's band director, who happened to be from Bethel. After sharing with his music students what he knew about Woodstock, the news spread like wildfire on RCC's campus. In the throes of the Vietnam War, during which

RCC had its fair share of protestors, three days of peace and music sounded heavenly—something even the most straightlaced teenager found tempting.

That evening after dinner, I asked Momma and Daddy if they'd join me in the living room. I'd invited Elaine to be with us too—for moral support, yes, but also because her parents had agreed to her going, offering another possibility, something she hadn't even told me about.

Elaine and I perched on the edge of the sofa, my parents facing us in their upholstered wingback chairs.

I cleared my throat. "Momma. Daddy. You've already said no, but I wanted to ask if you might reconsider the spring-break trip. And please, hear me out."

They stared at one another, and I fidgeted, tightened my ponytail.

Finally, Daddy spoke. "Okay. We're listening."

I grabbed Elaine's hand and squeezed. "We're wise enough to know we can't afford more than a couple days, but I have proof from the bank that I've saved enough money to pay for my part. Furthermore, I have a chance to further my education, possibly even my career." Would the Smith's Print Shop opportunity hinder my plan? "I mean, not everyone who graduates from RCC needs to work at Fieldcrest, right?" Fearing that the notion I might not want to linger in Eden after graduation would negatively affect my case, I turned from Momma to Daddy, then back to Momma. Since neither appeared concerned, I continued.

"Here's a letter from my professor." I handed Daddy the bank statement and an envelope addressed to Mr. and Mrs. Jim Jackson.

He eyed the bank information, his lips moving as he read the numbers. He then removed and unfolded the white paper and adjusted his glasses. He held the letter up for Momma to read as well, and both nodded as they took in Mr. Barnes's words.

After a moment, Dad spoke. "Ava, it does appear you're taking this quite seriously."

My head bobbed. "Yes, Daddy. I am. And Elaine is too. Elaine, tell them."

Elaine let go of my hand and smoothed the pleats of her plaid skirt before speaking. "Mr. and Mrs. Jackson, my parents agreed to my goin', and they even offered an idea. A possibility of sorts, though it's still uncertain. It'll depend on how ..." Elaine stopped for a moment. "Bobs is healin' up nice and doing well with his crutches. Mom said a little sun might do him some good, so they're talkin' about him goin' with us. At least, they're tryin' to encourage him to consider it. He's been a bit depressed ever since he came home."

I sucked in my breath. Bobby? Going with us? The notion had never crossed my mind.

"We know being back is a blessing, but it probably feels a bit like a curse as well, given all that happened." Momma's eyes glistened. "Honestly, I can't ..."

I knew. Momma was imagining JP, thinking of him all grown up. Wondering if he'd have chosen the military. Wondering what he'd look like as a grown man.

Daddy handed me the letter and bank statement. "Let your mother and me think about this overnight. Pray about it. We'll let you know tomorrow, Ava."

Momma cleared her throat before speaking. "Do try to understand, Ava. We're only thinking about you, your safety. It's because of love, dear. Only and always—"

"I know. I know. Love. I get it." I shrugged. "But Momma, sometimes—" I took a deep breath. "Sometimes love lets go."

Daddy's gaze was fixed on Momma, and he reached for her hand. Then he turned to me. "As we've said, give us until tomorrow."

I knew they loved me, but I hoped their love would be liberal enough, God's answer loud enough, to allow me to finally experience some freedom.

And the next morning, I wrote in my journal—

February 22, 1969

Dear Diary,
Well, Daddy and Momma said yes! Looks like this RCC Eagle is getting ready to take flight!

CHAPTER 9

AVA—FEBRUARY 1969

"Can you believe it, Elaine?" I washed down a bite of hamburger with a big gulp of vanilla milkshake. "I'm still pinchin' myself, to see if I'm dreamin'. I mean, they really said yes this mornin'"

Elaine nodded as she wiped her mouth, blotting her lips with her napkin, and leaving a piece of paper stuck to her upper lip. Making a face, she licked it off and spit. "Ew. I hate Circle's napkins. They're so thin. Like wipin' your mouth with toilet paper."

I giggled and pointed to my upper lip. "You've still got some right, right there."

This time, she used her finger to remove the remaining napkin, then flicked it on the ground. "Yuck." She slurped Tab from her red-and-white-striped straw, her gaze fixed on something behind me. "He's cute."

I glanced over my shoulder. At a table several yards away sat a group of teenage boys, though none were familiar. "Which one in particular?"

"The blond, curly-haired one in the striped velour pullover, Amsterdam on the front."

He was cute. "A tall drink of water, for sure." Turning back, I wagged my index finger inches from my friend's nose. "But Elaine McLeod, you shouldn't be lookin'. Not with a steady boyfriend and all."

"Now, Ava, no one said lookin's bad. Just no touchin' Anyhow, Glenn's not here." Elaine winked.

"True. Hey, how is ol' Glenn?"

"You know. Big man on campus. He seems pretty happy at Wake Forest. And don't you go thinkin' he never looks at pretty girls, 'cause I'm certain he does."

"I guess you're right. Checkin' out the merchandise isn't so bad." I wadded up the wax paper with only a small remnant of burger and several fries, then took another long slurp of milkshake. "Speakin' of good lookin', how's your hunk of a brother?"

"Bobs? You've always had a crush on him, haven't ya?" It was her turn to cluck. "Now, Ava Jackson. Spill the beans. How many times have you kissed Bobs? And don't forget, that cute, perky, freckled nose of yours will grow ten sizes if you lie."

My face warmed, the memory of that one-and-only kiss stirring warmth somewhere deep inside.

"Why, Ava, you're blushin'." Reaching into her cup, Elaine picked out several pieces of chipped ice, then flicked them in my direction. "Here, let me cool ya down."

I ducked. "All right. All right. So, I have a crush on Bobby. What else is new? It's not like you didn't know." Still blushing, I smoothed my hair, then tugged at my ponytail, tightening it. "But honestly, hope to die, I've only kissed him that once. Remember the time?"

"Yeah, that night in the pup tent, in my backyard."

I sighed. "Yep, that's the time."

"Blast him for scaring us. He busted in and almost made me pee my pants."

I snorted. "You mean you did pee your pants. Or, perhaps I should say, peed your petti-pants."

"Some things are between us. Anyway, we were readin' *Seventeen* magazine. And that book. What's it called?"

"*The Feminine Mystique.* I'd snuck it home from school after that hippy chick—What was her name?"

Elaine tittered. "Lyndsey the Love Child. Wasn't that what everyone called her? And how ironic, too."

"Yeah, that's her. Anyway, we had French together. Said it was the most enlightenin' book ever." I slurped up the last of my shake, then removed my straw to lick the remaining ice cream. "Somewhere around our sophomore year, she stopped wearing a bra. Ew!"

Elaine squeezed her eyes shut, scrunched her nose. "Ew's right. Got her a lot of attention though, didn't it? So much so, she wound up prego before her junior year."

"Whad'ya expect? With a name like Lyndsey Lovechild? Had to carry on the family tradition."

"Only, at least her parents ... you know. After she dropped out of school, rumor had it she went somewhere out West and ..." Elaine's pointer ran the width of her neck, and she rolled back her eyes, stuck out her tongue. "Put an end to her problem."

"Yeah, I heard that too. Probably in some back street alley, with a ..." A tinge of guilt regarding our assumptions interrupted the gossip. "This is morbid. Anyway, she's the one who told me to read *The Feminine Mystique.* And I'll never forget. The article was about predictin' the man you were gonna marry. I remember 'cause I already had mine."

Elaine laughed. "That's right. And Bobs got all cozy, sprawled his lanky self out like he was settlin' in for the night. Grabbed that magazine right out of your hands, but as soon as he read the cover

..." Elaine chortled again. "Funny, Ava. Sure did embarrass the poor guy."

"Ain't that the truth. I reckon Bobby wasn't keen on reading about a woman's bosom, was he? Turned five shades of red." I glanced down at my own chest, then at Elaine's. With a smirk, I said, "At least some of us have somethin' when it comes to bosom."

"Better not wish for it, 'cause it can cause all sorts of trouble, even with a bra." Elaine shifted in her seat. "Mom says I'll likely need a reduction before I'm thirty. Been wearin' a bandline C-cup since the fifth grade." She grimaced. "No, I'd much rather have your figure, Ava. So slender and petite."

"I guess we're never quite content with what we've got. But back to Bobby. When he read that title on the cover, he flung the magazine right back at me, like it was diseased. Did him in, I s'pose. Tucked tail and backed himself right outta there."

"But not before—"

"That's right. I kissed him. Fair and square, on the mouth." I puckered, lips full, then smacked the air. "Like that! And I told him, 'I have a prediction about who I'm gonna marry, Robert McLeod. Wanna hear?' Though I don't think he stayed long enough for the answer."

Elaine giggled. "Good times."

"The best. And ya know? He's been my only real crush, though I doubt he so much as thinks of me now."

"That's not true, Ava, though more in a sister sort of way."

"Yeah, Sarah Kramer's more his type. Said so, right there in his letter."

"In all fairness, they did date for a spell, but that was more than a year ago now. She went off to college. Joined a sorority and got all stuck-ity-up-ity. At least, that's the latest gossip."

"She never did care for me much. Probably knew I had a crush on Bobby. You know? Me, the threatenin' underclassman and all."

The sun slid behind a swirl of wispy clouds, casting a hazy glow in the late afternoon sky.

"Brr. I should've brought a thicker sweater." Elaine rubbed her arms, then blew on her hands as she brushed them together.

"Hey, before we go, can I ask you, whose idea was it to have Bobby come with us on spring break?" The thought of having him nearly all to myself for an entire weekend sent a shiver down my spine.

"I think it was Mom. She's been upset seeing how depressed he is. Ever since his return, since the accident, he barely says a word. Won't talk about what happened. Doesn't laugh. Rarely smiles." Elaine fixed her gaze on her lap. Without looking up, she continued. "It's been sad, Ava. I hardly recognize my brother."

I nodded, though I remained silent, thinking of what to say. "Maybe the sun and some time away will do him good. I hope so anyway."

Another beat of silence, and the pensive moment passed.

"Speakin' of spring break, we'll need to find a place to stay, and with Bobs possibly comin', we could split the cost three ways, right?"

"Not if he's getting his own room, which I'd assume he would." My eyes met Elaine's. "Right?" When tingles rose up my neck, then settled on my cheeks at the thought of being so close to Bobby, I knew. Momma and Daddy would never approve. "Elaine, he wouldn't stay in our room, would he?"

"It would cut on cost. More money for, you know, other things. Anyway, how will your parents know? We'd all be together, so it's not like ..." Elaine paused. "You know what I mean?"

I did. Still, the idea of outrightly deceiving Momma and Daddy didn't set well. "I'll ... I'll think on that. I guess I assumed—"

"That you'd have to slip out of our room and into his for some hanky-panky? Seems all of us bein' together's safer, if you ask me."

"True but ..." My insides stirred. "I just know Momma and Daddy wouldn't allow it. That is, if they knew."

The sun slipped further in the late afternoon sky, and Circle's neon sign buzzed to life, like an alarm.

"I reckon I should go."

Elaine glanced at her wristwatch. "Me too. I'll start looking into hotels. We're kinda last minute, so there may not be much available." She gathered her trash and stood. "And we need to go shoppin'. My bathin' suit from last summer won't do. And a new dress, maybe some new dancin' shoes."

"Yeah. Let's plan a day. I've got finals comin' up, and things are pretty stressful at school, but we'll find a time. Soon, I hope."

~

Later that evening, in the quiet of my room, I wrote:

February 22, 1969

Dear Diary,

Had a swell time with Elaine today at Circle Drive-In. We're both over the moon about our upcoming spring-break getaway. Still can hardly believe Momma and Daddy said yes. (Pinch! Pinch!)

Oh, and the idea of Bobby coming along. It's not set in stone, but just the thought. I have to admit, this is where I feel that tug in my heart, between what I believe to be right and know to be wrong.

It's a battle, that's for sure, because even though I know what I should and shouldn't do, I'm afraid, given freedom and my willful streak, not to mention, my huge crush on Bobby, I may not make good choices, which could get me in trouble. (Lyndsey Lovechild comes to mind.)

Honestly, even writing about it seems somehow wrong, but if I didn't put these thoughts down on paper —write my heart, as Momma says—I fear I'd bust.

Goodnight, dear Diary. Perhaps tomorrow I'll feel stronger.

CHAPTER 10

AVA—MARCH 1969

"MOMMA, I'M HOME."

I dropped my shopping bags on the parquet floor inside the front door, then hung my purse on the entry hook above the hall table. The smell of rosemary and thyme wafted from the kitchen, and I followed the mouthwatering aroma.

"Momma?"

Holding the phone receiver between her ear and shoulder, she stirred a bubbling pot with one hand and held an index finger to her lips, warning me to be quiet.

Walking up behind her, I leaned in, trying to decipher who she was talking to. Nudging me away with her hip, she narrowed her eyes and, once more, pressed a finger to her mouth.

I giggled as I removed the spoon from her hand and took over stirring the savory gravy. Stepping aside, Momma stretched the phone's cord as far as it would go, as if wanting to be out of earshot. Stopping by the bay window in the breakfast nook, her back to me, she nodded but said little. The conversation seemed serious.

Finally, she spoke. "Okay. Thank you, Doris. I'll talk to Jim and be back in touch …" A pause. "Yes, I understand …" And finally, "Okay, then. Goodbye."

"Doris McLeod?"

"Yes, she was calling to tell me a bit more about Bobby. How he's doing and so forth."

"And?"

"Seems they've gotten him to agree to go with you girls." Having returned the phone to its cradle on the wall, Momma slipped a potholder on her hand and opened the oven door, the fragrance of browning meat floating out into the kitchen.

Though my heart seemed to skip a beat with the news, I was nonchalant. "Oh, really? That's nice." Wanting to avoid further conversation about Bobby, I stopped stirring long enough to bend down near the open oven door and inhale. "Mmm, the aroma in here's heavenly."

"Roast, your father's favorite."

I stood again and resumed stirring, scraped the spoon along the bottom of the pan several times, then lifted it to my lips and blew before slurping the thick gravy. "Yum. This is perfect." I considered my words, fearing the tone of my voice might give me away. I tossed the spoon in the sink and replaced it with a fresh one. "Are we having mashed potatoes too?"

"Yes. I thought you might whip those up for us, sweets."

Having escaped further discussion about Bobby, at least for the moment, my breathing steadied, and with it, my voice. "Sure, Momma. I'd be happy to."

As I filled a pot and turned on the burner to bring water to a boil, Momma and I talked for a few minutes about our day—Elaine's and mine—in Greensboro. Always keen on fashion, Momma was curious about whether I'd found a dress.

"The perfect one. As soon as we can abandon dinner duty, I'll try it on and show you."

"Yes, please. What color?"

"The prettiest shade of lavender, with all these dainty, pearl-shaped buttons down the front."

"Oooh, sounds lovely." Momma retrieved several carrots from the refrigerator. After rinsing each one, she peeled them. I watched as each long, orange strip fell into the trash can. After a moment, she returned to the subject of Bobby. "What do you think about him going with you gals?"

Blast. A tinge of anxiety rose, flushing my face. How did Momma know I was thinking about that very thing? My honest thoughts on the matter I dared not share. At least, not if I wanted Bobby to accompany us.

"It certainly will make it safer, don't you think?" Guilt from the irony tugged at my conscience.

Momma considered her answer. "Yes, I believe so." A touch of hesitation rang in her response in the long pause that followed. "I guess my only concern ..." She hesitated again. "He's not the same since being back. Doris even said as much. Withdrawn. Depressed."

With a clang, she deposited the metal potato peeler in the sink, then laid the carrots on a bed of foil. Turning to face me, the lines etched on her forehead spoke her concern. "Ava, do you feel ... I don't know ... safe with him?"

The notion never crossed my mind. Safe? With Bobby? In truth, it was me—my intentions, what I imagined—that would have concerned Momma. That was, if she knew.

"Of course, Momma. It's Bobby we're talkin' about. He's no threat."

And with that, she said what she'd said so many times before. "You know, Ava. It's because of love, dear—"

"I know. I know. Only and always love."

Dinner over, Daddy scooted his chair away from the table and leaned back. "Now, that was a meal! And those potatoes, Ava. I do believe they were the best you've ever made. Did you add garlic?"

"Yes, and lots of butter, Daddy." I giggled. "Know why?"

His eyes narrowed, an eyebrow raised. "No. Why?"

"Because I'm tryin' to butter you up. Get it?"

"Ah-ha. So, there is an ulterior motive. I should've known."

Momma was curious too. "What is it, sweets?"

After Daddy's arrival home from a full day at Fletcher Ford, he and Momma had chatted, and I hadn't had a chance to show off my new dress. But as I'd peeled the final russet, I had known what I'd do.

"I'll start by excusin' myself to go and put on my new purchase. See what you both think."

"A new dress, I'm guessing."

"Yes. A lavender one. Ava told me, though I can't wait to see it too. Go! Get changed."

In less than five minutes, I returned. When I stepped into the dining room, Momma and Daddy were deep in conversation. I could decipher. It was about Bobby.

"That's what Doris said, for what it's worth."

"I suppose we need to take her word for it. Ava's got a good head on her shoulders, and Elaine will be there too. Of course, they'll have separate rooms."

A tug of guilt, and I cleared my throat.

"My, oh my." Daddy's eyes were tender, scanning me up and down, taking in his grown-up girl.

Momma agreed. "That is indeed the loveliest dress I think I've ever seen, Ava. Similar to a Nicole Lewis shirtdress but fancier. Feminine and so ... so modest."

It almost seemed she was surprised, like she expected something entirely different from her young-adult daughter preparing to take her first beach trip with a friend.

"Now, you two. See what good judgment I use. At least, when I have a mind to." I winked at them, then ran my hands over the front of the dress. "Aren't these buttons the sweetest touch?"

"Yes, they are, but please don't lose any, sweets." Momma's response sounded skeptical. "After all, a few missing in the middle would turn a modest dress into something entirely different."

I chortled. "You're funny, Momma." A change of subject was in order, so I dove right in and posed the question. "Any chance you might splurge and buy your wise-and-winsome daughter a pair of shoes? You know, to go with this lovely, modest frock? It could be an early Easter present."

The question out, silence filled the span of several seconds.

"Ava, I am very proud of you, regarding school and work. All of it. I believe I speak for us both." Daddy laid his hand on Momma's, a sign of solidarity. "I think your mother and I would be honored to buy you the perfect shoes, though you certainly don't want me helping you choose them. That's more up your mother's alley, isn't that right, Ellen?"

Momma nodded. "I believe another shopping spree's in order. Only, this time, it'll be you and me, Ava. How does that sound?"

My plan having worked, gratitude spilled out and over my face, and I hugged them both. "Thank you. Thank you so much. I'm very grateful, more than you'll ever know."

And with that, Daddy pulled his chair toward the table again, then reached up to tweak my nose. "And now, didn't I hear something about chocolate pudding for dessert?"

After helping clear the table, I escaped to my room for a few minutes.

I slipped out of my dress, then hung it inside the closet, nearest the front. The other packages from our shopping trip were still strewn about on my bed, and I carried them to the closet, then tossed them on the floor. I ran my hand under the sweaters on the shelf until I located the Keds box, then removed my journal and plopped down at my desk to write.

March 1, 1969

Dear Diary,
Today, Elaine and I had our much-anticipated shopping spree in downtown Greensboro. With so much to buy before our trip, which is only three weeks away, I've been pinching pennies, not to mention getting in as many hours as Ms. Cole will give me at the library.

I purchased my bus ticket yesterday, which broke the bank. (Not really, but I do still need to buy a new bathing suit—a two-piece, since Bobby's coming along.)

Elaine called a couple of days ago, having secured our rooms—yes, two!—at the Sand Dollar Bay Hotel and Resort, so that's taken care of. I have to admit, I breathed a sigh of relief when she told me Bobby would have his own room, a couple doors down. A little more money for me, but I think this is best.

Back to today and shopping. I had just enough to purchase the prettiest dress. Tried it on. Even twirled around the fitting room. Elaine exclaimed, "Ava, I can't take you anywhere!" (I think I embarrassed her.)

But I couldn't help it. It made me feel like a little girl. So giddy! So happy! Elaine loved it too, agreeing with me that the dainty buttons down its front were the perfect touch, making the dress unique.

Small and slightly iridescent, they're purple but with hints of pink, green, and blue in sunlight. The dress itself is modest, so Momma and Daddy approve. (And yet, with half a dozen at the top left undone, it reveals a little more of me, if you know what I mean. How will they ever know?)

And now, the only remaining necessity is that new bikini. Wish me luck!

I returned my journal and gazed again at the dress. It was lovely, the kind I imagined most young women dream about. Slightly formfitting, attractive puckers and darts, just below the knee, with capped sleeves and all those pretty, pearl-shaped buttons.

Downstairs once more, with only an hour or so of pale daylight remaining, I grabbed a cardigan from the hall tree and stepped outside. After an unseasonably warm day, the evening was cool. Birds sang their nighttime song, tucked in among the new buds of elms and oaks lining Glovenia. I turned right and walked past the houses of our neighbors, many I'd known most of my life, some who attended our church and others whose children were classmates.

Passing the third down from ours, I recalled the time I'd climbed a conifer in the Jenkinses' backyard. It was on a dare by their son Edward, who happened to be two years older but much less athletic.

"Bet ya won't."

"Bet I will. Watch me."

In thirty seconds flat, I was as high as I could get—lost in the dense arms of that vast Eastern White Pine. From my vantage point, I stared down at Edward, then spat, hitting him square on the forehead.

"Hey, that's nasty."

"It's what you get for bein' chicken."

And with that, Edward began to climb too, though he stopped after only ascending several yards. "Aw, climbin's not for me."

Now, that old pine was long gone, as were the Jenkins, the tree felled before grading the backyard. Later, an inground pool was installed by the new residents, the first of its kind for Glovenia. Edward's family had moved away.

Rumor had it, Mr. Jenkins had had an affair with one of the teachers from Eden High. Just like that, their family was gone, though I never learned where they landed.

I came to the end of the street and turned right onto Highland. From somewhere, the whir of a lawn mower and the chi-chi-chi of a sprinkler tickled my ears. The sky was a swirl of purple and orange, and the fragrance of hyacinth floated on a gentle breeze.

In a world of so much beauty, even in the simple things of early March, before the first clump of wisteria clung to its vine, what caused people like Mr. Jenkins to make poor choices, act in ways that hurt others? Destroyed families even?

And yet, I, too, was considering things I knew might have lasting consequences. Bad ones perhaps. Life-altering ones.

Where was God? Did he hear our prayers? Did he hear when Momma and Daddy, two of the most selfless, kind-hearted people I knew, prayed each time they discovered they were pregnant, fearful they'd lose yet another? Where was God then?

And yet, if one or more of those babies had lived, if God had answered their prayers, would JP ever have been born?

Would I?

The irony struck, and I sucked in my breath. I'd never asked Momma how many children she wanted. Three? Four?

Wanting to be home before dark, I turned around to head back and thought about those babies who'd been conceived and passed away without warning, each of the losses further fragmenting

Momma's tender heart. What would they look like? What might they have become?

Were they in heaven? I'd once thought this to be true, believing all life was sacred and loved by God. Had they been born, however, I'd likely not have come along.

With the dying day, streetlights flickered to life, one by one. I breathed deeply and detected the scent of fresh cut grass, the aroma of smoke from someone's chimney, and—what was it?

I inhaled again. It seemed a bit early, with spring not having officially arrived.

Passing a split-rail fence framing a portion of a Glovenia resident's flowerbed, fresh soil indicated new life would soon arrive to join that which was already in bloom.

Carolina Jasmine.

Made sense. After all, my questioning—which had quelled my otherwise cheerful spirit only a half hour earlier, the reminder that God and JP seemed far, far away—was what Carolina Jasmine symbolized.

Separation, plain and simple.

CHAPTER 11

AVA—MARCH 1969

"HEAVENS, ELAINE!" I stared at my reflection in my best friend's full-length mirror.

"Ava, what's wrong?"

"Where are my freckles? And those eyes—where'd those lashes come from?"

My best friend chuckled. "That's what a little makeup does, silly." She gave my hair a final tease with her comb, then sprayed White Rain to hold the hive in place. Stepping back, she nodded. "Yep. Perfect, if I do say so myself."

"Wow! You've come a long way in your cosmetology skills. But honestly, I'll never be able to do what you did. I mean, it's a miracle!" I patted the pile of hair, its height reaching high above my head. "And this, a different look than my typical ponytail. How ever will I replicate it?"

Again, Elaine chortled. "Don't forget, Ava. We'll be together at the beach, so I can help. And you? Promise to treat me to an occasional adult beverage, if you know what I mean. We'll call it an even trade."

I stepped closer to the mirror and, mouth gaping, batted my

eyes, then assessed my overall face. The mascara was thick, the makeup—foundation, powder, and creamy rouge—heavy. I pressed my naturally rosy lips together, then pursed them out.

Elaine giggled. "You look like a duck."

"Ducks don't have a bright fuchsia beak, do they?" I forced a smile. "I don't even look like ... like me."

"You'll get used to it. I promise." Elaine handed me a piece of paper. "Now, this is what you'll need to buy when you go shopping with your mom. I've written down each product, alphabetical by brand name. Pretty much all of it you can find at Revco or Woolworth's."

I scanned the list. "About how much?"

"Buy one of each. Makeup lasts a long—"

"No. I mean, about how much will this cost?"

"Right. Sorry." Elaine considered, lips moving as she calculated. "I'm guessin' you can get most everythin' for well under twenty dollars, and that includes nail polish, which I put right ..." She pointed to the paper. "Revlon. There. Didn't have time to do your nails today, but make sure you get some. I'm thinkin' the same shade of pink as ..." She giggled again. "Your beak."

"Haha." But rather than laughing, I sighed. Twenty dollars was more than I'd budgeted, and I still needed to find a new bathing suit. "Can I pay you my share of the hotel in about a week, after I've worked some? I'm scheduled for twenty hours before we leave, so I'll be good for it."

"Of course. No problem. Just make sure you get everythin' on this list. Hear me?"

Someone knocked on Elaine's bedroom door.

"Who's there?" Looking at me, she mouthed his name, her guess causing my insides to flip-flop.

"It's Bobs." His deep, husky voice hadn't changed.

"Come in, but be warned. Enter at your own risk."

At that moment, a surge of self-consciousness rushed over me, but where to hide? Wearing rolled-up jeans and a cream boatneck pullover, clothing-wise, I was underdressed compared to the fanfare of both my hair and face.

"Elaine. I ... I feel—"

But before I finished my sentence, the door opened, Bobby's frame filling the doorway.

"What'cha up to in here?" He smiled, sauntering inside.

"I was practicin' for my upcomin' cosmetology final. Ava said she'd be my guinea pig."

Bobby's gaze met mine, our first face-to-face interaction since—how long had it been? Since before he'd left for the navy the spring of 1967. Had it been that long? For a moment, neither of us spoke.

"Ava, sure seems you've grown up." He scanned my full length several times, a hint of a smile tugging the corners of his mouth, his lips partially hidden behind a thin mustache.

"Hello, Bobby." I grinned. "How are you? I mean, after ..." I reconsidered my words. "After all this time."

Elaine's brother avoided my line of questioning. Instead, he shifted a pile of clothes, then sat at the end of the bed.

"Man, women are messy."

"I warned you, Bobs."

Scanning the room, he chuckled. "Wowzers, sis. Are you packing for the beach? Or moving out?"

"Neither. But we were goin' through my closet and drawers, trying to figure out what I might still need."

My mind raced, searching for words. Why was I at a loss?

"I hear you're taggin' along for some fun in the sun." Moving closer to the bed, I detected English Leather. "And how'd we get so lucky?"

"You know. Wouldn't want two beautiful young women all alone at the beach, and, of all times, during spring break." Bobby laid back, hands behind his head. "Doing my duty, I s'pose."

"Big brother, we certainly wouldn't want to cramp your style, but that's mighty chivalrous of you."

With that, Bobby lifted his head, his gaze fixed on me. "It's my pleasure, ma'am." Sitting up, he ran a lean pointer finger and thumb along the brim of an invisible hat, then dipped his head, giving a quick wink in my direction. White gauze wound around the nubs of what had once been his middle and ring fingers, his pinky sticking out awkwardly. "And now, I'll leave you lovely ladies to your toilette."

With a formal wave of his bandaged hand, he stood, then bowed before stepping toward the door. One hand on the knob, he turned to look back, and our eyes met. Something in them stirred apprehension. Something I didn't recall from the past. What was it? Confidence? Anger? Though his words were those of a gentleman, something dark, ominous, threatened, not at all resembling the depressed, despairing person Elaine had described.

And again, Momma's echo from a week earlier—*Do you feel safe with him?*

Only, this time, her words sent a chill down my spine.

"Momma, wanna get lunch?"

We'd shopped all morning on Greensboro's Elm Street, purchasing last-minute items—a bright-yellow-and-orange-striped beach towel, as well as all the makeup from Elaine's list, at Woolworth's. Finally, in Kress's shoe department, we found the shoes to accompany my lavender dress, the slip-on beaded slippers a perfect match.

A quarter past noon, my stomach rumbled its displeasure.

"How about Kress's café?"

We rode the elevator, the cheerful attendant whistling "You Are My Sunshine."

At the fourth floor, the middle-aged man waited until we'd come to a full stop. The elevator jolted, causing me to take hold of Momma's arm, steadying myself.

First, the attendant opened the sliding gate and pulled back the heavier main door. Then, with a tip of his hat, he smiled, his white teeth a contrast to his dark, weathered skin.

Exiting, we thanked him in unison, and Momma handed him a quarter.

"Ain't that the nicest thing. Thank ye kindly."

As we strolled toward the café, the aroma of baked goods wafted through the corridor, its shiny oak walls waxed to a glisten. My mouth watered.

"Momma, do you recall much about those sit-ins that took place near here? In the diner at Woolworth's, I believe."

"Indeed, I do. Happened less than ten years ago, if I recall correctly. Created quite a fuss but eventually helped bring an end to segregation."

"Yeah. I remember. Everyone talked about it at school, even though I was only in the ... what? Third? Fourth grade? But still, I've never forgotten."

"I suppose those four men stirred courage in the hearts of others, and—"

"Made a difference." I leaned in and hugged Momma. "That's what you were gonna say, right?"

"Yes. For many, in fact. Even for that kindly elevator attendant. There'd have been a time a man of color wouldn't dare speak to a white woman. Isn't that sad? Not even to wish her a good day."

The attendant's merry tune echoed in my mind, and I hummed as we were seated at a table for two against the far wall, near a window. Sunlight spilled in, the divided panes reaching nearly as high as the vast ceiling. The warmth embraced me, and I removed my wool cardigan.

"Boy, shoppin' makes you hungry." I scanned the lunch menu,

determining what to order. "I think I'll get a grilled cheese and soup. Or maybe fries."

"How about instead we split onion rings and both get soup and sandwiches?"

"Sounds perfect. And Cokes."

After we placed our order, I leaned back in my chair and lifted my face toward the sun. "This is nice, Momma. Thank you."

"Why, of course, sweets. My pleasure." She unfolded her napkin, then draped it across her lap. As was typical for Momma, her strawberry-blond hair was coiffed to perfection, with several wisps framing her heart-shaped face.

Our gaze met across the table. "Momma, your eyes in the sunlight are the most glorious shade of blue. Cerulean, like the sky."

She laughed. "And yours, Ava, remind me of springtime, when everything comes to life." She paused. "That's what your name means. A derivative of Eve, the mother of life."

"Really? I don't think you've ever told me that." I stared at the beautiful woman before me, my own mother, the one who'd given me life. And John Paul too.

Dressed in a turquoise A-line wool skirt and matching turtleneck, she appeared more youthful than her forty-eight years. Though nearly thirty when I was born, she'd seemed youthful to me. How old had she been when she'd suffered her first miscarriage?

"Momma, I don't think I've ever asked you. How many children did you and Daddy want?"

She considered her answer, her eyes fixed on me, though they seemed to be looking beyond. "I don't guess I know exactly. We always hoped for a large family, but then ..." She stopped, pondering. "After our miscarriages, we sort of gave up. Didn't think children were God's plan for us. But then John Paul came along." Her eyes pooled.

I dug into my handbag and pulled out my hankie. Handing it to her, I cleared my throat. "Momma, how was it? I mean, to lose those babies and then ..." I took a long drink of my Coke, the icy bottle a cool relief in my hand. "What was it like to lose JP?"

Momma peered out the window, a ray of sunlight highlighting the right side of her face. "I suffered for some time, no doubt. Dark waves of anger and guilt, wondering if we'd done something different, perhaps he'd have lived. Were there signs we should've recognized? Something we could've done to prevent it?"

Momma dabbed her eyes, and I reached across the table to take her hand.

"I felt so guilty. I was his momma, after all. The one who should have protected him. Surely there was something I ... we could've done. But then, like that, he was gone, and with no clear reason. Deemed it crib death." She took a deep swallow of the cool beverage. "And you. I suppose you've suffered at times because of that fear and guilt." Her eyes met mine. "I'm sorry for that."

Tears blurred my vision. Though I'd never met my older brother, only knew him through photographs and memories shared through stories, I often sensed I lived in his shadow. Truth was, I battled resentment at times. His absence ironically filled our home with an elusive presence which, whether true or not, I blamed for Momma and Daddy's tight hold on me, when all I wanted was to wiggle free.

Rays of sunlight shining through the branches of an elm just beyond the window warmed our table, and dancing shadows shimmered across the tiled floor of the café. My heart overflowed with love for this woman who only wanted the best for me. To keep me safe.

"I'm sorry too, Momma. I can't imagine." I squeezed her hand, then released. "Hey, what did you tell me once, about a year after Chester died, and my little-girl heart was still broken over the loss of my best friend? He was only a dog, but I was so, so sad, and I'd asked you, 'When does the hurtin' stop?' Your response was somethin' I've never forgotten. 'It's grief. Just another word for love unendin'.' That's what you said."

Our conversation was interrupted by the arrival of our food, and after the server left, Momma said grace.

I dipped an onion ring in ketchup and took a bite, making sure the onion didn't separate from the crunchy outside. "Anyway, the same's true for you, isn't it? Your grief over the loss of JP? Yours—Daddy's too—is love unendin'. I get it now. And I better understand your protective nature with regard to me. It makes sense." I dunked a triangle of sandwich in the rich tomato soup, then concluded. "And Momma, I can't thank you enough for lovin' me the way you do but also for trustin' me, allowin' me this trip with Elaine. It means the world."

And with that, Momma said again what she'd said too many times to count. "It's because of love, Ava." She paused, but this time, I didn't interrupt. "Only and always love."

CHAPTER 12
AVA—MARCH 1969

March 9, 1969

Dear Diary,

Yesterday, Momma and I finished all my shopping. Besides finals and some much-needed library hours, I'm officially ready to take flight—soaring on the wings of a ... Greyhound bus. Ha! Still can't hardly believe it!

Friday, I spent a couple hours with Elaine as her hair and makeup guinea pig. Honestly, I hardly recognized myself, hair in a beehive. Freckles hidden under a pound of foundation.

But even more strange than how I looked—even more unfamiliar than my reflection—was Bobby. I don't know if I'll be able to articulate what I mean. Elaine's been describing him for weeks, making him out to be pitiful, depressed, vacant. Like the old Bobby was washed away somewhere in the South Pacific after the explosion.

What I witnessed was different. Overly confident, with an angry look in his eyes. Like he's searching for a fight, a way to release pent-up anger. He acted chivalrous enough, but that's just it. It seemed staged. And the way he stared at me made me uncomfortable.

I don't know. Perhaps I expected something—someone—else, especially after all Elaine said. Or, at the very least, the return of the humorous, somewhat aloof but goofy Bobby I once knew. After all this time, after not seeing him for nearly two years, I imagined I'd feel differently, but I was left unsettled. A sense of fear. Dread even.

On a bright note, Momma and I had a wonderful conversation at lunch yesterday, and I see her differently too, but in a good way.

Well, thanks for listening, faithful friend. I'm headed out the door with Daddy and Momma in a few minutes. Church and lunch after. Write more later.

~

"CAN YOU BELIEVE IT'S only a little over a week away?" I asked Elaine.

I'd escaped to the kitchen to sit cross-legged on the bay-window bench with my bowl of Jiffy Pop, the phone cord stretched far as it would allow. The sound of my parents' laughter brought a smile. How long had our Sunday evenings included *The Ed Sullivan Show*, sodas, and popcorn?

Cramming in a handful, I talked as I chewed. "And you'll love the bathin' suit we found yesterday. I'd planned on a two-piece, but this one's even cuter. At least, I think so."

In truth, after Friday's interaction with Bobby, I'd decided to go the more modest route. The way he'd looked at me stirred self-consciousness, but how to broach the topic with Elaine?

"I, for one, did buy a two-piece. A cute one, the color of buttercups."

"I'm sure you'll look splendid, especially with those matchin' yellow sunglasses. Don't forget to pack them."

"Already did. Been puttin' things in my suitcase as I think of them. Sure hopin' I don't forget anythin'."

I chewed another fistful, then washed the popcorn down with Fresca. "Elaine, can I ask you somethin'?"

"Shoot."

"It's about seein' Bobby on Friday."

"And?"

"After all you've told me, about how distant he's been, depressed and such, did that interaction surprise you?" After a moment, "Elaine?"

"Yeah, I'm thinkin' about my answer."

"I'm not tryin' to put you on the spot. I guess it just wasn't what I expected, that's all. Bobby seemed more forward than I remember him from two years ago, but in a strange sort of way."

"How so?"

"I don't know. Confident. Chivalrous. But somethin' about ..." I considered my words. "I guess it seemed almost like an act. Like he was tryin' too hard. And somethin' in his eyes that—"

"What are you sayin', Ava?" Elaine's tone held a defensive edge. "Did he look at you inappropriately? Is that what you're implyin'?"

"Never mind. I wasn't tryin' to stir anythin'. It's not that it was inappropriate, just ..." I paused. "I don't know. Let's drop it, okay?"

It was clear Elaine was ticked, and I fumbled to find a fresh topic. "Hey, tell me about the Sand Dollar Bay Hotel. And speakin' of, I'll have my share of the money to you this week. Thanks for givin' me time."

"No problem. I knew you'd come through." Elaine's tone indicated the tension had passed. "Regardin' the hotel, it's a resort, with a conference center and restaurant. I didn't think they'd have availability, seein' as we were so last minute, not to mention it's spring break. But they said a rather large group had canceled, so I reckon we got lucky."

"Wonderful. Thank you for takin' care of bookin' it. Is there a pool?"

"Yep. *And* an outdoor dance floor by the tiki bar. Best, the ocean's only yards beyond."

"Sounds heavenly. I can almost smell the salt water, feel the breeze off the Atlantic." I sighed. "I can't believe it! One more full week of classes, some exams, and work. It'll fly by!"

"Let the countdown begin!"

Later that evening alone in my room, I tried on my new swimsuit. Its pink bodice was covered with white polka-dots and had a padded cotton bra, giving the illusion of a fuller figure. The suit's pleated front was punctuated with four shiny black buttons, with a tie-behind strap for comfort. The bottom half was black, with boy-leg shorts and an adjustable black belt.

I stood before the full-length mirror and assessed my reflection, turning from one side to the other, fiddling with the straps to find where to tie them. I was no Elaine McLeod when it came to curves, but I was comfortable in my slender frame, appreciating the way my hips met my waist with a gentle slope.

After I'd taken off my suit and slipped on my terry robe, I added the swimsuit to my open suitcase. The Sears Cruisaire softside luggage had been a gift from Grandma and Grandpa

Schmidt for graduation, and I thought the Myrtle Beach trip the perfect time to break in its three matching pieces.

Graduation. How could it be a mere two months away? No sooner would I return from spring break than I'd be tying up loose ends. Graduation was at the end of May.

As I stood beside the bed organizing my new makeup and beauty products in the set's matching cosmetic case, soft fur brushed my leg.

"Hey, you." I bent down to scratch the orange-and-white tabby under his chin. "That's where you've been hidin'."

Aslan blinked at the sudden light, offered a pitiful meow, a few dust bunnies clinging to his whiskers, then he ducked back behind the dust ruffle.

I closed the case with a snap, then placed it by the larger piece of luggage, still open against my bedroom wall, and sat at my desk. Aslan took the opportunity to jump on my lap and kneaded the soft blue cloth.

"Makin' biscuits, eh?" I ran my hand down his spine, and he lifted his tail, purring his pleasure. "I haven't seen you much these last few days."

He rubbed the length of my hand as I extended my finger, marking his territory.

"I know. I know, sweet boy. I'm yours."

With that, he jumped to the carpeted floor with a gentle thud, then sauntered off to sniff my luggage.

"Don't even think about stowin' away. Too much water at the beach for you. Although, come to think of it, you might enjoy the sand, like one great big litter box."

Aslan jerked his head to one side, then licked his shoulder several times, as if the very thought of sand dirtied him. Satisfied, he sat up straight, curled his tail about himself, and closed his eyes.

"Yes, you are indeed handsome. Still, no matter how clean, I think they'd discourage you from visitin' the Sand Dollar Bay Hotel. You'll need to stay home. I'll only be gone a few days."

I turned again to my desk, then opened the front-facing drawer, but before taking out writing paper, I lifted the wooden lid of the tiny hideaway compartment the desk's creator had fashioned in the far-left corner. Feeling around, I touched a dried rose, fragile with age, then a smooth, cool stone. Finally, there—a small, pearl-like object.

I drew it out. The lavender button, an extra included with my new dress, shone in the dim lamplight. Attached to the manufacturer's tag, I'd clipped it off to save, just in case. Not to mention, it was so cute, the perfect keepsake to remember the gift of this upcoming trip.

And, if I ever lose one ...

I placed it back in the tiny chamber, then returned the lid and slid out a single sheet of pink stationery before closing the drawer. With pen in hand, I began.

Sunday, March 9, 1969

Dear Daddy and Momma,

I want to thank you for the gift of this trip with Elaine. For trusting me enough. It's hard, seeing your little girl grown up, especially given the fears, doubts, and insecurities that likely haunt you from time to time, causing you worry. I'm sorry for that. And I must say, I do sometimes sense JP's presence—like he's right here, with us still.

Forgive me for the times I've felt resentful, rebellious even. I'll admit, I'd even toyed with the idea of going against your wishes had you said no, finding a way to *stretch my wings and soar. But that's wrong, and I'd honestly never truly enjoy time away without your blessing. I believe that.*

Confessing this makes me feel better—lighter somehow. I can be willful at times, downright obstinate too, but I hope I mostly make you proud. Can you believe it? I'll have my two-year secretarial degree in less than three months. And then, who knows? The sky's the limit!

Anyway, I wanted to thank you again—for everything. Soon, I'll be breaking in those pretty dancing shoes, but I promise. I'll waltz my way right back to Eden … and to you.

Always your girl,
Ava

CHAPTER 13
AVA—MARCH 1969

I GATHERED MY THINGS as Mr. Barnes addressed the class.

"Attention, everyone. Prior to our departure and whatever break holds, I want to remind you: There's extra credit for anyone who returns with proof he or she took steps toward an interview, even a mock interview, or secured an apprenticeship."

My professor paused, his gaze scanning the lecture hall. "Take, for example, Miss Ava. She's meeting with relatives of mine in Myrtle Beach over break. They own and operate a small printing business and have agreed to hold a mock interview." His eyes met mine. "Miss Ava, I commend you for taking this step, and I assure you the experience will benefit you down the road." He cleared his throat before concluding. "And again, extra credit, which some of you need more than others."

With that, he dismissed class, but not without first asking me to linger a moment.

My teacher handed me a business card stapled to a piece of paper. "Ava, I've typed up directions to Smith's Printing in North Myrtle. You said you're staying at the Sand Dollar Bay Hotel, correct? They're only a fifteen-minute cab ride from there and are expecting you at nine o'clock sharp on Friday, March twenty-first. Please dress professionally, and be on time."

"Thank you, Mr. Barnes. I'm not sure that, without this mock interview, I'd have been permitted to go to Myrtle for spring break. It was the leverage I needed."

"Mr. and Mrs. Smith are fine folks, and I believe you'll enjoy meeting them and they you. Please give them my regards."

And with that, spring break officially began.

"Momma, do you have a suit I can borrow? We're nearly the same size."

In my excitement, I'd failed to ponder what to wear for my meeting at Smith's Printing. Though I'd considered applying to Spray Cotton Mill after graduation, that was still several months away, so I'd not yet needed to purchase a dress suit.

"My, sweets. I hadn't thought of that." She laid her book aside and motioned for me to follow her.

"What about that three-piece tweed ensemble you have, the one you wore for the auxiliary meetin' last month?"

"That's what I was thinking, though it may be a bit long."

"No worries. Wearin' heels will help."

Momma rummaged in her closet, then pulled out the royal-blue-and-teal-checked suit and removed it from its plastic cover. "Here. Try it on."

Moments later, I stepped out of her bathroom. "So? What do you think?"

She eyed me up and down, nodding. "It might work. Take off the jacket, please."

I did, then draped it across the bed. Momma stood behind me, then tugged the sleeveless black shell tighter.

"I believe I can take this in a bit."

"Do you think that's necessary?"

She moved to face me. "It's a little loose, don't you think? You are a tad less busty. It wouldn't take much. The skirt, however, is doable, and the jacket fits okay." Smiling, she nodded. "Yep, I think it'll work just fine."

"What about gloves? A purse?"

"No, not gloves this time of year. As for a purse, you can borrow my little blue one. Throw it in your suitcase."

It was settled. I'd take a piece of Momma—three pieces, in fact—with me.

March 18, 1969

Dear Diary,

Tomorrow's my last day to tie up loose ends. Our bus leaves at six o'clock Thursday morning, so we're leaving at four thirty to be in Greensboro by five thirty. Bobby agreed to drive us to the station, so that's taken care of. (Considered driving all the way to Myrtle, but since he's still healing, thought it better we take Greyhound.)

I'll try and finish up early tomorrow so I can spend plenty of time with Momma and Daddy, maybe even make a special meal for them.

For some reason, a Bible verse keeps running through my mind, one I memorized way back in Sunday school. Maybe I'm thinking of it especially now, given I'm soon to be at the beach, basking in sun and sand. From Psalm 139, beginning at verse 17: "How precious also are thy thoughts unto me, O God! how vast is the sum of them! If I should count them, they are more in number than the sand."

Is it true? And what does this mean exactly? I thought it meant that God's thoughts about me were precious and, if counted, would outnumber the grains of sand. But now, I'm not sure that's what it's saying. Isn't it saying God's thoughts are precious to me, no matter what God's particular thoughts might be?

And what are God's thoughts exactly? Yesterday at church, Pastor Wyatt reminded the congregation that God has a plan, a perfect plan. He used Jeremiah 29:11 as his text. "For I know the thoughts that I think toward you, saith the Lord, thoughts of peace, and not of evil, to give you an expected end."

Here, it seems God's thoughts are about us, so does that mean the thoughts he thinks about me are precious? That his thoughts of me outnumber the grains of sand? (I sort of feel I've gone full circle.)

I wish the Bible was easier to understand. Rereading my first entry back on January 13, I wrote—

If there's already a plan that God already knows—well, that bothers me. Confuses me. Makes me wonder why God can't keep me from sin.

And concerning my questioning—wondering why he allows bad things to happen when he clearly could stop them—I guess that's where my mistrust comes in. Do I believe: 1) God has a plan? 2) His plans are good? 3) He thinks of me more times than the number of grains of sand on the shore?

Why all this grappling?

Goodnight.

~

"Now that, Ava, was a wonderful meal." Daddy pushed back his chair, then placed his hands behind his head and closed his eyes with a smile. "You outdid yourself, dear. Thank you."

I had to admit. The fried chicken, macaroni and cheese, green beans, and rolls—with apple dump cake and homemade whipped cream for dessert—were divine.

Momma agreed. "That was stupendous, Ava. Wherever did you learn to cook like that?" She winked at me.

"I've learned from the best. Anyway, it's the least I could do, but how will you survive without me for the next several days?" I returned the wink.

After the dishes were cleared and the kitchen cleaned up, I phoned Elaine. "Are you ready?"

"I don't reckon I'll sleep a wink tonight, Ava. I've already loaded the Buick."

"How about Bobby? Does he seem excited?"

"To be honest, I haven't seen him much today. Left before I returned home from the hair salon, and that was this afternoon. Still isn't home."

"What do you think he's been up to all day?"

"Haven't a clue. Yesterday though—man, was he grouchy."

"Hopefully a little time away will be exactly what he needs. What we all need."

We hung up, and I finished packing. Besides the larger suitcase and my cosmetic case, I had the small tote. The trio, all tan with red-and-green trim and shiny brass hardware, matched perfectly, and after I zipped the carry-on closed, then placed it beside the other two bags on my bedroom floor, I stepped back to admire the lot.

Just then, Aslan appeared and wove figure eights around my legs, his soft fur tickling my shins. "Still considerin' an escape, boy?

I'm tellin' ya. You'll no sooner get to Myrtle than you'll wish you hadn't. You're fickle that way."

He meowed and, to prove my point, meandered from the room with several twitches of his tail.

It was almost nine o'clock, and I'd promised myself I'd attempt at least a couple hours of sleep. Like Elaine, however, I suspected it would be difficult, with the next day's adventure stirring.

Had I forgotten anything?

Ah, yes—one more thing. After slipping it from its hiding spot on my closet shelf, I slid my journal inside the tote, then zipped it again. Surely there'd be much to write about in the coming days, and I didn't want to forget a moment.

After I'd kissed Momma and Daddy goodnight, thanking them for the hundredth time, I climbed into bed. The clock read 9:45. In fewer than six hours, I'd be up.

As I rolled onto my side to turn off my bedside lamp, the door creaked, and light seeped in through the crack.

"Ava, you still awake?" Momma's voice was only a whisper.

"Yes, Momma."

She entered, then sat on the edge of my bed and stroked a strand of hair from my face. "Tomorrow's the big day."

I smiled. "Finally."

Momma chuckled. "You've been waiting for this moment a long, long time, haven't you, sweets?"

"A lifetime."

"It goes without saying, though I'll still say it again." She hesitated, swallowing a rise of emotion. "Be safe. Take care of you. Make wise choices." One more pause. "And remember, it's because of love."

And in unison, we said the words. "Only and always love."

CHAPTER 14

CASSIE—JUNE 2016

CASSIE'S FINGERS CEASED THEIR tap-tap-tapping, and she waited for Ava to say more. "Surely you're not stopping there, right when you're about to get on that Greyhound." She surprised herself with the abrupt comment, but she was so engrossed in the older woman's story, it seemed she'd only been transcribing a few minutes rather than several hours.

Ava said, "No, dear. That's it for now. After all, you still have quite a drive back to Greensboro."

Cassie didn't want to argue, though a forty-five-minute drive was hardly long. She was captivated by all Ava had shared. She knew some of the Stallingses's love story, but many of the details were new.

"There's more. Much, much more." Gideon's eyes were soft as he spoke, his gaze fixed on his wife. "You look tired, my love. Best I be getting you home too."

"Won't you at least stay until Brent returns?" Fiona glanced from her mom to her dad. "He shouldn't be late, and he'd love to see you both. Tell you about his golf game, Dad."

"We won't rush right out. Of course, we'll stay for a bit ..." Ava covered her mouth as she yawned. "Excuse me. I guess I am pretty pooped."

Cassie considered addressing the issue still on her mind. Would it be too much? "I'm not sure if Fi has told you about my recent diagnosis, my surgery, and the treatment."

Ava's furrowed brow spoke her concern. "Yes, dear. A little."

"Do you mind if I ask ... about your experience? Your battle with it. You had a mastectomy also, right? Underwent treatment, and ..." Cassie smiled. "Obviously, you beat it."

"Yes, that's true. And no, I don't mind." Ava relaxed again, leaning against the sofa cushions. "And exactly how many years ago has that been, Gideon?"

"Well now, it's 2016, and that was back ... in 1987? Am I recalling correctly? You were thirty-six, weren't you, my love?"

Ava's head turned side to side. "Funny how something seemingly so significant at one time blurs over the years. But yes, I think you're right." She directed her attention to Cassie. "Remind me. How old are you?"

Cassie smiled at Ava's inquiry. "Soon to be forty-seven. So almost ten years older."

Ava reached over and placed her cool hand on Cassie's. "And how are you, dear?" The tenderness in her voice, the genuine concern in her gaze brought tears to Cassie's eyes.

"Overall, I'm doing well. The scariest part is thinking I might not be around for my family, especially the kids." She focused on a loose thread on the hem of her T-shirt, fiddling with it before giving it a yank. She held it up for Ava to see. "Like this. Sometimes that's how I feel, like I'm hanging on by a thread. Does that make sense?"

"Yes. Yes, it does. And concerns for one's family—that is the hardest, most frightening part."

"May I ask, was it your left or your right?"

"My left, dear. The lump just inside my left armpit."

Cassie nodded, her questions regarding this shared experience put to rest.

"Amazing technology now, though." Cassie's hand landed on a lock of hair draped across her shoulder. "This, for example. Not losing much of it. Have you ever read about the cold cap?"

"What is it?"

"Something new. Actually, Grant learned about it, then shared with me. It's just that—a cold cap I wear during chemo. Not particularly a pleasant experience but doable. I mean, so far I've survived." She chuckled. "And it's working. Haven't lost much."

"My, oh my. The miracle of science." Ava shook her head.

They talked a bit longer, Cassie asking several more questions. When the clock in the foyer chimed three, she closed her laptop and slipped it inside her canvas bag.

"We need to do this again, and soon." Fiona stood and began gathering mugs, then arranged them on the silver tray. "Some things can perhaps be discussed via emails and phone calls, but does everyone agree that coming together another time is a good idea?"

Ava and Gideon nodded. Cassie believed talking face-to-face was best. There were questions and details she could certainly call about or email the Stallingses about, but another meeting was what she preferred.

"I'm all for that. Grant and I don't have much planned for the summer. A few camping trips with the kids and possibly a silver-anniversary trip for us."

"How lovely, dear." Ava patted Cassie's hand. "Twenty-five years is quite a feat in this day and age, and don't forget. Myrtle Beach is very nice." She gave Cassie's hand a final pat, followed by a tight squeeze.

"Let's say you've piqued my curiosity, but, shame on you. You haven't told me any details about your trip to Myrtle. Talk about building suspense."

"Good writers leave cliffhangers." Ava giggled.

How young she seemed, like a girl.

As if reading Cassie's mind, Gideon stepped toward his wife and helped her to her feet. "That's my girl. My beautiful, beautiful Ava."

The drive from Eden to Greensboro seemed like a timeslip, and Cassie, exhausted from the day, anticipated she'd step from the quiet of her Camry to the chaos of home. And before she got all the way through the front door—

"We got a puppy!" Her usually quiet youngest son smiled broadly, though his twin scowled.

"Hey, I thaid I would tell Momma."

Cassie stared at her son, then her daughter before turning her attention to Grant, who approached the trio, hands thrown in the air.

"What can I say?"

Cassie gaped for a moment. "You mean it's true?"

"I sort of made the mistake of taking the kids to an adopt-a-pet day in the parking lot of Tractor Supply, and—"

"You didn't."

"Oh yeth he did. A cute, little, fluffy—"

"Low-shedding, mixed breed who needed a forever home." Grant fought to redeem himself. "And we love adoption, right, Cass?"

Chester and Charlotte scampered from the room, their plans for the puppy spilling out in giggles as they closed the door to their playroom.

"Honey, we said we'd discuss this before going ahead and—"

"I know. I know. But Cassie, wait till you see him."

Just then, right on cue, their oldest daughter rounded the

corner, a tiny bundle in her arms. "Hi, Momma." It was a ball of fluff. "Meet Merle."

"Merle? That's his name?"

"Yep. After Merle Haggard. In his honor, really. When Daddy read on his paperwork that he was born on April sixth, he said we should name him after Merle Haggard."

Cassie raised an eyebrow. "I'm confused."

"Merle Haggard was born on April sixth and passed away on his seventieth birthday, this year, in fact. And ... he's my favorite country musician sing—"

"Ah-ha, I get it now. This puppy's a Merle in memoriam, is he? I see how it goes. I leave for the day, and you all conspire—"

"I suppose you won't be leaving us very often then, will you?" Grant puckered and smacked his lips, sending his wife an imaginary kiss. "Lannie, let Momma hold Merle."

Cassie took the small creature from her daughter and held him close. Leaning down, she inhaled as Merle snuggled in and yawned. "Ah. Puppy breath. I love that smell."

And as if that was the final bit of approval needed, the little dog yapped two times and closed his eyes.

"Merle, welcome to the family. You're as mongrel as my mixed emotions."

Later that evening, alone in the bathroom, Cassie opened her journal in Notes.

Saturday, June 25, 2016—

Well, today was more than I ever could have anticipated. Here I thought I was going to Fi's to hear about Ava and Gideon, to hear much of their story through her eyes, or at least as she knows it. I expected to leave with notes, then text and email Ava to get more info. But surprise of all surprises, Ava and Gideon were there too, and though we spent hours together, we only got through part of Ava's story. And that dirty dog, she left me hanging. (She must be a writer! Ha!) And speaking of dogs, guess what I came home to. A dog named Merle. Merle! Grant owes me big time. He knows I'm a sucker for animals, but I can't help but wonder if his timing's the best. I still have several chemo treatments to go, we have an upcoming family trip ... Oh, I don't know. Mostly, I can't wait for my next trip to Eden to hear more of Ava and Gideon's love story. I wonder if Ava ever wanted to kill her husband. Now that's a thought ... Until tomorrow.

CHAPTER 15

CASSIE—JUNE 2016

"MERLE? REALLY?" Cassie released her husband's hand as they strolled down James Street, past their neighbors' homes. The cheerful birdsongs contrasted with her irritability. With a humph, she crossed her arms.

"I told you. Merle Haggard's my favorite country singer." Grant reached over and poked at Cassie's ribs in an affectionate, playful manner as they walked, the setting sun casting a pink and orange glow across the sky, wisps of purple mixed with evening clouds.

"No, not his name. I'm talking about you getting a dog. And without even discussing it with me." She pushed his hand away.

Stopping, Grant turned to face her. "Hon, we've discussed it plenty of times. You know that."

"I know. But we decided it wasn't a good time. Dogs are wonderful, we both agree on that, but what about when we travel? The added expense of vet bills, food, and—"

"Cassie, stop." Grant pulled her close, then placed a finger over her lips. "Let's say I made an executive decision. I didn't imply to the kids you weren't on board. On the contrary, I implied we both determined it was the right time."

"I'm pretty sure my response earlier spoiled that. At least for Lannie. She's so perceptive anyway. Nothing slips by her."

Grant nodded. "Ain't that the truth! No one else has to know. As far as the others are concerned, we were on the same page. Are on the same page, I should say. Because we are, aren't we? You said so yourself—welcome to the family, Merle. Isn't that what you said?"

This time Cassie allowed her husband to tickle her. "Yes. But I still don't know what we'll do when we go on vacation."

"Merle's small, and he seemed to enjoy the car. I bet he'll love camping. Anyway, we'll figure things out as we go along." Grant kissed the top of Cassie's head. "You have to admit—he's cute, isn't he?"

Cassie smiled. "The cutest. And that puppy smell, I love it."

The matter settled, the two walked on. The happy sounds of neighbors enjoying a backyard barbeque, crickets, and tree frogs chirping, filled the quiet space between husband and wife.

Finally, Grant broke the silence. "Tell me about your day."

Cassie considered where to begin. "It was beautiful, for sure—though the Stallingses's surprise arrival threw me for a loop."

"They were there too?"

"Yes. Fi invited them. After the shock wore off, it was …" What was it? "Nice, and I learned so much. Took copious notes. The time flew, but so did my fingers." With a chuckle, Cassie raised her hands and wiggled them. "Boy, these babies can dance."

Grant, too, chortled. "I'll bet." He took ahold of her hand. "Have I ever told you I'm proud of you?"

"A time or two." Cassie squeezed. "You know, we've been holding hands for more than a quarter of a century. What are we gonna do for our twenty-fifth anniversary?"

"Hmm. Let's think on that. Right now, I want to hear more

about your day. I'm sure you're tired, so not too much until you've processed. A thumbnail sketch perhaps."

"Ava did most of the talking. We'll get together again soon. Until then, I'll organize my notes."

What specifics of the day to share with Grant?

"For one thing, Ava certainly left me with a cliffhanger." Cassie described much of what Ava had shared, right up to leaving on the Greyhound bus. "But I have a hunch, this is where the story gets good." She sighed. "Only now, I have to wait."

"Patience. It's a virtue." Grant jabbed lightly at Cassie's ribs.

"Yeah, well—it's difficult when there's a love twist." She smirked. "Hey, how much do you know about the USS *Enterprise*?"

"There was an explosion off the coast of Pearl Harbor, if I'm remembering correctly. January fourteenth, 1969."

"How do you hold all that information?"

Grant tapped his head. "Just that good."

"You're rotten, you know that?" Cassie giggled. "Anyway, seems something happened. Something perhaps difficult for her to talk about, even now, all these years later."

"Like?"

"I'm not sure. Tension was building, that's for sure. Between Ava and Bobby. She'd always had a crush on him, but then something happened." Ava described for Grant what had created Ava's discomfort, how Bobby had been injured, the questions that remained.

Grant's silence indicated he was thinking. Cassie knew. Being a physician, her husband was familiar with the human body, how it functioned, even if he wasn't a urologist or, in the case of the spinal cord, an orthopedic spine surgeon or neurologist.

"Yes. It is possible for someone to have an injury to the spine and therefore lose sexual function, yet still be able to walk and get on quite normally. The body—such a mystery."

"So remains Ava's story." Cassie sighed. "The woman's sixty-six but seems like a girl. Beautiful inside and out. We talked a bit about her experience with ... you know. She had a mastectomy too, though she was only thirty-six. I got to ask her some questions about all that right before I left, which was good."

Again, Grant stopped walking. Turning Cassie to face him, he drew her close. "Like I said, I'm proud of you—for all sorts of reasons." Lifting her chin, he kissed her.

The warmth of his mouth pressing against hers was familiar, comforting. "I love you. Thank you for all your support. For everything." Pulling back, she smiled. "And now, what about we plan our silver-anniversary trip. Go somewhere soon. I've heard it from a reliable source, Myrtle Beach is quite nice." Cassie chuckled. "Correction. Almost heard about it."

Millie Kate's screams rang in her parents' bedroom, awaking Cassie with a start, and she bolted upright.

"No. Not again." She threw back the covers and stood, but the room spun. Every ounce of her screamed for rest, the exhaustion from her latest chemo treatment hitting her particularly hard. Mustering all the strength she could, Cassie plodded to her daughter's bedroom.

"It's all right, love. Momma's here."

The toddler stood in her bed. Damp with sweat, her arms were outstretched. "Hol' me."

Cassie prayed her arms wouldn't give out as she lifted her little girl, then gently guided Millie Kate's head to rest on her shoulder. "There, there, lambie. Let's sit down. Momma will sing." Situated in the glider, Cassie gently swiped Millie Kate's damp hair to one side. "You're safe. Nothing to fear."

Jesus, tender Shepherd hear me,
Bless my little Lamb tonight ...

Cassie sang the song her own mother had sung to her and her brother when they were children. Millie Kate's breathing slowed, and she twitched several times, her tense muscles relaxing in her mother's embrace.

As Cassie finished the last stanza, something soft brushed her bare foot. She peered down to discover Merle. He whined, his dark eyes blinking up at her in the dim glow of Millie Kate's Peter Rabbit nightlight.

"Hey, how'd you get out of your crate? You truly are like the real Merle Haggard, with your prison breaks and all." She scratched the puppy's head. "Worried, are ya? It's okay. Millie had a bad dream."

Merle turned several times, then flopped down on the rug at Cassie's feet and smacked his lips. Cassie stood and stepped over him, careful not to trip as she returned her daughter to her crib. Leaning down, she whispered, "Jesus bless you, lambie."

She walked toward the bedroom door, and Merle curled up under Millie Kate's crib. "A guardian dog, eh?" Cassie smiled. "Okay. You can sleep here, but only tonight."

Back in her own bed, Cassie fluffed the pillow.

"Everything okay?" Grant yawned.

"Another bad dream. Sorry it woke you."

"No worries. I've got a little later start tomorrow." Grant reached out, then let his hand rest on Cassie's abdomen.

"Wanna have lunch tomorrow?" Cassie yawned, snuggling in closer to Grant.

"Got another lunch date with Peter. He invited me, which is good. But you could join us. I'm sure he wouldn't mind."

Peter Gentry, a physician's assistant at Orchard View had, like Grant, grown disillusioned by some of the other physicians' and

PAs' practices, especially regarding women's reproductive health. Though Grant never hid his beliefs concerning this, had even left Orchard View because of this disparity, others were less open about theirs. Some Grant believed to be conservative when it came to abortion in particular but justified their medical decisions based on their patients' desires, rather than following their personal convictions.

In the year since Grant's leaving, Peter had expressed, though in secret, an interest in understanding more about Dr. Billings's specific reasons for feeling the way he did. Why he'd left the practice he'd been part of, even having been named senior partner, after a decade of service with Orchard View.

Cassie had to admit—she'd been a bit upset when Grant had told her he was leaving. Worried for their future. For his reputation. She recalled questioning his decision, asking him if staying was the better choice. At least then he could stand up for what he believed.

Cassie checked the time, then yawned again. "It's almost three o'clock. I hate for you to be tired tomorrow. I'll think about joining you." She wondered if she should continue the conversation, given the hour. "But Grant, can I ask you something real quick?"

"Shoot."

"It was weird, but several weeks ago I was having coffee with Jane Freemont. You know, from the paper."

"Yes, of course. Her husband's an attorney, right?"

"I was sharing a bit about the kids, especially Millie Kate. She'd had a bad dream that day too, which woke her from her nap, and she'd snuggled with Jane at the dining table." Cassie smiled in the dark. "Then, right before she had to leave, Jane asked me a strange question. Something about whether you still kept up with anyone from Orchard View."

"And?"

"Funny. Before I could answer, the clock chimed, and she skirted out. Said we'd talk more next time."

Grant rolled over to face Cassie. "Hypothetically, how would you have answered?"

"That's just it. I'm not sure. I mean, there's nothing wrong with you remaining friends with someone you once worked with, right? Someone who shadowed you for a bit. Respected you. You tell me. What should I say if it comes up again?"

No answer. Had he drifted to sleep?

"Grant?"

"I'm thinking." Another pause as Grant took several slow, deep breaths. "I'm not doing anything wrong. I'm ... I'm trying to protect Peter, at least until he's ready to ..." He hesitated. "I guess, until he's ready to decide what he wants to do, based on what he believes."

A beat of silence fell between husband and wife. Soon, Grant's rhythmic inhale-exhale indicated he was asleep. But as Cassie lay there in the dark, his words echoed in her ears.

Based on what he believes.

And in the dark, Cassie imagined Ava as a young woman poring over her journal, and her words echoed. *What are God's thoughts exactly? And are his thoughts—those which outnumber the grains of sand on the seashore—about us? No. Are his thoughts ... us?*

CHAPTER 16

CASSIE—JUNE 2016

Cassie folded her legs under the picnic table, then took Grant's hand and squeezed.

"Thank you both for meeting me today." Peter Gentry peeled back the foil wrapper, and a plume of steam rose from the fresh burrito. "I asked Jenn to join us, but she had a prior commitment. Said next time for sure." He blew before taking a bite, then with a strand of cheese dangling from his bottom lip, spoke with his mouth full. "Man, I love José's taco truck."

Grant flicked a dollop of sour cream from his fork and shook Texas Pete onto a mound of shredded chicken, rice, and beans, then passed the hot sauce to Cassie. "Yeah, they've done well here in this pocket of Greensboro. Perfect lunch spot, that's for sure." He folded his hands. "Mind if I pray?"

Pete set his fork beside his paper bowl. "Not at all." He bowed his head.

"Father, thank you for this day. Thank you for this food. Bless the hands that prepared it, and bless us as we do your will today. Thank you for allowing Cassie to join us, and bless our conversation. May you be glorified. Amen."

Pete and Cassie echoed Grant's *amen* before digging in. The warmth of the sun and the gentle breeze stirred a sigh, and Cassie smiled. "I love summer."

"Speaking of which, any summer plans for you and your family, Pete?" Grant took a bite of beans.

"Camping in July. That's about it. Jenn's parents will visit from Montana. Oh, and the kids have camp later this month." Pete dunked a corn chip in salsa. "Anything new with your practice? Still liking it?" He popped the chip into his mouth.

"Honestly, even after a year, it's taking some getting used to. A different hospital system and management. The clinical staff's nice enough though."

"I, for one, will always miss you at Orchard View. Doesn't seem the same." Pete's fist pounded the wooden tabletop.

"I appreciate that, but we both know I had to go. Like I've said, if I hadn't, I'd have likely been thrown a without-cause termination and given ninety days to be out anyway. It was for the best."

"Probably true. Some are still pretty hot about it."

"There are always a few. Some like to complain, and others have professed personal convictions. If they're willing to practice medicine that contradicts what they say they believe, that's their prerogative. I couldn't anymore; that's all."

Peter took a swig of sweet tea. "If you don't mind me asking, what were the policies when you first signed your contract all those years ago? Did they change, or was it your beliefs?"

Grant's pause spoke volumes, and Cassie knew. Her husband was considering how to respond.

"I guess my convictions. Where I once didn't think much about certain aspects of a woman's reproductive health, how it meshed with my worldview, over time I began to have stronger convictions about ..." Would he come right out and say it? But before he could—

"About abortion, right?"

Grant's eyes lifted to meet Pete's. "Yeah, and now I do. Have strong convictions, that is. There will be the exceptions, like in the case of a woman's health. An ectopic pregnancy, for example. A woman will almost certainly die if her pregnancy isn't terminated. Her baby too. I'm not hard-nosed, but I do have some firm beliefs." Grant dipped a chip in guacamole. "Unfortunately, health providers don't always provide expectant mothers with all their options. You know, so they're fully informed. I couldn't continue keeping information from my patients that might help them make the best decision for them and—"

"Their unborn babies?"

Grant's gaze met Pete's, and he nodded. "Exactly. Let's just say, some information is kept undercover, so to speak." He squeezed Cassie's thigh under the table. "And don't even get me started with regard to some of the financial benefits." One more pause. "Personally, there's so much about this I believe to be wrong, but the bottom line? I couldn't be responsible for what I consider the taking of another human life."

"And you believe that? That the unborn, even in the first trimester, is human life?"

Grant nodded, taking Cassie's hand. "Yes. Yes, I do."

"So, let's say it is, or, at the very least, the potential for human life. Isn't the mother's life more valuable, given her age? Her standing in society? I don't know. Isn't she more valuable simply because she's ... alive?"

Grant wadded up the foil from his tortilla wraps. "Pete, it comes down to where one believes life begins. For me, based on my personal faith today, I think life begins at conception."

"But again, why?"

"First, science supports it. With the intricacies of cell formation, DNA, the human genome, and double helix. But also, I think the Bible supports this. Verses speak to such, though I'd be hard-pressed to come up with one, especially on a full stomach." Grant laughed.

Come on. Surely Grant could recall one supportive verse.

As if an answer to Cassie's silent plea, Grant said, "Psalm 139, for example. The writer—David, I think—says something about God forming all our inward parts, covering us in our mother's womb. He goes on to say we're fearfully and wonderfully made, that God sees our unformed substance and that we're written about in God's book even before we live a single day. Something like that. I'll find the specific passage and text it to you."

Grant dipped another chip, then popped it into his mouth and talked with his mouth full. "And that, Peter, is why I couldn't stay. Couldn't encourage women to use abortive measures of birth control, like the IUD, for example. Wouldn't tell her abortion is better than carrying to full term, even when ..." He paused. "I guess what I'm trying to say is, there are other options. And yes, I know. Who am I, being a man and all?" Grant smiled at Cassie. "But I'm married to a wonderful woman who was—"

What was her husband about to share?

Again, Grant hesitated. "Let's just say, this topic's important to me. To us. Not to mention, besides our two biological kids, we have three beautiful adopted children, each whose birth mother, despite personal, painful circumstances, chose life rather than—"

"Death." Peter's answer was like an exclamation point on his dilemma, as if he'd finally come to a conclusion.

"How did you feel about our lunch date?" Cassie peeled potatoes at the kitchen sink, a trickle of water running to rinse them. "Sure was a beautiful day. And man, José's was rockin'. Good thing we arrived when we did. That line was out to the street by the time we sat down."

Grant sat with Ben, helping him with fractions. "Now, try to reduce six-twelfths. Take your time." With the scrape of his chair, he pushed away from the dining table and came to stand beside Cassie. "In answer to your question, I thought it was good. Very good, in fact. Didn't you?"

"I did. I felt a little nervous a few times, on your behalf."

Taking the peeler from her hand, Grant picked up a potato. "Me too, especially when I couldn't recall a verse to support what I was trying to say." He chuckled. "I'd have blamed José's, all that good food and all. Thankfully, Psalm 139 came to mind and in the nick of time." He finished one russet, then rinsed it off and began with another.

"That should do it." Cassie counted the potatoes. "One per person and one for the pot." She snickered. "Funny, the things we remember from our parents. Mom taught me that way back when. Anyway, go on."

Grant faced her, kitchen utensil in one hand, a partially skinless potato in the other. "The best part, even better than the weather and the food, was Peter's response when I explained why I believe life begins at conception. Don't you agree?"

"I do. I was praying silently you'd say what was on your heart. You know, speak truth in love."

Grant nodded. "Sharing how I believe felt great. And pulling those words from Psalm 139 out of the blue like that ..." Grant chortled. "I guess God answered your prayers, Cass. Still, I hope I didn't butcher the passage too badly, which reminds me. I need to text him the full context." Setting the potato peeler down, Grant wiped his hands on his jeans, then removed his phone from his back pocket. "Siri, remind me at eight p.m. to text Peter."

"I thought it was interesting you chose that particular passage to share. That's the same one Ava talked about the other day. Something she was grappling with as a teenager, regarding God's thoughts for us or ..." What was it? "Said his thoughts toward us are precious, outnumbering the grains of sand, or something like that."

"Yeah, that's what Psalm 139 seventeen through eighteen says. You know it too, don't you?"

"For the most part. But I'd forgotten the part about the sand. That verse stood out to Ava, which was ironic because she was preparing to leave for Myrtle Beach. But I believe she even said as much. That this specific verse was probably running around in her mind because she was getting ready for her spring break beach trip. Anyway, I need to reread that psalm too. Glad God gave it at the right time today." Cassie squeezed Grant's forearm. "And thanks for finishing the potatoes."

"Of course. Happy to help." He tossed the metal tool into the sink and turned off the water. "And know what? When you excused yourself to run to the restroom, Pete told me he'd never heard it explained that way, regarding abortion, both the scientific and biblical support for being pro-life. Seemed to make an impact."

Cassie wondered what she'd missed. "Did you tell him that I—"

"No. Maybe there'll be another opportunity to share some of that, but I didn't today." Turning back to the table, Grant stood behind Ben's chair. "How we doing, son?"

Ben held up his paper. "Is this right?"

"One-half. Sure is. Good job!"

At that moment, Merle came into the kitchen, sat at Cassie's feet, and whined.

"See there, Cass. Merle's telling you, 'That husband of yours isn't such a bad guy after all. Even helps in the kitchen.'"

"No fraction pun intended, but I never said my other half was so bad, now did I?" After reaching down, Cassie patted the dog's head. "And don't you forget it, you mongrel pooch."

~

Before bed, Grant read the text he'd sent to Peter aloud. "How does that sound?"

"Perfect." Cassie yawned.

"I also shared a direct link to Psalm 139 and included a YouTube video with this psalm put to music. It's a time-lapse short film, showing the development of a fetus from conception to full-term baby boy. Peter knows the development of human life from a physician's perspective, but put these images to music—it's powerful." Grant ran a finger over his iPhone screen, then hit the side button, and his screen went black. "Thanks for coming with me. Maybe we should try and do something with Pete and Jenn as couples this summer."

"I'd like that." And she meant it. The conversation that day had cracked open a window, and too much time shouldn't pass.

There was still work to be done.

CHAPTER 17

CASSIE—JULY 2016

Cassie turned off the faucet, having filled a bright-blue water pitcher adorned with red poppies. Holding it up, she said, "To match the Spider-Man plates. What do you think, Bennett?"

Her son groaned. "But when can we start the party?" Ben scuffed his feet across the kitchen floor, then plunked onto a chair with a humph.

"Soon, son. Be patient."

The doorbell rang.

"I bet it's Grandma and Grandpa." Lannie sprinted from where she'd been arranging birthday favors on the dining table.

Cassie wiped her damp hands on her jeans and followed, though her pace was slower than her daughter's. By the time she reached the foyer, the three were chatting as Lannie helped her grandma remove her jacket.

"Hello there. So glad you both could come."

"Yes, lovey. Sorry we're late, but your father's appointment was longer than we'd expected." Cassie's mom held open her arms, inviting Cassie to step into her embrace. "Come, child." She took her face in her hands, then kissed her on each cheek. "Wonderful to see you. Today, has it been good or bad? I hope good."

"Fair to middling, I suppose. Just this doggone fatigue."

"I guess it could be worse. You still have nice color to your cheeks."

Cassie's dad wrapped his arms around the trio, then squeezed. "My girls. Three out of five anyway." Before letting go, he, too, kissed Cassie.

"Love you, Daddy. Love you, Mom. Thank you for coming to celebrate." Cassie led the way to the kitchen, Lannie holding her grandparents' hands.

"Lookie here. What a lovely group. And there's the birthday boy." Cassie's dad placed his broad hands over Ben's shoulders and squeezed. "How is it possible you're already a decade old?"

Ben peered around and smiled up at his grandparents. "Hey, Grandpa. Hi, Grandma."

"We were explaining to the ten-year-old that sometimes patience is necessary. Isn't that right, son?" Grant shook his father-in-law's hand. "Good to see you, Dad." Turning to Cassie's mom, Grant hugged her. "And you Mom. You're looking lovely, as always."

"Thank you. So wonderful to see you." Cassie's mom's hands were clasped in front of her, her smile expressing her delight. "You know how much I love togetherness. Nothing better in the world." Setting a brightly wrapped package on the table, she patted her grandson's head. "This is for you, Ben. It's from Uncle William."

"And Tante Ann too?" Ben looked excited. It wasn't often he received birthday presents from Cassie's brother and his wife.

"No. This one's specifically from Uncle William." Ben's grandfather flicked the bill of his baseball cap. "Though I'm sure Tante Ann wrapped it." He chuckled, then patted his wife's arm. "Isn't that right, Patricia dear?"

Everyone gathered in the kitchen, and Cassie handed a lighter to Grant. "Okay. It's time."

Her husband lit the candles, then hummed a starting note. Everyone sang—"Happy birthday, dear Ben. Happy birthday, to you—"

Cassie leaned her head against Millie Kate's, the toddler balanced in the crook of her hip. "Blow your horn, love. Wish your brother a happy tenth birthday before he makes a wish and blows out the candles."

Chester, Charlotte, and Lannie blew theirs as well, all the while jumping up and down in glorious pandemonium.

Ben inhaled deeply, then released, extinguishing all but one candle with a single breath.

"Did ya 'member to make a with?" Charlotte clasped her hands. "Huh? Did ya?"

Once more, Ben blew. This time the last flicker disappeared, and the birthday boy smiled. "Yes, Char. I made a wish."

"What wath it?"

"None of your business, sis."

Cassie sat her toddler in her booster chair, then turned to Grant. "Can you cut and serve, please? I'm exhausted." She fell into the chair next to Ben's. Managing to make his favorite chocolate cake from scratch was nothing short of a miracle. "Phew. I need to rest a moment."

Grant picked up the knife. "Looks delicious. It was a labor of love, I know." He sliced it, then placed sizable hunks of cake on Spider-Man plates and added a scoop of Breyers vanilla bean to each.

"Son, does ten feel any different?" Cassie tousled the top of his head.

"Nah. Not yet anyway, but maybe if I get my wish."

"Is that so?" Grant leaned in toward Ben, cake-covered fork in one hand. "Do tell."

"If I tell, it won't come true."

"That's not quite accurate. After all, there are exceptions to the rule." Grant turned his fork over as it reached his mouth. "I believe"—he talked with his mouth full, his tongue covered with thick frosting—"somewhere it says birthday boys can tell their parents. It's in the fine print."

"Mom, is that true?" Ben's crescent-moon eyes spoke skepticism. "Or is Daddy teasing?"

Cassie giggled. "No, son. I believe he's telling the truth."

Ben turned to stare at his dad, who leaned in, then pointed to his ear. "Whisper it right in here. Your secret's safe with me, Bennett Jonah Billings."

Adequately convinced, he cupped his hand around his mouth and whispered into his dad's ear. When he'd finished, Grant's face broke out in a smile, though Cassie noticed his eyes glistened.

"Now that's some birthday wish, son!" Grant patted his son on the back. "One day."

"Aw, no fair. Tell uth too." Charlotte rose and stood between Grant and Ben. "Tell me, pleath!"

"Now, Char, you know they can't. Some things must remain a secret, at least for the time being." Cassie kissed the top of her daughter's dark, curly head.

"Char, tell me. Have those two front teeth come in?" Cassie's mom pointed to her own mouth. "Open up."

From across the table, Charlotte smiled broadly. "Not yet, Grandma. But thoon, I hope. I can't eat pitha very well, and itth my favorite."

"Yes, dear. We'll celebrate with a big pepperoni-and-cheese as soon as you can. How's that for a deal?"

"Me too?" Chester also smiled, revealing two permanent front teeth, though he was still missing a lower incisor. "I love pizza."

"Of course, dear. We'd never leave you out."

"How's William?" Grant scraped his plate, then licked a bite of cake from his fork. "Nice of him to send a gift."

"He's fine. They all are. Been busy with the new house. Moved in ... when was it?" Cassie's mom nudged her husband.

"Memorial Day weekend, I believe. Yes, May twenty-eighth. I've never forgotten because it was three weeks and a day after my procedure."

Cassie asked, "Speaking of, how was your appointment today, other than long? Any news?"

"Nope. Doc said I'm doing well. Heart's tickin' like a champ."

"That's great!"

"Yes indeed. Ever since the stent, he's been good to go." Cassie's mom leaned in to rest her head against her husband. "Michael Bennet's a keeper, that's for sure."

"Likewise, sweetheart." He kissed his wife's head. "Now look what I've done. You've got a bit of chocolate in your crown of glory."

With that, Millie Kate, her hands covered with frosting, tapped the top of her own head. "Messy Millie."

Laughter erupted around the table.

Grant's phone rang, interrupting the festivities.

"Hello ... Hey there ... Yes, that's correct. Ten as of today ... He's right here if you'd like to speak to him ... okay. Good to talk to you. Hello to Ann and the kids."

Grant extended his phone toward Ben. "It's for you. Uncle William."

Ben took his father's phone. "Hi ... Thank you ... Yes, she did. It's sitting right here. Want me to open it?"

Cassie leaned in. "You could FaceTime if you like."

"Mom said we could FaceTime. One minute." Ben fiddled with the phone, and William's face appeared on the screen. Ben held the phone up for everyone to see.

"Hey, bro." Cassie waved.

"Now that's what I call a birthday party." Cassie's older brother smiled and waved back. "Hey, everyone."

"Can I open it now?" Ben's face beamed with anticipation. "Please. Can I?"

Grant laughed, then took his phone. "Let me hold it while you open the gift." He rose and stood behind Ben's chair. "Go ahead, son."

Ben tore the wrapping paper, revealing a cardboard box. With another rip, the paper fell away.

Ben held the box for William to see. "Wow! Baseball cards. Were they yours?"

Cassie's brother nodded. "Sure were, and now they're yours. Someone gave them to me a long time ago, and I'm giving them to you."

"I love them! Thank you so much." Ben set the box on the table and thumbed through the cards, pulling one out at a time.

"Hunter told me to tell you hello. He'd love to come see you play. Is your season still going?"

"A few more games. I'll have Mom or Dad text you the schedule."

"Sounds good. Glad you like the gift." William waved. "Enjoy your party, everyone. Thanks for letting me barge in."

Everyone returned his wave, then said goodbye.

"That's a thoughtful gift." Cassie leaned over to get a good look at the box. "Vintage too."

Ben picked out a card and held it up. "Neato! Jim Gentile of the Baltimore Orioles. Do you think they're worth a lot?"

"Definitely, son. But you're not thinking of selling them, are you?"

"Nah. Just thought it might be fun to know what they're worth. Haiden's grandpa gave him a bunch of baseball cards once, and he had them ... what's the word?"

"Appraised, son. The word's appraised."

"Yeah, that. Anyway, he found out they're worth lots of money."

"They're definitely a treasure, and how nice of Uncle William to part with them." Cassie stuffed the wrapping paper in a trash bag.

"Guess Hunter didn't want the cards since he's not into baseball like I am." Ben held up another one, read the front, then turned it over to read the backside. "This is the best gift!" He slipped it back in its cardboard box. "And don't forget to text Uncle William my summer schedule. I want Hunter to come watch me play."

Later, after her parents had left and the kids were in bed, Grant and Cassie rocked on the front porch. Crickets chirped, and an Eastern whip-poor-will serenaded them from somewhere in the neighborhood.

"Phew. That was a day." Cassie took Grant's hand. "Glad you were able to get off early and so thankful Dad's cardiology appointment went well, though that office seems to run a bit late most of the time."

"Yes, it's poor management. They're going through a transition with new office staff." Grant leaned back and sighed. "I'm pooped, so I'm sure you are. Thankfully, we can sleep in tomorrow. That is, unless someone decides to have a baby at two in the morning. Then everyone will sleep in except me."

Cassie tittered. "Let's hope that doesn't happen." She sighed. "About Ben's wish."

Grant squeezed her hand. "Honey, we tell each other everything, but this time, I think this needs to remain a surprise. Even for you. What was it you said to Char? Some things must remain a secret, at least for the time being, or something like that." He met her gaze. "Will you trust me?"

Cassie let out a humph. "Very well. I trust you."

She rocked for several minutes, enjoying the evening sounds, the indigo sky. The suburban neighborhood their family had called home for the last five years was a welcome relief compared to the hustle and bustle of Greensboro's downtown.

"Those baseball cards, what a wonderful gift. Do you recall who gave them to William?" Grant tucked his hands behind his head, rocking with his eyes closed.

"No, I don't, but I can't remember a time when William didn't love baseball. Played first base, I think. Good ol' Billy!"

"And you, always the cheerleader."

"Excuse me. I was a tumbler, thank you very much. Not to mention, I was on the dance team—a very different thing than a cheerleader." Cassie stopped rocking and stood. "Haven't forgotten our school's fight song either." She hummed the tune, shaking her hips and throwing her arms, concluding with what was intended to be a high kick. "Ouch! I think I threw out my back with that one." She fell into her rocking chair. "Man, I'm not as limber as I once was."

"Come here." Grant held out his hand, helping Cassie back to her feet. He pulled her onto his lap. "I love you. You know that, right?"

Drawing her knees to her chest, she leaned against Grant as he rocked. "Yes, I know."

He brushed her hair aside and kissed the nape of her neck, then buried his face between her shoulder blades. His voice was soft, filled with emotion. "You weren't up for an anniversary getaway, with the side effects and all. But we'll still go somewhere, I promise."

With her eyes closed, Cassie inhaled deeply, then spoke in the exhale. "Yes. Yes, we will." Shifting to face him, she placed her forehead against his. “We still have another eleven months before our next anniversary. Maybe after chemo’s over.” Turning back, her head rested against his shoulder, and a long sigh spoke her weariness. “I’m so tired.”

“Hold on, my love. Hold ...” Grant’s voice broke, and he swallowed. “Hold on.”

Cassie only mustered two words. “I will.”

But was that true? Did she believe this trial was working something good within her?

A gentle breeze brushed her face and, breathing in, Cassie recognized the fragrance. Gardenia, like a whisper, offering hope. Affirmation.

Refinement. That was what this season was. She offered a silent prayer. *What are you up to, God?*

CHAPTER 18

CASSIE—AUGUST 2016

July 31, 2016

Dear Cassie,

Oh, where has summer gone? I honestly don't know. Please accept my apologies for only now getting back with you to set a new date for visiting. There's still so much for Mom and Dad to share, and they're looking forward to it. Besides, Mom left you with quite a cliffhanger, if I remember correctly.

Dad gave us a little scare the early part of the month. They called it a ministroke, but there haven't been any long-term side effects that we're aware of. It took him a spell to get back to himself. Was tired most of July.

I should have written to tell you, and I'm sorry I didn't. Anyway, all is well now, and our big family trip to Yellowstone is over. You'll be happy to know I survived in a camper for ten days with three children, a large goldendoodle, and an extroverted husband, who would admit he's seen enough geysers and mud pots for a lifetime. (Can you ever see too many?)

Anyway, did you get that silver-anniversary getaway with Grant? If so, where did you go?

Texting would be easier and faster, but I love receiving snail mail, and—given we're still sort of meandering in the late 1960s with Mom and Dad—writing seems more appropriate. (But ... feel free to text me back instead!)

Hope to talk soon.

Thoughtfully,
Fi

Cassie folded the letter, then slipped it into its envelope. Fiona had written only five days before, but now August and the beginning of a new school year was upon them.

Where had time gone?

Having a definitive date felt—urgent? No, but pressing just the same. She didn't want to wait.

Cassie checked her desk calendar. Besides several appointments for the kids and one for her, not to mention the start of school on the sixteenth, she was free. Furthermore, she'd been feeling better, more energetic than she had in early July.

She retrieved her cell phone from her purse, then texted several options during the last two weeks of August. Though it seemed far away, it would roll around quickly.

In only moments, her phone pinged. *How about Thursday, August 18?*

Yes. Perfect. 10 a.m.?

Another ping. *Yep. See you then!*

Cassie jotted it on the calendar. It was a date, an opportunity to continue Ava and Gideon's love story. She felt a flutter. Not so much nervousness but excitement, like continuing a good book or a movie whose ending—

"Mom, where are you?" Lannie's voice came from the foyer, and the front door slammed.

"In here, Lan. At my desk."

Lannie appeared at Cassie's desk within seconds, her face was rosy, and beads of perspiration dotted her upper lip. She leaned down to give her mom a hug. "Phew! It's hot out there."

"Did you get the lawn finished?"

"Yep. Just need to pick up some sticks from the willow tree. Guess we had strong winds the other night."

It was true. Two nights earlier they'd lost power in the middle of the night. Millie Kate had awoken frightened and confused in total darkness, discovering her white noise machine and nightlight weren't on. It took an hour, with the dim glow from a camping lantern, to finally coax her back to sleep.

"Thank you for doing that. We'll be leaving in about twenty minutes to get Ben from baseball practice. Hunter's coming today too."

"Who's bringing him? Tante Ann or Uncle William?"

"I think his mom. Will probably have Courtney with her too."

"Yay! Maybe she'll let me take her out back to play."

Cassie's older brother and his wife married later in life, though they'd known one another as kids. Ann had been married previously, a marriage that sadly ended in divorce. With her first husband, she had a daughter. Courtney, though nearly eighteen, had Down Syndrome and was like a little girl, only bigger. Lannie loved her.

"I'm not entirely sure who all's coming."

"Is Hunter staying for the weekend?"

"Yep. Ben has a game tomorrow and another Saturday morning, so we'll probably meet halfway on Sunday afternoon to get him home. With school starting, this is our last opportunity to have him."

"I'm glad Ben gets to spend some time with Hunter. Hopefully they won't be too squirrely though. You know how boys can be!" Lannie rolled her eyes. "Okay, I'm gonna finish up outside. Be ready in fifteen."

~

Laughter from the backyard floated in through an open window while Cassie and Ann sat at the kitchen table. Cassie pressed her fingers to her temple and massaged.

"Headache?" Ann's eyes held concern.

"Yeah. Been nursing one most of the day. I'm just so tired, and it never seems there's a moment's peace in the summer, though I do enjoy having the kids home." Cassie sensed rising guilt. "It's this blasted treatment, the lingering unknowns. I'm ... I'm sorry."

"Hey, no apologies. Hear me?" Ann patted Cassie's free hand. "And thanks for inviting Hunter." She chuckled. "Adding fuel to the fire though, don't you think?"

"Actually, gives the kids—Ben especially—more to do. And Hunter's always good with the little ones. He's never any trouble." Cassie managed a smile. "And Courtney too? So glad you brought her along."

"Are you kidding? When she found out, you should've seen her face. She sure loves Lannie, and she's so good with Courtney. So many girls Lannie's age are, I don't know, intimidated, I guess. You know, by someone with special needs."

Cassie nodded. "Lannie's definitely unique, in lots of ways." She sipped her sweet tea. "Speaking of unique, the gift William gave Ben for his birthday was so special. Didn't Hunter want those baseball cards?"

"No. He could care less. Watching Ben play, that's the only thing about baseball Hunter cares about. And that's because he loves his cousin and knows he'll get snacks at the concession stand." Ann laughed. "William asked him, but he told him to go ahead and give them to Ben."

"I've been on him to write a thank-you note for weeks, but you know. It's easier to bathe a cat." It was Cassie's turn to chuckle. "Hey, you wouldn't recall who gave the baseball cards to William, would you? Ben said he mentioned they were a gift, from long ago. Did he tell you who? Because I can't recall. Only know he's had them for ages."

Ann shook her head. "Haven't a clue."

More girlish giggles from outside, followed by a string of whoops and hollers from the boys. "Wonder what that's all about." Cassie reached to lift the curtain, then peeked behind. "Seems Ben and Hunter are demonstrating how to properly pass a football, only ... it's Lannie's shoe they're—"

The shoe hit the window with a thud, and Cassie's chair screeched as she pushed it back, then stood. But before she could reach the door, Ben and Hunter burst through, panting like puppies, sweating like piglets.

"Boys?" Cassie's hands met her hips.

"Aw, we were just playing football, Mom. And the shoe barely hit the screen." Ben swiped his forehead with the back of his hand. "Can we have a soda? It's blazing out there." He didn't wait for his mom's answer before rummaging through the fridge, sending bottles clinking.

"I believe there's some SunnyD in there, maybe some Sprite too. Help yourselves."

"Gee, thanks, Aunt Cassie. And thanks for letting me come to stay. Your backyard's the bomb!"

After Ben and Hunter raced outside again, cold beverages in hand, Cassie said, "Boys. Wouldn't it be nice to have that kind of energy?"

Ann reached across the table. "So tell me. How are the treatments going?"

Another sigh. "You want the honest answer or the everything's-gonna-be-all-right response?" Cassie leaned her head on her hand, her elbow resting heavy on the oak tabletop.

"Cass, this is me."

"Yeah, I know, I know." Cassie's gaze met her sister-in-law's. "I'm tired. And scared. And, did I mention, tired?" She half sighed again, half laughed. "But hey, what's the saying? What doesn't kill you makes you stronger. I'm banking on it."

The crinkles around Ann's eyes spoke her sympathy. "Hang on. You're almost there, right?"

Cassie nodded, then took another long swallow of iced tea. "Did I tell you I've been commissioned to write a book?"

"Really?" Ann's eyes reflected her curiosity.

"Fiona Davis asked me. Remember her?"

"I think we met once, at a cookout ages ago."

"I'd forgotten that. After Lannie's baby dedication, I think. Anyway, I'm in the process of writing her parents'—Ava and Gideon's—love story."

"How wonderful!"

"I've already met with them once, and we're meeting again in a couple weeks."

"I love a good memoir. You're perfect for this job, Cass."

"This one's pretty special, given—"

"Momma, Char won't share Merle." Chester was in tears. "And she's had him all afternoon. Dressed him up in clothes." He sniffed. "He looks so sad."

"Miserable Merle." Cassie chortled. "Poor thing. Tell Char to come here. Have her bring Merle too."

Her son darted from the kitchen. "Char. Mom wants you."

Cassie snickered. "Chester Conrad sounds a little too happy about that."

"Do they get along most of the time?"

"They're best friends. Still, they have their squabbles."

"That's the only thing about Courtney and Hunter. The age difference, her disabilities ... they're not close."

Right then, Charlotte entered, holding a bonnet-clad pup, the brim of the hat flopping over, covering Merle's eyes.

"Char, what are you doing?" Cassie held out her hands, and her daughter placed the dog in her grasp.

"I was pretending he was Laura Ingalls—you know, like in *Little House in the Big Woods.*"

Cassie snickered. "I'm glad you're enjoying the book, but that bonnet's tight. Let's loosen it a bit." Cassie untied it, and the puppy shook his head, sending the headpiece to the floor. "Oh, well. How about we give your brother a turn now, okay?"

Charlotte pouted. "Do I have to?"

"It's Chester's turn with Merle. Why don't you go play with Lannie and Courtney in the backyard. Show them how you've mastered a cartwheel."

"A cartwheel? Now, this is something I need to see." Ann tousled the top of Charlotte's head.

"You can watch from the window, Tante Ann." With that, Charlotte skipped out the back door.

Things quieted down, and Ann asked, "When do you suppose the book will be finished?"

"By fall 2019, for their fiftieth wedding anniversary. At least, that's what I'm hoping."

"And do you have a publisher?"

"We're thinking of self-publishing, with so many good companies out there, software and such. Grant says he'll help me."

"How exciting! I'll definitely want to read it, so keep me posted."

The kitchen clock chirped four o'clock, the song of a robin filling the space.

"I love that. Where did you get it?"

"It was a Mother's Day gift a year or two ago. The kids know how much I love birds."

"Birds and flowers—that's what I've known about you, Cassie. You're an expert in both."

"I love all things symbolic, I suppose. And both hold so much meaning, at least for me." Cassie fingered the flowers adorning the table, a gift from Grant several days earlier. She'd arranged them in a bright-yellow Fiestaware pitcher. "Take these Gerber daisies. Cheerfulness, that's what they stand for."

"And the robin? Does it have a special meaning?"

"Indeed. It stands for renewal. Hope."

"If that isn't perfect!" Ann drank the last of her tea, then dabbed her mouth with a blue-and-white-checked cloth napkin. "You amaze me, Cassie. With all you're going through, you still find time to do for others. Write a book even. You remind us to live with eyes open, to look for beauty all around, even in the simplest of things. Like flowers and birds." Ann smiled warmly at her sister-in-law. "In my daddy's native Dutch, he taught me to say *Verwondering*, meaning you live with wonder. Wonder at each mirakel."

Heat rose on Cassie's face as she considered how to respond. "Thank you? No, wait. Let me say that again—Thank you. Really. Your words mean a lot."

And once more, the kids' laughing tickled their ears.

"You're welcome, Cassie. I mean it. I truly do." Ann rose and pushed in her chair. "I best be going. With traffic, it might take me more than four hours to get back to Greenville. Thank you again for having Hunter. Meet up on Sunday?"

Cassie also rose, then hugged Ann. "Yes, indeed." Squeezing harder, she kissed Ann on her cheek. "I'm thankful to have you as a sister. Wish we had more time, that we lived closer."

"Me too. Gezellig. It's Dutch for togetherness." Ann also gave Cassie a quick peck.

"Tell that big brother of mine hello." After taking a daisy from the pitcher, Cassie handed it to Ann. "Here. A little cheerfulness for the ride home."

And right on cue, Courtney burst through the back door. Her smile lit up the room. "Momma, this the best day ever!"

But Cassie wondered. Could she continue discovering joy in simple things, especially in the dark throes of chemotherapy, with the ultimate outcome still unknown? After removing another daisy from the pitcher, she held it up, twirling it between her index finger and thumb. Joy in the coming days? She hoped so.

CHAPTER 19

CASSIE—AUGUST 2016

Cassie shifted on the hard examining table. All she wanted was to get out of there with her hope intact. The pink paper gown crunched under her weight, though, at less than a hundred pounds, a stiff breeze would threaten to topple her. "I'm so looking forward to having an appetite again and putting on some weight." She squeezed Grant's hand. "Dr. Spencer, what can you tell me?"

The gynecologist perched on a chrome stool and scanned Cassie's records on the computer screen, reading silently. Her face shifted to accommodate her reading glasses.

"Let me see here." She uh-hummed several times but gave no indication whether what she read was positive or negative. "Okay. So ..." She turned from the computer, then spun to face her impatient patient. "Let's say ..." She cleared her throat.

Was she stalling?

"Let's just say—and this is only my opinion—from your oncology notes, one more round of chemotherapy and then, my guess? You'll be ringing that bell."

Grant whooped, then embraced Cassie, kissed her, and hugged her again. "Babe, you've got this beat!"

Tears welled. She was almost finished with treatment, and—despite weighing fewer pounds and having a little less hair—she'd succeeded in walking through this difficult season without losing what mattered most.

Hope.

With you, I can do all things—

The silent prayer was interrupted. "That does not mean we're out of the woods entirely. You'll need to return to Dr. Evers every few months the first year for check-ups and scans. There's always a chance—"

"Dr. Spencer. As a physician myself, I'm aware. Cassie's aware. But ..." Grant, too, choked on rising emotion. "We're gonna celebrate this victory, if you don't mind."

She smiled, then turned to Cassie. "My apologies. Right now, congratulations are in order." She leaned toward her patient. "May I?"

Cassie nodded, then extended her arms to receive a hug from the physician. "Thank you. Thank you for everything."

"You've been a joy, and I'm thankful to have been part of your care during this journey. Even though I'm not the specialist here, since our first visit back in April when I referred you to Dr. Evers, I've held you close in thought." She placed a hand on Cassie's shoulder, then leaned in and smiled. "I appreciate your upbeat spirit, with a pinch of sass." Dr. Spencer winked. "Right, Cathy?"

"Ha!" Cassie returned the wink, remembering the physician's mistake at her first appointment. "Correct, Dr. Spinster."

"Hey, no old-age jokes. I'm not that old." She snickered, then turned her attention to Grant. "Speaking of the practice, did I hear correctly? You used to work here? Senior partner, in fact."

Cassie's insides flip-flopped. She'd been nervous on her husband's behalf. Though Grant was faithful to accompany her to appointments at the oncology center, he hadn't been back to Orchard View since his resignation.

"Best doctor this place ever had. Kindest. Most compassionate." Cassie's gaze met her husband's as she spoke.

Grant smiled at Cassie. "Thank you." He turned to the doctor. "That's right. Practiced here for ten years. Good years too. Lots of fine folks at Orchard View."

"And are you still practicing? Elsewhere, I mean?"

"Been with Piedmont Women's for a little over a year."

"And are you happy there? Plan on staying?" Dr. Spencer eyed Grant from head to toe. "You don't look to be more than, what? Midforties? Lots of years ahead of you, I'm guessing."

He guffawed. "Midfifties actually. Hope to retire in the next five to ten years. Do some traveling." His eyes met Cassie's. "And now, we have even more reason to take that celebratory trip. Isn't that right, Cass?"

He was referring to their deferred silver-anniversary vacation. "So much to celebrate."

"Cassie, I'm thrilled with your prognosis. Truly. You've done wonderfully, all things considered. Didn't even lose much of that beautiful auburn hair. How lucky!" Dr. Spencer picked up a manilla folder and tucked it under her arm. "Heard you used a cold cap. Pretty new technology, but from what I've read, it seems to work well. Were you happy?"

Cassie's hand instinctively went to her hair, pulled back in a ponytail. She tugged on it, tightening it. "Yes. Very."

"Good. Glad to hear it." The physician smiled. "As I said, after reviewing Dr. Evers' notes, likely one more chemo treatment, and ..." She pointed at something unseen. "Can you see that? It's the light at the end of the tunnel. Keep walking. You're almost there."

They said their goodbyes, and Dr. Spencer left the room. Cassie remained on the examining table for a moment.

"Thank you for coming with me. It means a lot, even though it must have—"

"Are you kidding? It's all good. Really. I wouldn't have missed this for the world." Grant touched the paper gown at Cassie's shoulder. "I don't think anyone was ever so beautiful, even in one of these."

She mustered up her best southern drawl. "This ol' thing?" Fanning her face with an imaginary fan, she giggled. "Why, that's mighty kind of ya, sir. And now, didn't I hear somethin' about you takin' me out to lunch?"

"Yes, ma'am. We'll catch the next stagecoach as soon as you can tighten that bustle, and we hustle on outta here."

Grant leaned in and kissed Cassie. Pulling away, his gaze remained on the pink paper gown. "May I?" His blue eyes pooled.

Cassie knew what he meant. "Yes."

Gently, Grant tore the paper, beginning at the left shoulder, exposing his wife's arm and chest, where her left breast had been. Peering down at the vacant spot, seeing the scar, Cassie instinctively lifted her right hand, tried to cover her nakedness.

"Don't." Grant took her hand in his, then kissed it. "No shame, my love. Your scar, it tells a beautiful story. A story that might change the world."

Cassie understood. Grant meant more. He was referring not merely to any physical scars but those with which she'd been born. Ones that couldn't be seen but were there just the same.

And at that moment, a whisper—words she'd heard before, long ago. They emerged from somewhere deep, floating up from the depths of some vast ocean.

Every scar holds a story.

CHAPTER 20

CASSIE—AUGUST 2016

Standing at the kitchen counter, Cassie tipped her mug and downed the last swallow of coffee.

Grant joined her and set his mug in the sink with a thud. "How are you feeling about the day? Ready for the time warp?"

Cassie assessed the items on the kitchen table. "Laptop. Check. Notebook. Check. Pens and phone. Check. But my, oh my! Have you seen my time-travel space suit?" She giggled, then remembered. "There is one more thing." She walked to the half bath off the kitchen and grabbed a wad of tissues. Returning, Cassie held up her hand. "Might need these."

"Good thinking." Grant stepped toward her, then wrapped his arms around her middle and clasped his hands behind her. "I'll be praying for you. This is a big day. One you've been waiting for, for what? A lifetime?"

"And for more than one reason. It will be my first book, after all. But promise me something."

"Anything."

"No new pets."

Grant kissed the top of her head. "I promise. Besides, I'm going to work, and the older kids are in school, so little time for shenanigans. Good planning, making this visit on a weekday rather than on the weekend." He kissed her again. "And speaking of pets, I'm taking Merle with me today. The office staff's been begging me to bring him, so he'll hang out in the break room and behind the reception desk."

"He'll love that, I'm sure. And you'll be able to get the kids? Three o'clock. I'm dropping Millie Kate at Mom's. I can get her when I get back, or you can get her after you've gotten the others. Text me and let me know."

"Will do. And again, breathe. Enjoy today. You were made for this."

"Thank you for having Mille Kate, Mom." Cassie knelt and sat her toddler on the carpeted floor of her parents' living room. "Momma will be back later this afternoon. Evening at the latest." Before standing, she kissed her daughter's wooly head.

"How are you today, lovey?" Cassie's mom reached to squeeze her daughter's forearm.

"Pretty good. My energy's been up lately, though I'm still losing a hair or two. Doctor says that should stop soon." She smiled. "Man, that cold cap sure did the trick."

"So thankful your energy's returning, and your hair looks great, but I was referring to the task at hand."

Cassie chuckled, realizing she'd misunderstood. "I'm good, but how about you? Are you thankful I'm doing this? You were a bit worried at first. Dad too."

The older woman's eyes grew soft. "Yes, I ... we are fine. Of course, we were a bit concerned when we first learned of Fiona's request. Seemed a lot to ask. And we are your parents, after all. We knew it would be ..." She hesitated. "You know. But we prayed, and

God gave peace. So yes, we're thankful. And having increased energy and an almost full head of hair, that's icing on the cake." She hugged Cassie. "Millie Kate and I are going to have a big day, isn't that right?"

Playing with the television remote, Millie Kate glanced up at the sound of her name. "Bear?"

Cassie's mom laughed. "Of course Grandma Patricia will watch *Brown and Friends* with you. But first, let's see your momma out the door. Maybe get some juice."

Cassie hugged her mom, then stooped to kiss her daughter once more. "Love you, pumpkin. Momma will see you later."

When Cassie rang Fi's bell, she heard approaching footsteps and sensed that familiar flutter. She breathed a silent prayer. *Be with me, with all of us. Establish the work of my hands, and may your favor rest upon me.*

This had become her frequent request, having discovered this verse in Psalm 90. Words of Moses, they spoke her heart too. Since her conversation with Grant a couple months earlier, after their meeting with Pete Gentry, she'd made a point of reading through the book of Psalms, reading one or two almost daily.

The door opened. Fiona stood behind it, a broad smile bringing crinkles to the corners of her blue eyes. "Come in!"

The two hugged. When Fi stepped back, she eyed Cassie up and down. "You look wonderful. Just wonderful."

"Thank you. Feeling pretty good too. Almost finished with my treatments, something I found out earlier this month. Best news I've received in a long, long time."

"I bet. I'm so happy for you, Cassie." She led the way to the kitchen, where three children sat at the table, books and iPads spread out over the oak surface. "Our big news—we're homeschooling after years of public school. Made the decision mid-summer. Don't ask the kids how they feel about it right now. They're smack dab in the middle of ancient civilization and none too happy about it. Isn't that right?"

Three middle-grade children, two boys and a girl, moaned their reply but didn't look up from their studies. Still in sweats and T-shirts, hair mussed, they were the perfect picture of home education, at least how Cassie imagined homeschoolers might look.

"That is a big decision. I'll wait to talk to them about it until PE or something equally fun." Cassie leaned over Fi's youngest, her daughter Bethany, and read aloud from her open notebook. "'Mesopotamia, the region near the Tigris-Euphrates River and in the north of what is called the Fertile Crescent.' Yeah, I don't blame you for having sour faces." Stooping, she whispered, "If you need a field trip, Lannie would love to see you. I can come up with some sort of permission slip."

The twelve-year-old turned for the first time. A slight smile tugged at the corners of her mouth. "Thanks, Ms. Cassie."

The two women settled themselves on the living room sofa, and Cassie took a throw pillow and hugged it to her chest. "It's nice to be here again. When do your parents arrive?"

"They'll be here around ten thirty. I wanted to visit with just you for a few minutes."

"Perfect." Cassie reached over and patted Fiona's leg. "Tell me about your Yellowstone trip. Sounded amazing! At least for you."

Fi giggled. "It was, but by day five, Brent was itching for some ESPN with the guys down at Howie's. All things considered, he was a trooper, and we survived, so that's a positive." She thumped the pillow Cassie held. "And how about your twenty-fifth anniversary getaway? Where'd you go?"

Cassie sighed. "Nowhere ... yet." She hugged the pillow closer. "I wasn't up for it in June. The twenty-second came and went, but we promised we'd make up for it soon. Now that I'm feeling better—"

The chime of the doorbell interrupted their conversation.

"Must be Mom and Dad. Early as always." Fiona rose to greet them.

Once more, Cassie squeezed the pillow to her chest and inhaled. Grant's words rang in her mind. *Remember. Breathe. Enjoy this.*

Fluffing it, she placed the pillow back in its spot and smoothed her skirt. Another deep breath, and she removed her laptop from her bag and opened it. The screen came to life with a photograph from Ben's tenth birthday, and the memory brought a smile, quieting the butterflies.

She was made for this.

Voices drew nearer as Fiona and her parents rounded the corner from the foyer, Gideon's deep voice further calming her flutters. Today was his turn to share part of their love story. To pick up where Ava left off.

"Hello, dear." Ava approached Cassie with open arms. "You look lovely."

"So do you. How are you?" After rising from the couch, she stepped into the arms of the elderly woman. "Wonderful to see you again."

Turning to Gideon, she held out a hand, but instead, he enveloped her in an embrace. "We're fine, Cassandra. Couldn't be better."

Formalities aside, the trio gathered on chairs and on the sofa. Fi excused herself, then, moments later, returned with a tray.

"Here you go. Coffee and cookies. Peanut butter blossoms, to be precise. Bethany Lila made them as part of her science class yesterday. I told her, 'Not all homeschool assignments are bad, and some are downright yummy.' She agreed. Anyway, help yourselves."

Ava leaned in to get a closer look at Cassie's screen saver. "How beautiful! A birthday party, am I right?"

"Yes. Ben's tenth, last month."

"My, my. Is he a decade already? How can that be?"

Gideon came to peer over Cassie's shoulder, standing behind the couch. "What a strapping young lad. And a baseball player too, I hear. Is his season over?"

"Just. A couple weeks ago. My nephew, Hunter, came for a weekend in July to see the playoffs. Those two about drove our Lannie crazy. And she's not one to have her feathers ruffled easily."

"How nice, dear, and I'm sure Lannie survived." Ava patted Cassie's arm.

Gideon returned to his chair adjacent to the sofa. "Did Ben receive any special birthday gifts?"

"Funny you should ask. He received the nicest gift from William. A well-kept cardboard box packed full of vintage baseball cards. Mostly from the sixties."

Gideon's smile broadened. "Your brother, he's the most generous person. And the work he does down in Greenville. Transforming lives, that's for sure. Builds more than bridges and buildings, if you know what I mean." Gideon winked.

Cassie nodded. "I do. He's touched a lot of lives through his work with Habitat for Humanity, not to mention his own nonprofit. Community Connections has provided housing for countless people, helping them get their feet back on the ground and start fresh." Cassie bit into a cookie. "These are good." She chewed, then swallowed. "And for as long as I can recall, my big brother has had a thing for architecture and playing baseball. Guess that's why he finally decided to go by William. Too many B's in the sentence, Billy loves bridges, buildings, and baseball. Although I, for one, appreciate alliteration." Cassie chuckled at her own humor. "On a more serious note, are we ready to get started? I think Ava left me hanging near the bus station, did she not? March 1969."

Gideon's gaze fell on Ava. "That's correct. You rascal, that's where you abandoned Cassandra." He winked at his wife, then turned his attention to Cassie. "But today, I'm going to take you to where the story began. No more backstory. Not the bus station, not spring break. Because our story actually starts in a hotel room. Room 212, to be exact. My hotel room in June of that same year, when I visited the Sand Dollar Bay only months after Ava." Gideon again gazed tenderly at his wife. "And where did it all begin, my love?"

Ava smiled. "In a book."

Although Cassie was a bit confused, a bit disappointed even, there was no time to question. Instead, once again, her fingers danced on the keyboard, waltzing right back to 1969.

GIDEON STALLINGS'S STORY

O Joy that seekest me through pain,
I cannot close my heart to thee;
I trace the rainbow through the rain,
And feel the promise is not vain,
That morn shall tearless be.

—George Matheson's
"O Love That Wilt Not Let Me Go"

CHAPTER 21

GIDEON—JUNE 1969

I CINCHED MY SEATBELT TIGHTER and shifted in my seat, then tapped the smoldering butt of my cigarette in the metal ashtray on my armrest.

Right on cue, the stewardess's voice blared throughout the plane's cabin. "Please extinguish all cigarettes, and make sure tray tables are in their upright, locked positions. We'll be landing in Myrtle Beach shortly. On behalf of your flight crew, it's been a pleasure serving you."

One last drag. Inhaling long and deep, praying the nicotine would do its job. With eyes closed, I pinched the Marlboro between pointer and thumb, then focused on my breathing. One slow inhale, then exhale. Inhale, exhale.

"Hey, mister. Don't you need to put that out?" A little boy in a blue baseball cap poked my right arm. "Said it was time. We're almost ready to land."

Blast. I opened my eyes. The child seated between me and a woman I assumed to be his mother stared at me. Funny. For the entire flight from Charlotte to Myrtle Beach, we hadn't exchanged a single word.

"Y-yes. Thanks." I tamped the butt in the ashtray on my armrest, then flicked closed the tiny metal compartment.

The boy cocked his head. "Why do you talk like that?"

Rarely embarrassed, something about the way he stared at me made me squirm. So straightforward. "Because I have a c-condition that makes me s-stammer."

"Oh." Satisfied, he rested his head against his seat, a slight smile spanning his fair, freckled face.

When I lifted my gaze from him to the woman beside him, our eyes met. Blushing, she mouthed, "Sorry about that."

A slight tip of my head told her it wasn't a problem. A distraction, in fact. Exactly what I needed.

I tossed back the dredges of my gin and tonic, shook the glass, then lifted it to my lips once more, draining what remained of my liquid comfort. The clink of ice startled the boy, and he glanced at me again.

"You been to Myrtle Beach before, mister?"

"No. First v-visit. You?"

"Naw." He turned to the woman. "Mommy, how many times we been here?"

The woman was applying lipstick, but with her son's question, her compact snapped closed and she rubbed her fuchsia lips together. "I believe this makes three, son, but we'll ask your daddy when we've landed, okay?" She rummaged in her purse, then pulled out a tissue and blotted her bright mouth. Leaning over to see past the boy, the attractive woman's gaze met mine again. "Never gets old, does it? Flying, a miracle to me, how we get from one place to another in no time 'tall. Like time travel." She smiled, revealing two rows of perfectly straight, milk-white teeth, then extended her manicured fingers. "I'm Patti. This here's Billy."

I reached to take her petite hand, enveloping it in my own. "Deon. N-nice to meet you."

"You here on business?" With her question, she ran a comb through her blond pageboy.

"Yes. A c-conference."

"What do you do, if you don't mind me asking?"

"I'm an architect. Civil engineering's my b-background."

"Hear that, Billy? An architect." She tousled his auburn hair. "Kid sure loves to build. Can't hardly pull him away from his erector set, ain't that right, son?"

Billy nodded, his blue eyes wide as he met my gaze. "Gee, mister. Have you built any bridges?"

I chuckled. "Several, but I'm not b-building them much these days. More a designer. I draw up the plans, then work with builders who do the actual c-constructing." I tossed back my cup one more time. A cold stream from melted ice and a hint of lime wetted my throat, which grew more parched with every foot of the Boeing 727's descent.

The stewardess appeared beside me. "Anything to discard, sir?"

As I handed her my glass, she smiled at me before addressing Billy. "How about you, young man? Any trash?"

He shook his head. Turning to his mom he said, "Can I ask her?"

"Go ahead, son."

"Ma'am, do you have any of those little wings? You know, the kind I can wear to show everybody I flew on a plane."

"I might. Let me finish this job, and I'll go see what I can find. How's that?"

"Gee, thanks. Hear that, Momma? Said she'd check."

"How nice, Billy. Now, we're almost down. Can you gather your things? And don't forget to zip your backpack."

While the boy stuffed papers, crayons, and a book inside his bag, he whistled a song, something I couldn't quite decipher, his melody a little off key.

"Tell me, what's that t-tune?"

"'Take Me Out to the Ballgame.' You know that one, don't you?"

"Of course. One of the b-best songs ever, about the greatest sport. You like b-baseball?"

"Do I like baseball? Momma, he asked if I like baseball."

Patti giggled, and Janet, the woman I'd managed not to think about for the last fifteen minutes, came to mind. So much for a reprieve.

"Let's just say, Billy eats, sleeps, and breathes baseball. Isn't that right, son?"

"Sure is." Turning to me, his eyes were saucers. "Did you play baseball, mister?"

"You can c-call me Deon, and yes. In high school. First base, but that was l-long ago."

Patti craned her neck to face me. "Surely not that long ago. What? No college ball?"

I shook my head. "No t-time for that, not with my s-studies and—"

"Girls, no doubt." Patti winked. "You married?"

Rising emotion warmed my cheeks. Almost. Nearly. But instead, my answer was shorter, like a staccato. "N-no."

At that moment, we touched down, and the occupants of row E lunged forward a little. I breathed a deep sigh.

"Flyin' make you nervous?" Patti snapped closed the clasp on her cosmetic bag, having returned the tissue, lipstick, and comb, then slid the pouch inside her black leather purse.

"Let's just say, I haven't d-done it a—"

"Welcome to Myrtle Beach, South Carolina. We hope your time here, whether for business or pleasure, is safe. On behalf of the flight crew, we appreciate you flying the friendly skies. Please watch as you open the overhead bins, as some bags may have shifted during flight. You are now safe to unbuckle."

"It was nice meeting you. Hope you enjoy your conference, Deon. Billy, do you have everything?"

"Yes, Momma." Billy stood up. Stretching his neck, he appeared to be searching for someone in a row farther back. "There he is." He waved. "Hey, Daddy."

As passengers filed out, I unfolded from my seat. "Can I help you with any b-bags?"

Patti smiled. "No, my husband will get them, but thank ya kindly."

At that moment, a tall man, the beginnings of a five o'clock shadow peppering his chiseled jaw, reached Row E.

"Hello, sweetheart. Hey there, son. Good flight?"

Patti nodded. "Yes, it was. And we met this very nice man who was gracious enough to receive a reprimand from our eight-year-old."

"You don't say." The man extended his hand. "Thank you for that. I'm Mike, father to a precocious child, I hear."

We shook. "Nice to meet you. I'm Deon, D-Deon Stallings, and he was fine, really."

"Mix-up with our tickets put me way near the back. But I got to sit by the window, so it was all okay." Turning to address his wife, he chortled. "Didn't have to fight me for it, did you?"

Patti giggled. "Not this time anyway."

Janet.

"Again, it was nice meeting you. I h-hope you have fun playing in the s-sand, Billy. Build a castle for me."

"Daddy, Mr. Deon's a builder. He was a builder. Now he's an arch ... archi ... archite ..." Billy stopped, and his freckled face turned a shade of pink. "I wasn't trying to stammer. I ... I just can't say the word."

I patted the bill of his baseball cap. "No worries. Architect. And who kn-knows? Maybe you'll be one someday."

"An architect? You don't say." Mike Bennett's head bobbed up and down. "Me? I'm an attorney, near Greensboro." He paused. "Ever hear of the Farnsworth House?"

I chortled. "Hear of it? Had to s-study it in grad school. Now, there's an architect's n-nightmare for you."

"Yeah. My grandfather—Mom's dad—he was from Illinois. Worked with the prosecution team for that case with ... what's his name?"

"Who? The architect's?"

"Yeah. Ludwig Mies van ... what is it?"

"Van der R-Rohe. One of the most talked-about lawsuits out there, architecturally s-speaking, that is."

Mike lifted Patti's yellow leather carry-on from the overhead bin. "Got everything, Billy? Patti, I'll carry this." He turned to me. "Sure was nice to meet you, Deon. Billy, what do you say?"

The boy smiled up at me. "Nice to meet you."

"Likewise, Billy. Keep p-playing b-baseball. It's the greatest sport—"

"In the whole wide world." His eyes crinkled as he finished my sentence. "Bye, Mr. Deon."

"Got an address?" The nub of a cigar stuck out from the cab driver's lips, and he chewed it while he waited.

"Yes. One m-moment. It's in here s-somewhere." I dug in the pocket of my leather satchel, searching for the Sand Dollar Bay's address. "Ah, here."

The driver took the slip of paper, then wadded it. "Know right where it is. Don't need this none." He tossed it over his right shoulder, and it landed on the floor at my feet. "Stutterer, eh? Had a nephew who did that. Years ago. Grew out of it though." Pivoting in the driver's seat, he stuck out his hand. "Name's Sam. Glad to have ya aboard."

I shook. "D-Deon. Thank you." My hand free again, I leaned down and picked up the wadded address. "L-leave things neater than when you arrived, that's what Mom always s-said." I chuckled. "How far is it?"

"About fifteen minutes. Twenty max, depending on traffic." He thrust the gear into drive, craning his neck to see behind him, then huffed. "We're off."

Neither of us spoke for a mile or so. I occupied the time reading billboards until one advertising Chesterfields, with a slender woman dressed in a short navy skirt and pink jacket, brought Janet to mind again. I shook my head. Blast. Couldn't get away from her, even with all these miles between us.

"Where you from?" The driver startled me. His gaze met mine in the rearview mirror, the cigar nub still lodged between his lips, like it had been born there.

"Ohio. S-small town. Probably never heard of it. L-Lima. Right off I-I-75."

"A Buckeye, eh? Me? I'm a Wolverine. Go Blue!"

"Gu-guess we'll be s-seeing you in the f-fall, in maize-and-blue's neck of the woods."

"Yep, that's what I'm told. Course, I'll be watching on the telly."

A second-generation graduate of Ohio State University, I was a die-hard Buckeyes fan. Didn't miss a game. "Prefer w-watching from the House that H-Harley Built rather than the couch. Can't say I've ever been to Ann Arbor's B-Big House though. Probably won't this year either. Be there in spirit. I'll f-flick you a wave from my s-sofa when OSU scores their first touchdown."

The driver snorted, his cigar nub bobbing. "I'll wave back, or maybe send you another gesture. Depends on if the Wolverines score first." He snorted again.

In fifteen minutes, we arrived, the resort and conference

center's parking lot full to capacity. The driver pulled up to the curb, and a bellman opened my door.

"Welcome to the Sand Dollar Beach Resort."

I unfolded from the backseat, making sure I had my jacket and satchel.

"May I help with your bags, sir?"

"No, th-thank you. I only have one s-suitcase. I can get it." I thanked him again. With a nod, he turned to assist someone in a blue Plymouth Fury.

The cab driver stepped up beside me, then opened the trunk and removed my suitcase. "Here ya go. And don't forget—Go Blue!"

"How about f-five bucks the Buckeyes w-win big?"

"You're on!" The cab driver winked.

I paid him the fare. "Thanks for the ride. Stay s-safe."

He chortled, sending the wet cigar nub bobbing once more. "Now, what's the fun of that?" He pointed at me. "And hey, I hear walking uphill with pebbles in your mouth helps with stuttering." Then, as he ducked back in his cab, "Or was that for hiccups?"

Turning to face the hotel, my home for the next several days, I breathed deep, then stepped up to the revolving door. Funny. Had I ever used one before? No recollection.

And, just like that, my thoughts revolved right back to Janet, her face flashing across my mind. "Okay, you c-can come too."

She might as well. After all, I couldn't seem to shake free from her. Probably couldn't, even if I were a million miles away.

CHAPTER 22

GIDEON—JUNE 1969

SUNLIGHT PEEKING THROUGH DRAWN curtains sprinkled signs of morning on Sand Dollar Bay's room 212. Small dots dancing.

After tossing back the covers and standing, I followed them, stumbling through darkness. Where was my suitcase? Reaching the end of the bed, I cursed as my toe collided with the wooden bench that served as a luggage rack. Blast it anyway!

After hopping on one foot to the desk, I fumbled around for the lamp. With a click, light flooded the room, and I blinked, then leaned to rest on my elbows, holding my head with both hands. Pulsing throbs from too many drinks at last night's tiki bar cleared the cobwebs of my early morning confusion.

Myrtle Beach. The engineering conference. What a way to begin.

Shielding my eyes, I managed to find the bathroom, then blindly reached for a washcloth, sending several to the black-and-white tiled floor. Cold water—that was what I needed. Finally, I held the stiff cloth under the flow, feeling it go limp in my hands. I wrung it out and sat on the closed toilet, pressing it to my eyes and forehead, then counted.

Before I reached ten, Janet's face flashed again, pulsing with the tempo of each throb, and I cursed. Why couldn't she leave me alone?

I stood. With the washcloth still over my face, I stepped toward the wall where I knew the switch would be. After running a hand over cool tiles, I located it, then flipped it on. Even with my eyes closed, still covered, I sensed it. Light.

Easing the cloth from my face, I pinched my eyelids shut. Then, one by one, slowly, I forced them open. After all, I had to find my toiletry bag, find the aspirin I knew it held.

Back in the main part of room 212, I discovered my suitcase right where it should be, on the rack at the foot of the bed. After rummaging around, I pulled out a clean pair of cotton Bermudas and an Ohio State T-shirt. Last, I drew out my toiletry bag.

Having fallen into bed fully dressed half a dozen hours earlier, I had awoken still in what I'd put on the morning before. Back in the bathroom, I peeled off my wrinkled khaki pants and unbuttoned my plaid oxford, then stood before the mirror in my open shirt and drawers. Bloodshot, hazel eyes stared at me, and I blinked. At nearly twenty-six, why did I do this?

I brushed my teeth and changed into clean clothes, then threw back three aspirin with a feeble petition. *Headache, go away.*

In the main room once more, I slowly drew the curtains to get a better look at Myrtle Beach. Though the tiki bar below me was only yards from the sand, less than a football field to the water, it was dark when I'd sat on a bar stool the night before. But with the morning light, I could see it. Stretched out before me, the Atlantic.

I'd only visited the ocean one other time, when I was a boy, before Mom had passed. We'd taken a summer trip to Florida, spent time on the Gulf side, in Siesta Key.

What I remembered most was building sandcastles, digging

moats, and being buried from neck to toe by Dad, covered in the soft, white sand. At first, I'd been afraid, but he'd encouraged me. "You can pull up at any time, son." As usual, he'd been right.

I stepped out onto the postage-stamp-size balcony enclosed with wrought-iron railing, and heat struck my face, a stark contrast to the room's air-conditioning. I inhaled the salt air, breathing deep.

Gulls cried in the distance, echoing one another as they sought breakfast in the breaking tide. To me, they were hecklers, poking fun at my tippling. My negligence.

Below, a family of five arranged their swimming gear by the pool. A man struggled to open a table umbrella, dodging children who danced around him like impatient puppies.

"You're it." One child tapped another, then darted off toward the deep end.

"No horseplay." The man wrestling the umbrella cursed before continuing. "Someone's gonna fall and crack their skull. We don't need a trip to the emergency room today."

A girl in a yellow cover-up called back, "Dad, you're a poet and didn't know it," followed by a belly laugh.

A woman in a floppy sun hat and two-piece floral bathing suit applied sunscreen to a fair-skinned toddler who bellowed his disapproval.

Janet.

Shaking my head, I opened and closed my dry mouth several times, tasting again the stale remnants of bourbon and Coke from the evening before. Hadn't I just brushed my teeth? My stomach clenched.

Returning to the coolness of the room, I closed the door to the sounds of morning beach activity. Coffee. That was what I needed. Hot and strong. I scanned the spartan space for a hotel guide, hoping to find a room-service menu, then walked to the desk to check its drawers. Nothing. Maybe in one of the bedside tables. I checked one, then the other. No guide, only a notepad and telephone atop the one on the right, closest to the sliding door, a Bible in its drawer.

I dialed zero.

"Good mornin'. How may I help ya?"

The voice on the other end was perky, my answer gruff.

"It w-would be a good morning if I could order some coffee. Can't seem to l-locate the room-service menu."

"I'm sorry about that, Mr...." A pause as the woman, someone who sounded more like a teenager, confirmed to whom she was speaking. "Yes, Mr. Stallings. Room 212, is it?"

"That's right. Second f-floor, ocean-side."

"Sir, did you check the desk drawer or the bureau perhaps? It might could be there."

Might could? "H-hold on." It was only three strides to the bureau. I opened one, then two drawers. Without checking the third, I returned to the phone. "Not there."

"I do apologize, Mr. Stallings. Certainly should be a hotel guide in one of them. Not sure why it's missin'. How about I send a room attendant right up to bring one to y'all, okay?"

I was irritable and in need of coffee. The young woman's pronunciation of the word *guide* sounded more like *god*, and I sneered my response. "I'm not l-looking for God, you know. And, for c-clarity, there's only one of me."

"What? What's that?" Her voice registered confusion. "I'm ... I'm not sure—"

"N-never mind. It was a j-joke, that's all." Who was I to poke fun at another's manner of speaking? "Yes, please send someone up. Th-thank you."

"Okay, Mr. Stallings. He'll ... he'll be right up, no more'n five minutes, I reckon."

I returned the receiver to its base and sat on the edge of the bed, then resumed holding my head. The pulsing throb at my temples reminded me I was alive, though at that moment I wasn't sure I wanted to be, especially with my—

The phone rang, interrupting my self-deprecating ponderings. "Hello."

"Hello. Mr. Stallings?"

"That's me."

"Yes, sir. I'm Mr. Johnson, hotel manager. I understand you're missing your hotel guide, and I wanted to be sure you have your conference packet, which I made certain myself was placed in your room yesterday afternoon. Should be a red folder. Inside you'll find your name tag and meal ticket, not to mention other conference materials. The itinerary and such."

I scanned the room from my perch on the bed but didn't see it. "Where was it p-placed, and I'll l-look."

"I believe I instructed Jonah to lay it on top of the bench. He confirmed as much."

"Hold on." At the foot of the bed, I lifted my suitcase. Not there. After reaching down between the bed and the bench, I felt around until I touched something. A folder? Yes. I pulled it out, then inspected its contents. My name tag and meal ticket were included.

I picked up the handset again. "Yes, sir. It's h-here, like you s-said. Thank you."

"Very well. And you should receive that hotel guide and an in-room service menu shortly. I hope you have a good day, sir."

"Thank you."

As I replaced the phone in its cradle, there was a knock at the door. "One m-moment."

I opened it, and a hotel room attendant dressed in a crisp, white button-down and black slacks stood before me. The shirt was in stark contrast to the middle-aged man's dark skin, as were the whites of his eyes.

As if to confirm my thoughts, he smiled, revealing two rows of perfectly aligned white teeth, minus an eyetooth. "Good mornin', sir. I have your guide and menu."

I extended my hand to take the spiral-bound book, and our fingers touched. "Th-thank you."

His smile broadened. "You're most welcome, sir. Anythin' else I can do for ya?"

Could he? My mind raced. "Yes, there is. How about you answer a question for me p-perhaps."

"Yes, sir. I'll certainly try, sir."

"Why do people in the S-South say y'all, even when there's only one of m-me?"

The man laughed. "Is that right, sir?" He paused, considering his response. "I reckon it just be the way we folks here say things." He laughed again, his chuckle deep and hearty, the sort that shook his shoulders, turning his dark eyes into half-moons.

Leaning forward, I read his name tag. "J-Jonah, is it?" I extended my hand again. "I'm D-Deon, from up n-north."

Jonah nodded. "That right? Where 'bouts?"

"A s-small town. L-Lima, Ohio. Heard of it?"

"Can't say that I has. Never been further north than ..." Jonah's eyes darted upward as he considered, then returned his gaze to meet mine. "I guess never been north of Ke'tucky. Reunion some years back. Ms. Forney's side of the fam'ly."

It was my turn to nod. "That right? Lima's about five hours from L-Lexington. Famous for being the home of a-astronaut Neil Armstrong. From a town n-nearby. Wapokenta."

"Wapa what?" Jonah belly laughed. "Now that be a name." He swiped his eyes.

I couldn't quite explain it, but, right away, something about Jonah settled quietly, calming me. Like a brother. "Thank you again. For the guide and m-menu."

"You're most welcome. And if you need anythin' else ... y'all let me know." Jonah winked.

"Ha. Sure will." Suddenly, I remembered. "Wait one m-moment."

Stepping away from the door, I walked to the desk chair where I'd tossed my khaki pants, then dug in the pocket for loose change. After pulling out a quarter, I flipped it once, then caught it as I reached the door. "Here you g-go, Mr. Jonah."

His smile returned, slight at first, then wide. "Thank ya kindly. That's mighty nice of ya." Jonah dipped his head before taking a step back. "You let me know if I can be a'service, ya hear? You have a good day now."

I closed the door. Sitting on the bed, I flipped through the menu and decided on a meager breakfast of black coffee and wheat toast, not sure my stomach could handle much more.

The same young woman answered when I phoned the front desk, though her voice sounded curt. "Yes, Mr. Stallings?"

"I'd like to order coffee and wheat toast, p-please. To the room. Room 2—"

"I know your room number. Wheat toast and coffee. That all?"

I could hear her scowl. "Yes, ma'am. Th-that's all. Thank you."

She hung up without another word. Had I hurt her feelings?

Again, Janet. "Go away."

While I waited, I considered watching television but knew I'd only find game shows or morning news programs. I recalled hearing *Today* was to feature interviews leading up to Queen Elizabeth II's crowning of Charles, making him Prince of Wales. When was that? His coronation wasn't until July sometime.

Maybe sit on the balcony, soak up some sun? But I might miss the delivery knock. Instead, I opened the bedside table drawer again. Inside was the Bible, its pale gold cover embossed with a simple floral design. *Placed By the Gideons* was pressed in the lower right corner. *Holy Bible* was above, more central on the front.

As I scanned the cover of the book, it wasn't Janet who flashed across my mind. Instead, it was Mom, and her voice echoed.

Gideon, son. That's who God's calling you to be. Like the man in the Bible, the one God knew was greater than he himself could ever have imagined. Yes, called to do great things.

And though the sliding door was closed, a seagull's cry pierced right through, the bird's heckle another reminder. Only this time, once more Janet's face flashed—and the gull's message?

You're a loser.

CHAPTER 23

GIDEON—JUNE 1969

DISMISSED FROM THE MORNING KEYNOTE, I—along with several hundred conference attendees—filed out of the auditorium. The din of too many voices made my head throb.

Even with only a few bites of dry toast and a cup of coffee several hours earlier, I wasn't hungry. Still, eating might ease my headache.

I grabbed a turkey club and chips from the hotel diner, then headed outside. With an hour until the afternoon's sessions, perhaps I'd have time for a quick swim.

I located a lawn chair at the far end of the pool and unwrapped my sandwich from wax paper, tearing a piece of wilted lettuce poking out from rye bread. Leaning back, half a sandwich in hand, I closed my eyes and reflected on the morning.

The keynote was a retired army soldier. He'd shared how his architectural expertise had been used to help restore bridges in rural Vietnam. Prior to that, I'd attended a session on the business aspect of owning a firm. A real sleeper. I wondered if those at Robbins and Ray—two senior partners who'd sent me to the conference to "bring back fresh ideas"—would regret this decision. After all, wasn't owning my own firm a conflict of interest?

After finishing half my sandwich, I popped a potato chip in my mouth, then took a swallow of Pepsi. Its fizz burned my throat, making my eyes water. Not quite a hair of the dog, but the thought of anything alcoholic turned my stomach.

I rewrapped the other half of my club and slipped it into the brown paper bag, then put the bag into my leather satchel before climbing the steps to the second floor. Would my room be clean? If so, had Jonah been the one to freshen it?

After turning the key to room 212, I pushed open the door. Coolness from air-conditioning met me. Plenty of chill to keep my sandwich for the next forty-five minutes or so. Perhaps I'd feel like eating the rest later, after a swim.

The room had been cleaned, the bed covers pulled tight, pillows fluffed. Peeking in the bathroom, I noted the towels and washcloths piled high, and none were missing from the folded stack placed above the toilet on a chrome rack. All the fixtures sparkled, the scent of disinfectant lingering in the spotless bathroom.

Laying my room key and satchel on the bedside table, I noticed a note written on Sand Dollar Bay stationery.

Friday, June 20, 1969

Dear Mr. Deon,

It was my pleasure to freshen your room this morning. Even more, it was a pleasure meeting you. I'm sorry it wasn't me who brought your breakfast. I was attending to a room down the hall, where it seems the occupants had a food fight of sorts. Either that or someone was sick. Times like that, I have to pray the preacher Paul's good words, something about rejoicing in all circumstances and doing everything as unto the Lord.

Anyhow, I was called to a different duty but finished in time to clean your room. I hope your breakfast was to your liking, as I'll admit, it didn't appear you ate much.

Should be me delivering your meals from here on out, that is, if you order room service. I sure do hope to see y'all again. (Wink! Wink!)

Your friend,
Jonah Forney

PS I wondered if Deon is short for something? Gideon, perhaps? Do you know who that is? (Check the Bible by your bed, where I stuck a bookmark. And notice too, it's a Gideon Bible.)

I read the note twice, marveling how this humble hotel attendant would take the time to write, given his many duties. Surely he didn't do the same for guests in every room he cleaned?

After opening the drawer, I removed the Bible. And there was the bookmark— a business card, Smith's Print Shop across the top, an address and phone number below.

The passage he'd marked was from the book of Judges. The two pages in front of me were labeled—Judges 5 on the top left and Judges 6 on the right. Had I read this Old Testament book before? I had no recollection, nor did I recall specifically reading the story of Gideon, only that Mom had told me about him.

I sat on the bed and ran my finger down the pages until I located my name, discovering Gideon was first mentioned in Judges, Chapter 6, verse 11. I read: "And there came an angel of the LORD, and sat under an oak which was in Ophrah, that pertained unto Joash the Abiezrite: and his son Gideon threshed wheat by the winepress, to hide it from the Midianites."

Further down, I recognized my name again and read more of the passage, learning that, though Gideon was considered the least in his family, God called him to do great things—to be a warrior, to rescue his people.

A warrior? A rescuer?

I laughed out loud, then closed the Bible with a snap before placing it back in the drawer. That didn't describe me. Dad, maybe. The man who'd shared in the opening keynote session, perhaps. But me?

I rubbed my temples, realizing my headache hadn't eased, even with half a sandwich. A hair of the dog—a Bloody Mary?—that was what I needed.

Grabbing my room key, I figured I'd spend the remainder of my free time at the tiki bar down below. Make small talk with fellow architects. Ignore Mom's voice, Janet's face. Even if for only twenty minutes.

And maybe, maybe, I'd forget.

The remainder of the afternoon's sessions didn't impress, though my headache finally subsided after two gin and tonics. "Hairs of the dog." I'd chuckled to the man already five drinks deep when I sat down at the bar. "Because one hair's never enough."

After the closing keynote, I returned to my room to change into swimming trucks and lace up my sneakers. A quick jog and a swim, then I'd shower before the organized dinner in the dining hall, something I dreaded. Mingling, insincere chit-chat—not my style.

Outside, I made my way to the beach, then chose the more firmly packed sand nearer the end of the wooden-plank walkway but making a mental note to at least dip my feet in the ocean prior to going to the pool.

I'd only jogged several yards when the sun slipped behind an inky cloud, and I shielded my eyes to inspect the sky. A blanket of gray hovered in the distance, threatening rain. No matter. Unless it thundered, I'd be getting wet anyway.

A quarter of a mile from Sand Dollar Bay, the crowds were thicker, with more children to dodge and sandcastles to avoid. Beyond the many lawn chairs and beach umbrellas was a weathered wooden pier. Fishing poles, held by men and women, boys and girls, were attached to lines cast in the water. Shouts of "I got one" or "That's a doozie" were carried on the breeze.

Watching a teenage boy hold tight to his bent pole, the line taut in the water, I stumbled on something.

"Hey, watch it, mister."

Startled, I stopped. "Oh, I'm s-sorry." Below me was a boy. The boy, the one from the airplane. "B-Billy, it's you."

He lifted his chin to peer at me from under his Yankees cap. "Mr. Deon?"

Just then, Patti approached. Dressed in a turquoise and white-striped two-piece, clearly, she'd been sunbathing. The scent of Coppertone wafted around her. "Deon?"

I laughed. "What d-do you know?" I patted Billy's head. "Small world, isn't it?"

Billy stood, a bright-blue spade in his hand. "Wow, Mr. Deon. What are you doing?"

"Remember, Mr. Deon told us. He's attending a conference. Isn't that right?"

"Y-yes. Done for the day though. Thought I'd c-catch some exercise."

"Better watch where you're going because you almost smashed my castle."

I inspected the boy's work. "Glad I d-didn't. Mighty fine work, if I do s-say so myself."

Mike approached, a bright-green beach towel cinched around his waist. He laid a heavy hand on my shoulder. "Hello there. Deon, right?"

I nodded, then shook Mike's outstretched hand. "That's right. As I was saying, s-small world."

"Indeed it is." Bending to speak face-to-face with his son, Mike lifted his chin. "Look at me, Billy."

The boy's gaze met his father's. "Yes, Daddy."

"You need to watch yourself, son. Show respect to adults. What do you say to Mr. Deon?"

"But he stepped on it ... almost." Billy scuffed the sand.

"Even so."

Turning to look up at me, the boy bit his lip before speaking, his words barely a whisper. "I'm sorry, Mr. Deon."

"No harm done. To my f-feelings or, and more important, to your castle. It's quite a masterpiece. Don't forget. B-build on solid ground. That's m-most important." I flipped the bill of his cap and thought of Mom, how she loved to tell me that biblical story. "And you're right. I do need to w-watch where I'm going."

"How's the conference?" Patti tipped her sunglasses as she spoke, revealing her blue eyes, her mascara-covered lashes.

"Good. Day one's d-down. Two more to go. One and a half really. Conference ends l-late Sunday morning."

"Where you staying?" Mike lifted a Pabst to his lips, then dipped it in my direction. "Beer?"

Though I wanted to say yes, I shook my head. "No thanks. Had a d-drink earlier." I licked my lips. "I'm at the Sand Dollar Bay Resort. Y-you?"

"No kidding. Us too." Mike gave a swift pat to my back. "And with all these hotels to pick from." He chuckled. "Room 411. Call us if you want to hang out. When do you leave?"

"Not until M-Monday morning."

"So soon?" Patti sipped something from a straw the color of her fuchsia lips. "Hey, Mike, you two should exchange home telephone numbers. Seems the universe is linin' things up so you and Deon can be friends." She giggled.

"I b-best be on my way. Nice to see you again. Mike, Patti." I flipped a wave toward them before bending to speak to Billy. "I'm serious, k-kid. You're good. Keep up the excellent work." One more flip of his bill. "A Y-Yankees fan, eh? Me? Reds all the way." I smiled, then stood, directing my attention once more to Mike. "Maybe I'll g-give you a call. Tomorrow?"

"Sounds like a plan. Have fun. And hey, don't go smashing any kids' dreams out here on the beach."

After a quick swim, I returned to my room to shower and dress for the evening, but before I did, I checked for another note. Why was I disappointed there wasn't one?

But instead of keeping the Bible in the bedside table drawer, before showering, I removed it and placed it on top of the nightstand, beside the telephone.

It was my turn.

Jonah,

Thank you for the note earlier. It was nice. And likewise, I enjoyed meeting you. I'll likely order room service again, so hopefully no more food fights down the hall.

In answer to your question, my full name is Gideon Joseph. My mom loved to tell me about the biblical characters for whom I'm named, though I don't recall ever reading Gideon's story in the Bible. Thank you for showing me where his is located. I hate to disappoint you, but I'm not much like this mighty warrior in Judges, so maybe Mom messed up when she chose my name.

Anyway, I do look forward to talking again.

Your friend,
Deon

After I closed the door to room 212, preparing myself for the socializing that was to ensue, I remained a moment in the hall. For the first time in as long as I could remember, I breathed an actual prayer.

I'm not sure what you're up to, God, but I'm game for finding out. And while you're at it, could you please help Janet know I'm sorry. At least until I get a chance to tell her myself.

CHAPTER 24

GIDEON—JUNE 1969

THUNDER ROLLED. Yellow streaks of lightning zig-zagged in the distance. Still, no rain fell as I sat on the nearly empty beach. The Gideon Bible, a folded piece of paper tucked in its pages, lay beside me on a towel I'd confiscated from my room.

Yawning, I stretched and sipped my to-go coffee from the self-serve station in the resort's lobby. Though the sun was up, it stayed hidden behind a thick blanket of clouds.

How Jonah acted with such intentionality, though his duties were many and most not pleasant, baffled me, yet I was grateful for his response to my note, left, I supposed, when he'd tended my room the evening before. When I returned from dinner, I found the letter atop the bedside table.

Jonah, his handwriting in near-perfect cursive, had written—

Friday, June 20, 1969—P.M.

Dear Gideon,

Why is it that I hear a hint of sadness in your voice? Insecurity? Regret? What has happened that makes you feel this way? Or is this the result of words someone has spoken to you? I wonder.

We all come upon hard times. Me? I've had more than most. But I don't think, not for a moment, your mama made a mistake. No, sir! Gideon Joseph is a right fine name.

Sometimes—many times—we gotta grow into our names. But God knows from the start, and he doesn't make any mistakes. No, sir!

You may not have the time or feel inclined, but I'd like to offer an invitation. I get off early tomorrow, and I'll likely be fishing off the pier down from Sand Dollar Bay. You can't miss it, as it's the only one for quite a spell. Tomorrow afternoon. Likely, I'll have my kids with me. Maybe my beautiful Ms. Forney too. You could meet my family. Again, you'd be more than welcome. Would give us a chance to chat.

Anyway, maybe I'll see you tomorrow morning, if you order breakfast. But in case you don't, I wanted you to know you're welcome to join us.

And Gideon Joseph, I'm praying for you—asking the good Lord to show you his plan. Fill you up with his Spirit. Yes, sir. he's got work for you to do, of that, I'm certain.

No need to let me know. Show up if you like, say three thirty.

Yours truly,
Jonah

I folded the paper, then tucked it back in the Bible.

The Bible. Holding it in my hand, I ran my index finger along its edge, traced the small lamp embossed in the bottom-right corner, above *Placed By the Gideons*.

I recalled hearing about Gideons International, an organization whose aim was to distribute Bibles to schools, and to those in jail, in the military, and in the hospital. I did not, however, recall Mom telling me about any association with them and my name. She'd named me for the biblical Gideon, that was all.

Thinking about Mom stirred a memory. A Gideon Bible at the doctor's office where she received her medical treatments before—

A clap of thunder jolted me. Should I find cover? Still, no rain fell.

Why'd you take her?

This, a second sort of prayer, and in only two days' time. Truth was, I blamed God, blamed him for her leukemia. Blamed him for her pain. Blamed him for her death almost five years earlier.

And yet, even in her absence, she was with me, her words—affirmations, exhortations—echoing in my mind, sometimes waking me from sleep.

How I'd wanted her with me when Janet—

Another clap of thunder, this time coupled with a large raindrop that landed fair and square on the Gideon Bible's cover, directly on the lamp.

Fitting. When you took her, seems my light went out too.

Tucked away at a table in the farthest corner of the Sand Dollar Diner, I used a handful of napkins to blot my face, neck, and arms. Before I had been able to gather my things, make my way to the safety of the hotel, the sky had opened, releasing the fury of God.

I'd managed to protect the Bible from pelting rain by wrapping it in the towel before sprinting for cover. Now, in the air-conditioned restaurant, goose bumps erupted on my arms and legs, and I shivered. Only an hour before the morning's keynote, and I needed to shower. But for some reason, I was avoiding my room, avoiding room service. Avoiding Jonah.

"May I take y'all's order?" Pen in hand, the young woman standing beside my table snapped a wad of pink gum. "Today's special's a fried egg san'wich, side a hash browns or grits, and coffee. A dollar fifty."

I recognized the voice. "They h-have you working the front desk and in the diner, eh?"

Her furrowed brow spoke her confusion. "What?"

"I think we s-spoke yesterday. I called the front desk to ask for a hotel guide. An in-room service m-menu."

The woman shifted. Squaring her shoulders, she tucked the pen behind her ear. "Oh, it's you."

"I s'pose I owe y-you an apology. Not from 'round here." I thought my choice of words, with a hint of feigned southern drawl, a nice touch. "Anyway, I w-was only playing with ya. I'm sorry."

Her posture eased as she removed her pen. "Accepted." Holding a pad of paper in her right hand, she twirled the pen with her left. "About your breakfast?"

"I'll take the s-special, please. Coffee, black. Thank you ..." I squinted to read her name tag. *Loraine*.

The blond waitress smiled. "You got it. Be back in a smidge."

I unwrapped the Bible from the damp towel, then dropped the sandy, wet bundle on the floor. Jonah's note still stuck out from near the front, and I turned to that page. As soon as the Bible lay open before me, Mom's words echoed. *Start each day with a small portion of God's Word, son. Doesn't take a lot, but see what a difference it'll make. A lamp to your feet. A light to your path.*

How many times had she said that? Too many to count, but hers weren't merely empty words. She'd lived by example, demonstrating her convictions daily, right up until her passing. And for a season, when I was younger, I'd heeded her encouragement, but then life had stepped in. Sports, school, and—

I shook off her image, the girl who'd been my steady almost entirely through high school, well into college, even grad school. We'd planned on spending our lives together, but then she had gotten—

"Coffee." Loraine laid the ceramic saucer and matching yellow cup down with a clang, then popped her gum again. "Say, tell me about the way you talk. I mean, if you can poke fun at me, at least you can tell me why you …" She paused, and her blue eyes softened at their edges. "Stammer."

You certainly don't beat around the bush. "I don't know. N-neuro-o-logical disorder of some sort, I guess." My gaze met hers. "But hey, has its p-pluses. Kept me out of Vietnam, I suppose."

It was true. Though men, some women even—at least a dozen I knew—had shipped off for Asia, I had been told I couldn't serve. And I wasn't entirely disappointed, though it only added to my sense of—

"Insecurity? Embarrassment? Do ya ever feel any of those, 'cause ya sure don't seem to." Loraine scratched her head with the capped end of her pen and snapped her gum. "I mean, I don't want to come across rude or anything. I just reckon, if it were me, I'd be embarrassed to open my mouth, afraid of how I'd sound." Another snap of her gum.

How to respond? "I g-guess you kind of get used to it. I've been this w-way all my life."

She uh-hummed before turning around. "Y'all's breakfast will be out shortly." Stopping, she turned her head. Meeting my gaze, she winked. "Me? I think it's kinda cute." Another snap. "Ha, stammerin'? Who'da thunk?"

Had that happened? Furthermore, the young woman I'd spoken with on the phone only twenty-four hours earlier had seemed more professional. This same person, my waitress, was sassy, straightforward. Maybe came with territory, depending on the job.

The Bible still lay open before me, and I scanned the two pages Jonah's letter had marked. At the top was *What the Bible Says About*.

Mom's face again. The only oncology appointment I'd ever

accompanied her to, we'd sat in the waiting room, an office copy of a Gideon Bible between us. Pounding the book with my clenched fist, I'd asked, "Why, Mom? Why would God allow this to happen?" But before she could answer, a woman in white came to the door and called her name. Jocelyn Stallings.

Ironic, because that visit had been the one marking the beginning of the end. Two words from her physician, which she'd shared through tears once she returned through that same door no more than thirty minutes later.

Three months.

Despite the small, bronze placard requesting all reading material remain in the doctor's office, I recalled taking a *Time* magazine from the waiting room. Slipped it inside my jacket. An act of rebellion, like stealing it somehow flipped the bird to Mom's sickness, to the doctor's prognosis.

Now, the words blurred on the pages in front of me, and I swiped my eyes with the backs of my hands. Reading further, down a bit, were Scripture references—particular places to turn in the Bible. As my finger traced the rows of references, there. Under a section with Christ—His Work, below Isaiah 53:5–6, two phone numbers were written in faded pencil, each with a different area code. Why would—

"Your breakfast, Mr.—"

Startled, I bumped my coffee, spilling some. After grabbing a napkin from the chrome holder, I sopped up the black liquid before its thin stream reached the Bible.

"Deon. Y-you can call me Deon." I cleared my throat. "Sorry about that. I was just—"

"Readin'? Looks like it, anyway." Loraine leaned over to get a better look. "Of all things, the Bible? Why, Deon Stallings, didn't take you as the sort who—"

"W-would read the G-Good Book?" I chuckled. "Why? What does a B-Bible reader look like?"

It was her turn to laugh. "I don't know. You just said yesterday you weren't lookin' for God, but I reckon that's 'cause you've already found him." She giggled. "And me? Guess I shouldn't be judgmental."

Ironic. "G-guess we're even." I closed the Bible, making room for the plate Loraine still held in her hand.

"Here ya go. Enjoy."

Before I took my first bite, Mom's words echoed once more. *Begin with prayer.*

"Okay, okay." I bowed my head and, in her honor, did what I knew she'd want. Though only a whisper, I prayed aloud.

"Thank you, God, for this food. Thank you for the hands that prepared it. Amen."

Funny thing. I didn't stutter. Not once.

After a keynote and several small group sessions, I made it back to room 212 that afternoon. It was obvious someone had come to tend it. The bed was made and the trash removed, including my remaining turkey club and chips from the day before. I'd discovered them, the bread stale and stiff, in my satchel earlier that morning.

I changed out of my smart-casual conference attire into the same Bermudas, shaking out wrinkles before pulling them on. Rummaging in my suitcase, I chose a Cincinnati Reds T-shirt. As I slipped my arm through the second sleeve, my phone rang.

"H-hello?"

"Is this Deon?"

"It is."

"Hey. This is Mike. Mike Bennett. You know, from the beach." He snickered. "And from the flight. You know, father to a precocious eight-year-old."

"Hi, M-Mike. What's up?"

"I know you're leaving on Monday. Was wondering if you might like to meet at the tiki bar later. Share a beer. Patti's got some kids' activity she wants to do with Billy. A movie or something. Said she didn't mind if I skipped out. That is, if you'd like to join me."

I considered the evening ahead. I'd decided to jog the beach, see if Jonah was on the pier like his note mentioned, perhaps take him up on his invitation to visit. Figured I could run right on by if I chickened out. And then, an organized conference dinner at—

"Hey, if you can't, I understand. Thought I'd check, that's all."

"No. I was t-trying to recall what time dinner was. I think a beer would be fine. Before supper, right? What t-time?"

"Five o'clock sound good?"

"Yeah. See you then."

I hung up, then sat on the edge of the bed to tighten my sneakers. The Bible lay closed beside me. I opened to where the note from Jonah was still tucked inside and noticed again the faintly legible phone numbers. Comparing the numbers with the one included on the hotel telephone, I noticed the first one had the same area code as that of the Sand Dollar Bay Resort. The other, however, was different.

Making a mental note to call the numbers later, I opened the Bible mindlessly, allowing it to fall open wherever it would. It was a section near the middle. The Psalms.

I scanned for a page number, locating it in the upper left-hand corner. Five hundred eighty-four. Flipping back a page, Psalm 139 began on the bottom right, but on the next, where the majority of the passage was, something caught my eye.

In the margin, faintly with pencil, someone had written a date and some words. More, there was underlining. But strangest of all was the way the pages were wrinkled, like they'd been wet, then dried. Had someone spilled something on them? I knew it wasn't from the rain earlier, as I'd taken care to keep it covered.

I read the first underlined portion: "Surely thou wilt slay the wicked, O God: depart from me therefore, ye bloody men."

In the next column, more words were underlined, words near the end of that particular psalm.

"Search me, O God, and know my heart: try me, and know my thoughts."

In the margin, right beside the first underlined passage, beside verse nineteen, someone had written *March 21, 1969*. Then, below, *Where were you, God?*

What in the world? The fact that someone had opened the Bible's pages, read these words, and written in the margins, not to mention writing two phone numbers, was bewildering. Was it the same person who wrote both, and was there more? If so, why?

After closing the book, I returned it to the bedside table. This time, however, I placed it inside the drawer, then slid it shut.

I'd investigate more when I returned. After grabbing my room key, I headed for the door. But first, I turned around and eyed the space of room 212.

What had happened here, and who'd shared this room—a mere three months earlier?

And once more, much to my surprise, I silently prayed: *A lamp to my feet and a light to my path, huh? Well, guide me, God, like Mom promised you would.*

CHAPTER 25

GIDEON—JUNE 1969

DESPITE THE EARLY-MORNING THUNDERSTORM, the afternoon, though hot and muggy, was beautiful. Like the day before, the beach was crowded. Heeding Billy Bennett's admonition, I paid attention as I jogged, making sure not to smash any sandcastles.

In no time, I could see the wooden pier in the distance. Again, it was lined with fishing poles held by people as varied in sizes and shapes as those sunbathing or beachcombing on shore. I scanned its length, looking for any with dark skin.

But the question remained. Did I want to visit with Jonah and meet his family? I'd only met the man once, only briefly. Still, he seemed somehow kindred, but why? What was it?

I sat, then removed my shoes. Tracing a circle in the sand with my bare foot, I considered my options. I wasn't scheduled to meet Mike for another hour and a half, which would give Jonah and me plenty of time to talk. But was that what I wanted?

His note had mentioned hearing sadness in my voice, in my words. Insecurity. But how could he know? Not one to open up quickly, I feared I'd say too much. Did it matter though? Perhaps

Jonah was the one I could talk to, be honest with. After all, he lived in South Carolina. I'd leave on Monday, return to Ohio, and that would be that. No strings attached.

As I sat there, the ocean spread out before me, Janet's face flashed again. This time, it was her tear-streaked face, the way her mouth drew downward when she cried. Ugly crying, that was what she'd called it. She'd tried to hide behind her hands, which I'd peeled away before kissing her on the lips. That was right before—

A seagull startled me. It flew low, then landed only several feet from where I sat. On black feet, it walked one way, then the other, all the while keeping a beady eye fixed on me. The bird's head moved with little jerks as he cocked it to the side, then back up, then to the other.

"Sorry, I don't have anything to eat." I chuckled. Conversing with a seagull? With a flick of my hand, the bird lifted, flying upward a few yards before landing again, this time, even closer.

I scanned the area. Several feet behind me, I spied a crust of bread. Reaching for it, I saw that it appeared to be the remains of a peanut butter and jelly sandwich. As I touched it, something caught my attention. Right beside the crust ... was it a shell? I picked it up.

Small, somewhat iridescent in the sunlight, it was a button. A pearl-shaped, purple button.

I held the object in my open palm. Turning it over, I blew, dislodging several grains stuck in the button's hole. No more than an inch in length, a single lavender thread remained. Secured by a knot, it was proof that, at some time, a seamstress had woven her threaded needle in and out, attaching the button to a garment.

The seagull walked uncomfortably close.

Tucking the button in the front pocket of my shorts, I reached behind me again, this time picking up the crust. "Here you go, fella." I tossed it toward the bird, and he gulped it down. "That's all I have, buddy."

I stood and brushed myself off. Once more, I allowed my gaze to wander from the farthest end of the pier toward the entrance. And there, I recognized them. A family of five, each member with dark-brown skin. Two boys and a girl, a woman wearing a colorful dress, some sort of scarf wrapped around her head, and ...

Jonah.

And at that moment, I decided. After all, what did I have to lose?

"I'll be! If it ain't Mr. Gideon Joseph." Jonah pumped my hand several times, his handshake firm, his smile spanning from one ear to the other. "Georgia, children, I want you to meet my new friend. Goes by Deon. Deon, this here's my beautiful Ms. Forney."

I extended my hand, which Jonah's wife took, her fingers long and lean. "Very nice to make your acquaintance, Mr. ...." Her head tipped to one side. "I'm sorry. I don't know your last name."

"Stallings. It's G-Gideon Stallings, but y-you can call me Deon."

"Very nice to meet you, Deon. Children, say hello."

A trio of voices rang out. "Nice to meet you, Mr. Deon."

"Nice to m-meet you also. All of you." Turning my attention to Jonah, I smiled. "You were right. You have a lovely family." I felt a tug on the hem of my T-shirt. I glanced down.

"Mr. Deon, wanna, wanna see me twirl?" Jonah's daughter smiled up at me.

I knelt down. "Now, wh-what's your name?"

"Beatrix. But most call me Bea." She batted her thick brown eyelashes. "I take dance."

"You d-don't say." I leaned toward her. "And you t-twirl?"

"Yep. I can twirl twenty times before I get dizzy and fall. Wanna see? Huh? Do ya?"

"Bea Bug, let's keep it to five twirls today. I don't want to see you twirl yourself right off this here fishin' pier." Jonah rubbed the top of his daughter's braided hair.

"Yes, sir." And with that, Beatrix twirled as if the weather-beaten planks were her stage.

I clapped when she stopped, and her smile grew wider. "That was f-fabulous. Tell me, how old are y-you?"

"Five. Be six in September." She cocked her head. "Why do you talk funny?"

"Now, Bea, that's not polite." Georgia tapped her daughter's shoulder. "Where are your manners?"

"It's o-okay, Ms. Georgia." As I turned to Bea, our eyes met. "It's c-called stammering. It's the way my brain works. Some s-say it's because I think faster than I c-can get the words out, though I'm not so sure about that." I chuckled. "Anyway, I'm g-glad you asked." I rose to face Jonah again. "And who are th-these strapping young l-lads?"

Jonah's sons hadn't spoken a word since *nice to meet you*. One was clearly older than the other, his height reaching nearly my own and the spitting image of Jonah.

"Boys, please introduce yourselves. You first." Jonah pointed to the shorter of the two.

"I'm Eli, short for Elijah. I'm headin' to fourth grade in the fall." The boy leaned close to me and whispered, "But I hope to get Ms. Eller as a teacher. Momma's strict."

I turned to Georgia. "A t-teacher? My dad's a teacher. Or, I should say, w-was one. High school."

"As Eli explained, I'm elementary. Fourth grade for the last five years. Before that, first."

"Momma, that means I mighta had you next year if you was still teachin' first." As she spoke, Bea slipped her hand in mine. "I love my momma."

"I c-can see why."

The little girl's tiny hand was warm in my own. Had I ever held the hand of someone whose skin was brown?

"Anyway, my d-dad retired some time ago, after more than th-thirty years." Directing my attention to Eli, I reached out. "Nice to m-meet you, Eli."

"And how about you, son?" This time Jonah pointed to his taller child.

"I'm Joe, short for Joseph."

After he extended his hand, we shook, and I noticed how firm his grasp was, like his dad's.

"I'll be in seventh."

Joe Forney's demeanor was different than the others. More serious, curt even, not warm like Jonah's. Why was that?

"V-very nice to meet you, J-Joe. My middle name's J-Joseph." Abruptly, my hand was empty again, still hanging in the space between me and the young man. "Has anyone ever t-told you how much you f-favor your father?"

He humphed before answering. "Taller though. Take after Momma's side, I reckon."

Although Jonah wasn't particularly short, I had a couple inches on him. Georgia was tall for a woman, about the same height as her husband.

She laughed. "Yes, my people were indeed tall. My daddy, at least six feet, six inches. And Momma too, nearly six foot herself."

It was Jonah's turn to chortle. "Yeah, I didn't get much in the height category, but I like to say I make up for it in matters of the heart." He scanned our group before continuing. "What'd ya say you and I go fishin'? The boys can man their own poles, and G's gonna take Bea for ice cream. I got cold drinks in the cooler, plenty a' sandwiches made up fresh this very morning, compliments of G."

"I helped too." Having released my hand, Bea clapped several times. "Didn't I, Momma? Spread the butter just so."

"You certainly did, Bea Bug. Now, how about we go and find us some ice cream? Gentlemen, we bid you farewell, for now. Jonah, boys, go catch us our Sunday dinner, hmm?"

"Yes, ma'am. Nothing finer after a good mornin' of worship. We'll do our best. Promise." Jonah tipped the brim of his fishing cap in Georgia's direction. "Boys, head on down the pier a piece. I hear the fish are bitin' real good on that there side, close to the end. Atlantic skipjacks. More'n you can count. A quarter for the first one to catch us our supper, if'n you can."

"You're on, Dad." Pole in hand, Eli turned and ran, dodging people as he made his way to the far end of the wooden pier. Joe, pole in one hand, a tackle box in the other, sauntered, taking his time.

"N-nice young men."

"They certainly are. The best, though I'm a bit biased. Here, help me unfold these chairs, won't'cha? This spot's as good as any."

We each unfolded a red-and-white-vinyl-webbed aluminum chair. Then Jonah moved a large red Coleman between us. "Side-table." He smiled, then handed me a pole. "You like fishin'?" A matching green Coleman sat to the left of Jonah, shoved up against the wooden rail.

"Can't say I've d-done it much in the last ten years or so. Used to f-fish a lot, before my mom ..." I stopped short, considering whether or not to jump right in with such an intimate detail of my life.

"My momma too. When I was but a child of ... five or six. Her momma, my Bibi, mostly raised me and my brothers and sisters. We kept her on her toes, that's for sure. When did your momma pass away?"

So much for withholding. "Almost f-five years ago. Around the time I turned twenty, right after I g-graduated from OSU."

"A Buckeye, huh? Fine football team, though I can't say I'm much of a fan. Baseball's more my sport."

"Mine too. P-played in high school. F-first base."

"Ya don't say. Never played myself, leastways for a school team. Street ball as a kid. You know, neighborhood sorta stuff." Jonah wove a small, wiggly baitfish onto one hook, then wiped his brow with a navy bandana he'd pulled from his back pocket. "Mighty hot out here. Prob'ly hotter tomorra though." He handed me the pole, then continued baiting his. Placing it between his legs, he opened the cooler. "Cola?"

"Sure." As Jonah reached in, I snuck a peek. Did the Coleman contain anything more than soft drinks? A beer perhaps? All I could make out, however, were Pepsis and RCs arranged on shaved ice. After taking the bottle Jonah handed me, I wiped it across my brow. "Thank you."

Jonah cast his line, then reeled in the excess before propping his pole against the wooden rail of the pier. I followed his example, then leaned back and took a long swallow of the ice-cold Pepsi.

Though no one spoke for several moments, the silence wasn't awkward. Rather, an aura of peace, something unfamiliar but good. Safe.

Finally, Jonah spoke. "Gideon Joseph. Yes, indeed. Quite a name your momma gave you." He guffawed. "My momma too, I s'pose. Jonah. Ha!"

I nodded. "Apparently we've b-big shoes to fill."

"Yes, indeedy. For you, Gideon and Joseph, both the Old and the New Joe. Men called to do hard things, I reckon. Humble men too, leastways Gideon and the carpenter Joseph. The son of Jacob, well, I s'pose he had to learn his humility." He chuckled. "Learnt it the hard way, like that there Jonah in the Good Book. Like me." He took a long drink. Then, leaning back, Jonah closed his eyes. "Not much finer than this, if'n I do say so myself."

Something inside nagged me to share. About what? Mom? Janet? Our—

"No one will tell ya I'm real smart, but my Bibi, she raised me to love the Lord. To fear him. That is, to respect him, to know my place in his presence, so to speak." Jonah turned to meet my gaze. "I don't know why bad things happen, but it ain't how God intended. No, sir. If'n anyone's weeping, I reckon, most of all, it's him, seeing how those of us made in his image have gone and done the world a lotta hurt." He shook his head, his gaze fixed once more on the water.

How could it be? It was as if Jonah, this man I barely knew, could read my thoughts, could hear my silent bantering, my arguments with God. With myself.

"You ever hear the verse in Psalms, the one in chapter fifty-six, I believe. Something about God collectin' all our tears and keepin' them in a bottle?" Holding up his near-finished cola, he shook his head. "Bigger'n this one, that's for sure. I reckon God has a pretty huge storage space to have all them vessels and vials and water tanks." He laughed. "Yes, sir."

Without thinking, I opened my mouth. "B-but why would God take someone so sweet like my mom? Someone who l-loved him her whole life, did for others before herself? Never d-did a mean thing?"

"Now hold on a minute, son." Jonah's eyes met mine again, his gaze intense, his brow furrowed. "Not a one of us is perfect. Not a one. Not even your momma, sweet and gentle as she may have been. That's why Jesus died. Because we all sinners, in need of grace. Saved by grace, yes, sir." He turned to focus on the water. "Ever hear that passage about God throwin' all our sins into the sea of forgetfulness?"

Had I?

"It's somewhere in the book of Micah, I believe. Says God takes the wrong things we do and hurls 'em out into the depths of the ocean, like this'n right here." He pointed. "All's we gotta do is ask him. Tell him we're sorry, that we want to be forgiven. That's it."

Winding up as if to throw an invisible baseball, he laughed. "Like this," and he flung his arm toward the water. "Gone, just like that."

And I couldn't help but wonder. Did Jonah know more about me than I'd shared? Did he know that, more than being angry with God for taking Mom, more than questioning the call he had on my life, especially with a name like Gideon, I had done the unthinkable? And to something—someone—I should have loved?

Did Jonah know about Janet?

CHAPTER 26

GIDEON—JUNE 1969

I JUMPED WHEN I HEARD her voice, then turned to see mother and daughter approaching, ice cream cones in hand.

"Daddy! Daddy!" Bea ran toward us, melted vanilla trailing down her brown arm. "Momma and I saw a juggler."

"That right, Bea Bug? Where was that?"

"By the confession stand, where we got our ice cream. He was juggling beach balls."

"You don't say." Jonah motioned for his daughter to come closer. "You sure are cute as a button, even when messy. Here, let me clean that up for ya." He ran his finger up the stream, starting at her elbow, then licked his finger. "Yum, but Bug, it's con-cession, not con-fession." He slapped his knee and whooped.

Bea giggled. "You're silly, Daddy." Sidling closer to me, she held out her cone. "Want some?"

Leaning toward her outstretched hand, I pretended to take a bite, then smacked my lips. "Like your d-daddy said, it's good."

"You didn't eat any." The little girl's tone registered her disappointment. "I mean it. Here."

Once more, Bea held out her cone. This time, I licked it. "There. How's that?"

"Good, ain't it? Vanilla's my favorite. Joe likes strawberry, and Eli likes chocolate. Not me." She scrunched her nose.

Georgia arrived and stood behind Jonah's chair. "Any luck, Mr. Forney?"

"Not yet, G. But be patient. Ain't many a fishin' trip where I come home with an empty Coleman, now is there?" He chuckled.

"True enough. Bea, let's you and me go check on your brothers. Leave these two to visit some more." She kissed the top of Jonah's head. "Gentlemen."

I watched for a moment as the tall woman and her petite daughter walked toward the boys. Georgia's posture was erect, her shoulders squared. She carried herself with confidence and poise. Her manner of speaking, refined. As Jonah had said, she was indeed beautiful, inside and out.

"You do have a w-wonderful family." I turned back toward the ocean. "How long have you b-been married?"

"Near twenty-two years, I reckon. Let's see. I'm soon to be fo'ty-two. Married when I was about twenty. That right?" He rubbed his chin. "Georgia, she wasn't yet nineteen. Almost two years younger'n me." Nodding, he gazed out over the water, his attention seemingly fixed on something in the distance, like he was remembering. "Helped lift me up outta the pit of despair, that one. Yes, sir."

What did Jonah mean? What pit of despair?

As though reading my thoughts, he continued. "As I was saying, Bibi, she raised me and the others. Did the best she could. But I had a wild hair. Prob'ly more'n one." He turned to face me. "Turned to drinkin', runnin' 'round. Got into all sorts a' trouble, for a spell, leastways. Dropped outta school. Eighth grade, I reckon." He tipped up his bottle, finishing the last of his soda.

After wiping his mouth with the back of his hand, he took out his bandana again and swiped his brow.

So, that was what he'd meant in his note, when he mentioned everyone going through hard times. But Georgia, she had saved him somehow.

"How did you m-meet Georgia?"

"Ha. Now, if'n that ain't a story." He slapped his knee. "My Bibi, she had a friend, a woman she knew from church. I didn't step foot in church in them days. No, sir. But this friend—Beverly was her name—she had a granddaughter. Played piana. Sang like a bird too." He chortled. "Sings like a bird, I should say." Jonah nodded, his gaze fixed again, looking out at the water to something beyond. "My Georgia, Beverly's granddaughter. Bibi and Bev ... they schemed. Somehow planned it so G'd be where I was fixin' to be on a Friday night. Down at the local pool hall, which, I might add, was no place for a lady. But G and a girl pal—what was her name?" Jonah rubbed his chin again. "Penny, that's right. Penny tagged along, and the two of 'em, they strolled in and sat in a booth, tucked in a corner like, chatting away, sipping on sodas and—"

Overhead, several seagulls cried, and Jonah's pole bent, the line suddenly taut. Jumping up, he grabbed it with both hands, then reeled. The pole bent more, the line tighter with each reel and pull, reel and pull.

"Looks like a d-doozie!" I, too, hopped to my feet. "N-need help?"

"Naw, just cheer me on. Maybe come tomorra for Sunday dinner, and help us eat this gift from the sea."

Was that an actual invitation? Dinner at the Forneys'?

After several minutes, the large Atlantic skipjack was flopping on the wooden planks of the pier. Jonah worked to free the tuna from the hook, then placed it inside the green Coleman. "Welp, one nice-sized skipjack. That's what's for Sunday supper at the Forneys'."

Without hesitating, I posed the question. "Did you m-mean for me to come to your house? Tomorrow?"

"Yes, indeed. Welcome to join us for church too, if'n you have the time."

Did I? Part of me wanted to experience worship with this family, each member seeming like a longtime friend. Still, part of me was uncertain. And the conference.

"Let m-me see what's on the schedule for tomorrow. They're wrapping up around noon, in time for lunch. M-maybe I can skip out altogether." Speaking of which ... "What time is it?"

Jonah glanced at his wristwatch. "Four fifteen already? How can that be? Time sure flies."

Sitting again, Jonah opened the cooler and pulled out a dripping RC. Holding it up, he nodded my way. "You?"

"Please." I handed him my empty bottle, then took the cold drink, cracked it open. "Thank you." After taking a sip, I said, "Continue with how you and Ms. Georgia met."

"Oh right." Jonah also took a swig before putting fresh bait on his line. After he cast again, reeling in the excess, he rested his pole on the rail. "Where was I?"

"Georgia and her friend were at the pool hall, sipping sodas, I think."

"Ah yes." He took another long drink. "Welp, I seen her over there, thought her the prettiest thing from the start. She smiled at me a couple times. I guess she knew who I was from Bev's and Bibi's description. Or maybe she'd asked round. Anyways, after a spell, I walked over'n introduced myself. Offered her a beer, which she declined. 'Don't drink the stuff,' she said. I asked her if she'd ever heard how Miller High Life beer's—"

"A sign God loves us and wants us to be h-happy. Is that what you said?" I couldn't keep from interjecting the line I'd said too many times to count, something I'd read once, a quote of Benjamin Franklin's. About hard drink, of all things.

With that, Jonah threw back his head and whooped. With tears in his eyes, his gaze met mine, and he wiped his face with his bandana. "If that ain't the funniest thing I ever ..." He snorted again, then blew his nose. "That's not what I said, though I wish'n I had." One more blow, and he wiped, then returned the hankie to his pocket. "No, I asked if she knew it was 'the champagne of bottled beer,' to which she replied, 'I don't drink that neither.' And I knew. Somehow, I knew. With all my shenanigans, not even thinkin' I wanted to give up my ways, one look in those eyes." Jonah paused. "It took some time, but, as I said, she lifted me up outta that pit I'd put myself in. Yes, sir."

Something in the way he said it left me suspecting more, but what?

"And you g-got married when? Right away?"

"Not long after, I s'pose. Had some unfinished business I had to take care of. Felt it was only fair, to G and ..." He stopped short of finishing his sentence, seeming to question whether or not to say what was on his mind, a lingering memory. "You see, I had another girl. She was ... she was with child."

I sucked in my breath. Jonah? But—

"Thing is, I was in no place to be a father. Never had one of my own to even know to be one proper-like." He turned his head side to side. "No, I had no business doin' all I'd been doin'. But as we know, things happen."

"Did you t-tell Georgia?"

"I did. But it's not what you think." Again, Jonah stopped. Scratching his head, he cleared his throat. "You see, the girl, she weren't more'n fifteen. And me? I was no support. So she went somewhere, never knew right where, and ..."

I knew.

"When I met G, I was still tryin' to figure out what to do.

Tryin' to forget, usin' booze to do it. Was runnin' from God. The whole of it, just a mess. And yet, she seen somethin' in me, believed in me." He shook his head. "That was more'n two decades ago now. And she still with me. Poor gal." Jonah chuckled. "Best woman I ever known." He patted my knee. "And that's what I mean when I say we all hit hard times. But ain't no pit deep enough where God can't reach down and rescue. Yes, sir."

The silence that followed, despite noise all around us on the crowded pier, stirred up all I'd been holding back. Without even thinking, I spoke. "The s-same thing happened to Janet."

Jonah turned to meet my gaze. "Janet?"

"My steady g-girlfriend, all through high school, even into c-college. Thought she was the one, that we'd marry, have a f-family. Even our parents were c-close friends. But then ..." How to explain? But Jonah, he knew. "When we f-found out she was pregnant, Mom had already passed away, and Dad was suffering. I didn't know how to t-tell him. And I didn't want to be a parent. Janet, she thought we could figure it out, but I told her no. I wouldn't. And so she went somewhere, even though it wasn't yet legal, and ..."

Jonah's head bobbed up and down as he offered empathetic clucking.

"After that, our r-relationship wasn't the same. I guess Janet didn't trust me. Why would she? She'd given me her h-heart, her body, and I—"

"Took." For the first time, Jonah's tone sounded like a reprimand. But he was right. I had taken. Taken and then ... took.

The irony struck, and for the first time in a long time, tears welled. Not over missing Mom, but over what I'd done—what I'd demanded—of and from Janet. "Yes, yes, I d-did."

Jonah handed me his damp handkerchief, and I wiped my face, blew my nose. "How do I l-let the pain go? How do I make things right?"

"You ask, then receive. The Good Book says it. 'Ask and you shall receive.' Ask for forgiveness, then receive what God promises." He wound up his arm again, then pretended to throw. "He'll toss it all into the sea of forgetfulness, remember it no more." He patted my knee again. "Wanna do that? Right now?"

I nodded. But was it that easy?

As if reading my mind, Jonah continued. "And you'll have days where you wonder if'n God really did forgive, but that's when you do what the Good Book says, right there in the words of the preacher Paul. You wrap up all them there thoughts, take 'em captive. Then give 'em to God. His Son died for all the sins of this world, past, present, and future. He died for yours."

I didn't recall hearing that particular passage. I'd look it up later, but right then, I bowed my head. "W-would you pray?"

"'Twould be my pleasure." Jonah cleared his throat. "Dear heavenly Father, this here be your boy. You made him in your image, planned good things for him to do with the time you give him. Yes, sir. His momma didn't make no mistake when she named him Gideon Joseph. And I reckon he's learnin' more on this trip than he 'spected."

How true that was proving to be.

Jonah continued. "More than just about building bridges and such. You've called him, Father, to be a builder-up of people. To lift 'em up outta the pit of despair, like my Georgia did. Yes, indeed. I pray you show him the way, Lord, but first, he comes to you with all his burdens. The loss of his momma. The loss of his girlfriend. And yes, the loss of a child, a precious one also created in your image." Jonah paused, cleared his throat. "We know you hold this child in your keepin' now and forever. Yes, we do. That is one thing we can be a'certain of."

Jonah paused once more. After a moment, I opened one eye. Jonah rubbed his chin. Was he recalling something? Struggling with his own rising emotion? Finally, he nodded.

"Yes, sir. Thank ya, God. Thank ya for that image. I see them. I do. Two little ones up in heaven with Jesus, the best a' friends. Yes, indeed."

I knew what he meant, what he'd envisioned. I reached to pat his knee, and he took my hand.

"Now, Lord, hear Gideon's prayer." Squeezing my hand, he asked, "What would you like to say?"

I cleared my throat. "God, I'm s-sorry for how I treated Janet. I hope to have the chance to tell her. I want to say I'm sorry." What else? "But even before that, I'm sorry for w-walking away from you, for not doing what Mom encouraged. The path took me to wrong choices, selfish choices. Please forgive me. Forgive me and m-make me clean, I pray. Forgive me for giving Janet no choice but to ..." I couldn't bring myself to say it. "I know now. We had other options, and the choice she made has d-damaged her too. Please heal her."

After a beat of silence, Jonah squeezed again. "Anythin' more?"

Was there? What was it I wanted? "God, please help me to live up to my n-name, even though I can't imagine how you'll do it. I'm a c-coward, but you've called me to be courageous. With you, maybe I can be. Forgive me for d-doubting that you have a plan. Help me walk in trust, with you. Amen."

For a moment, it again seemed we were alone on the pier, that no one else was around. I was enveloped in a peace I couldn't explain, didn't want to diminish.

"Ready?" Jonah motioned with his right arm, and I held up my left. We wound, then cast. "There now. Gone."

It had to be nearing five o'clock. I didn't want to leave, but I didn't want to keep Mike Bennett waiting. "Jonah, I have a c-commitment soon, but can you call me later? You know my room number, of course, and by the time you r-ring, I'll know my plans for tomorrow. I'd sure love to join you and your family."

"Yes, indeed. I sure will. Say eight thirty?"

I stood, then stretched. As I handed Jonah his damp bandana, I scowled. "Sorry about that."

"No worries 'tall." He patted my back. "One more thing. I was wonderin' if'n you noticed that the Bible by your bed had ..." He paused. "That it had been read by someone before?"

I nodded. "I did. I found s-several places where someone had written in it, underlined passages and such."

"Indeed. Somethin' not uncommon, that is, in one's personal Bible. You should see mine." He chuckled. "But a hotel Bible? Sad as it is to say, I don't think most folks even crack the covers of those Gideon Bibles, most times anyways."

"Do you know s-something about who it was?"

Jonah hesitated. "Let's say, I don't think God makes mistakes. He plans things for a purpose." His gaze was intense. "I reckon you've stepped into a part of his purpose."

What did he mean? "So you do know something. There w-was a date, in the Psalms." What was it? "Three m-months ago. March twenty-first, I believe." And near the front. "Two phone numbers inside. I was going to call them, see who answered."

Jonah's head bobbed up and down. "Yep, reckon ya should. And the business card? The one I used to mark Gideon's story?"

"Yes."

"I s'pect you should call that number too. Ask 'em about that date, the one in the Bible. Ask if there was anything about that particular weekend in fact. Maybe they know somethin' too."

Why would Jonah have a business card but not know its purpose? "It was f-for a print shop, if I'm remembering correctly."

"Yes. Smith's Print Shop."

"Was it n-not your card?"

"No, I found it. Saved it." Jonah ran a hand over his jaw. "I'll tell you more. Tomorra, I hope. Will call you later tonight, see what you think. Okay?"

We shook hands. "Tell your f-family goodbye for me. That I

hope to see them soon. After all, you've a large tuna to eat. How can I m-miss that?"

"Ha. Yes, indeed. And I'm not done fishin' yet. Boys neither. You may need to stay a month."

I laughed, then waved goodbye as I made my way off the pier and turned in the direction of Sand Dollar Bay Hotel.

Picking up my pace, I tucked my hand in the pocket of my Bermudas, and my fingers brushed something inside. The button.

And again, Bea's face flashed. Beatrix Forney, the girl who was, as Jonah called her, cute as a button.

Who might the button belong to? No telling, with the hordes of people combing the beach. Still, finding it seemed fortuitous somehow. At the very least, it was a sort of souvenir, something to remind me of my fresh start.

But was it true? Did God forget all our sins, never think of them again?

Then help me to forget, too, God. Because, well, it certainly is hard.

Maybe, when I was home, apologizing to Janet, making things right, would allow me to finally start over. But where would starting over take me? And with whom?

CHAPTER 27

GIDEON—JUNE 1969

"SORRY TO HAVE K-KEPT YOU WAITING." I pulled up a wooden stool, then plunked down, thankful for the shade under the thatched roof of the poolside tiki bar, though the stale, windless air was stifling.

A tinny steel drum and the rattle of maracas somewhere on the beach gave the sensation of the Caribbean, and the low-volume muffle of a sports commentator droning on about the previous week's PGA tour mixed with laughter from around the bar. *Defending champ Lee Trevino blames injured knee for missed stroke.* Something like that.

Mike turned his attention from the mounted television above a plethora of amber bottles behind the bar to me. With a thump, he set his beer on the bar, then ran his fingers through his dark, damp hair, which had a few silver stragglers here and there. "No worries, man. Just got here a few minutes ago myself. Took a quick swim with Billy, then sent him off to watch *The Love Bug* with his mom. He's been dying to see it."

I guffawed. "What'll they think of n-next? A major motion

picture, about a Volkswagen B-bug?" Lifting my finger to catch the attention of the bartender, I continued. "And a love story, at that?"

After ordering my beer, I turned my stool to face Mike. "Are you and the f-fam having a good time?"

"Yes, and the weather's been great. Not like last year."

"Do you come here o-often?"

Mike tipped back his bottle and swallowed down the rest of his Pabst. "We've been here several times. Three, four maybe. Last year? The weather was terrible. Rained almost the entire time."

"Not much f-fun for a child with his heart set on playing in sand. That Billy, he's g-got skills."

My Miller High Life arrived, and I took a swallow, then, wiping my mouth with the back of my hand, read the label—The Champagne of Bottled Beer.

Jonah.

"I take it Billy's your o-only child."

Mike shifted on his stool. Forearms resting on the bar, he held his empty bottle with both hands and stared ahead. Had I touched a nerve?

Finally, his gaze met mine. "Yeah. So far. Patti, she'd ..." He paused. "She'd love more kids, at least one or two more, but ..." Again, he stopped. "Sadly, hasn't happened."

I understood. "I get it. I'm an only ch-child too. My parents tried for another after me, but ... things never ..." I took another swig. "Being an only ch-child has its perks though. How does Billy feel about it?"

"Doesn't say much. Sometimes comments on how a friend at school has a brother or sister. How he wishes he had a playmate. That sort of stuff. Mostly, he seems content."

I finished my beer and considered another, but Jonah's voice interrupted my thoughts. "Trying to forget ... using booze to do it ... runnin' from God."

"How about another?" After picking up my empty bottle, the bartender wadded my napkin, then wiped the counter in front of me.

"No. I'm g-good, thanks."

"One'n done, eh?" Mike chuckled. "I'll take one more, please."

"You got it." The bartender laid out a fresh napkin.

"How about you? Any plans for a wife? Kids?" Mike fiddled with a plastic stir-straw, twisting it, then tying it in a knot.

I shook my head. "Not n-now. Had a girlfriend, for a long time, in f-fact. But it ended."

"Too bad. I mean, you seem like the sort who'd love a family. You're great with Billy and all."

"Yeah, I suppose. Maybe one d-day." But what did I want, now that Janet was gone and—

"Say, why don't you plan to come see us in Greensboro sometime? Patti loves to entertain, and Billy ... he already thinks the world of you." Mike pulled a pen from his front pocket, then wrote on his napkin. He handed it to me and smiled. "I mean it. We'd love to have you. Like Patti said, meeting on the plane, then on the beach ... it seems the universe or God or something is scheming." He chortled. "We're not so far from ... where'd you say you live?"

"Lima, Ohio. C-cow and corn country."

Mike snickered. "That's right. Quite a piece away, I reckon, though not by plane. And we have our share of cows and corn too. You'd feel right at home. Lots of options for flights, and we'd have the guest bedroom waiting for you."

Visit the Bennetts? Jonah was right. This trip to Myrtle Beach was proving to be full of surprises. Seemed I'd be heading home with not one but two invitations for friendship. Not what I'd expected when Robbins and Ray booked this trip. Fresh ideas, yes —but friends?

The napkin in hand, I read Mike's address and home phone

number, then folded it and tucked it into the front pocket of my shorts. "I may d-do that. But maybe you should ask Patti f-first."

"Naw. Like I said, she loves to entertain."

Before parting, we shook hands. "Nice to m-meet you, Mike. Be in touch."

With a slap on the back, he made a suggestion. "And who knows. I've got some lovely single ladies who work down at the firm. Might pick one out for ya. That is, if you don't mind. A double date perhaps?"

"M-maybe."

But even then, it was Janet who crossed my mind. Only this time, her face brought a smile.

After dinner, having stayed awake through what was a sleeper of a speaker, I visited the hotel gift shop. If I was to be a guest of the Forney family, the least I could do was be the bearer of gifts. I perused the children's section, and it struck me. There weren't any dolls with darker skin. Only faces with a variation of peach skin tones, like my own. Finally, I decided on a stuffed dolphin, Flipper on its tag. For Eli and Joe, I chose two Strombecker car kits—a Cobra GT and a Cheetah.

Now, what for Georgia? I laid my selections on the counter and dug in my front pocket for my wallet. What? After pulling my hand out, there, once more, I saw the purple button. This time, I inserted it inside the coin compartment, then snapped it closed.

"May I help y'all?"

I glanced up and met Loraine's gaze. She winked.

"You?" I snickered. "They have you w-working everywhere."

"It's Saturday. I work in the gift shop on weekends." She said it as if I should know.

"I was s-surprised, that's all." I brushed my hands over the items between us and continued. "I'll take these. But first, I wondered if you're open in the morning? To get fresh flowers?"

"Open at seven thirty sharp. Be me unlockin' the door." Loraine pointed over her shoulder. "Got a fresh batch of flowers this afternoon. You can take your pick."

"Perfect."

"Want me to hold these back, and you can pay for everything at the same time? Tomorrow mornin', that is?"

"Good thinking. Not sure yet when I'll b-be here. Definitely not right when you open. Will you be around at, s-say, nine thirty?"

"Be here all day." She smiled. "Been doin much reading this trip? You know, the Good Book and all?"

"In fact, I have." It was my turn to wink. "Thank you, Loraine. See you in the m-morning."

Back in my room, it was obvious someone had come to freshen it while I was out, replacing towels and such. Everything sparkled in the bathroom, the scent of Clorox lingering in the air. It hadn't been Jonah, I knew. He was spending time with his family.

His family—the Forneys. How nice they each were. That was, except Joe. It wasn't that he was rude but not warm, not friendly, like the others. Why?

The clock on the bedside table told me Jonah would be calling in thirty minutes. Before he did, I needed to finalize my plans. Did I want to attend worship with them or just join them for Sunday dinner?

I perched on the edge of the bed, then reached in and removed the Bible. With both hands, one on each side of its cover, I held it up on the corner of its spine, lengthwise, its gilded pages faced me. With one hand on either side, I allowed it to open randomly, to see where it fell.

Once again, it opened to those same water-marked pages, to Psalm 139. March 21, 1969. "Where were you, God?"

Who had written this? What did Jonah know?

He'd encouraged me to call the two numbers near the front of the Bible and to call Smith's Print Shop too. But it was after eight o'clock. Surely this business would be closed, and with the next day being Sunday, would they even open again until the first of the week?

I flipped to the front. There they were, the two numbers, right under Isaiah 53:5 and 6. I read the Old Testament passage. "But he was wounded for our transgressions, he was bruised for our iniquities: the chastisement of our peace was upon him; and with his stripes we are healed."

What did it mean? The passage fell under the category Christ —His Work. Was this speaking about Jesus?

I picked up the telephone's handset, then dialed the number with the same area code as the hotel. My heartbeat quickened, anticipating who would answer. After several rings—

"Myrtle Beach Police Department. Is this an emergency?"

The police department? My heart thumped. "No. No, I'm s-sorry. Wrong number." I hung up, fumbling as I attempted to replace the handset on its cradle.

Why would someone write the Myrtle Beach Police Department's number in the Bible? I wasn't getting answers, only more questions. What about the other number?

Reading it again, I saw that it had a nine-nineteen area code. Where was that? The only way to find out was to call the operator. Or call the number, but that could be costly. I'd need to use the pay phone in the lobby.

Only fifteen more minutes and Jonah would be calling. I dialed zero and waited for a moment.

"Operator. How may I assist you?"

"Yes, ma'am. Could you p-please tell me the town area code nine nineteen services?"

"Nine nineteen, you say?"

"That's right."

"One moment." There was a pause. "That would be Eden. Eden, North Carolina."

"Okay, thank you." I hung up.

Did I have time to get to the lobby, make the call, and get back to the room for Jonah's call at eight thirty? Yes, if I hurried.

After grabbing the Bible and my room key, I sprinted to the door and down the hall. In less than a minute, I was standing at the pay phone, panting like a tired dog.

I rolled my neck several times, then took a couple of deep breaths. Why was I nervous? Who would answer, but why did it matter?

Jonah's words rang in my ears. *I reckon you've stepped into part of God's purpose*, or something like that. Was that what this was? Part of God's purpose? And did I want to take that next step, call the number, find out who was at the other end?

I opened the Bible. After removing my wallet, I unsnapped the change compartment. There. That button again, right there among my dimes and quarters. I rifled through the change and pulled out a dime, then inserted it in the pay phone. The handset wedged between my ear and neck, I punched in the numbers written in the Bible, beginning with nine one nine.

One ring. Two. As I waited, I toyed with the idea of hanging up.

"Hello. Jackson residence."

Jackson. "Yes. I'm sorry. This m-may sound strange. My name is D-Deon. I'm in Myrtle Beach. I found this number in my hotel room. I wondered who—"

But before I could say another word, there was a click, then a dial tone.

Standing in front of the phone, Bible in one hand, handset pressed to my ear with the other, I pondered. Who had answered?

Someone named Jackson. Yes, a young woman. A young woman with the last name of Jackson. But who was she?

Maybe Jonah knew more. The only way to find out was to say yes, and seeing as God was somehow in all this, joining the Forneys for church seemed the right thing to do.

CHAPTER 28

GIDEON—JUNE 1969

"I'll take that m-mixed arrangement of long-stemmed flowers, those, right ... there."

Loraine removed the colorful bundle—an assortment of daisies, roses, and irises—still dripping from their plastic holder in the refrigerated compartment behind the cash register. "Any baby's breath? No charge."

"Sure. Th-thank you."

She wrapped the flowers in green mesh netting she had cut from a hanging roll on the wall beside the refrigerator, then tied them with a bright-blue ribbon. "How's that?" She reached under the counter and pulled out my gifts for the Forney children. "Anything else?"

What for Jonah? I scanned below the counter, where the candy options hung from metal hooks attached to pegboard. "How about these?" I laid a package of Chuckles and Neccos beside the other items. "That'll d-do me."

Loraine rang me up. I handed her the cash, then thought about the Bible I had in my leather satchel, the one that had been by my bed, the one I needed to take with me to Jonah's. Was it stealing?

"Since you work here, I thought I'd let you know I'm leaving for part of the day. Going to visit a friend. Wondered, is it okay if I take the Bible from my room off hotel property? I mean, it belongs to the Sand Dollar Bay, right?"

Loraine stared at me, her blue eyes wide. "Do you know? That was the longest I've heard you speak without a single stutter. Not a one."

Really? "That so?" I shrugged. "Maybe it's this good salt air."

Loraine giggled. "So you're sayin' you wanna take the Bible? I don't reckon it'll be missed, and besides, I think that's the Gideons' intention. I mean, that's kinda the point, right?"

Deon considered her words. "Hadn't thought about it that way, and no. I don't check out until t-tomorrow." Blast.

The corners of Loraine's mouth tipped up. "Almost. Guess you'll need to stay a little longer. You know, soak up more of this good sea air. That, or come back more often. Anyway, you take it. Keep it, fact. My grandpa's a Gideon. I'll have him bring another by this week, after you're gone. No trouble 'tall." Her smile broadened. "It'll make him happy knowing someone actually cracked the Bible's cover, since so few do."

Keep the Bible? What was God up to? Seemed he was literally using the Good Book as a lamp to my feet, a light to my path, like Mom had said.

Question was, where would it guide me?

"If'n it ain't Gideon Joseph. Lookie here, Bea Bug. It's our friend, and don't he look spiffy?" Father and daughter stood just outside the revolving door in the hotel lobby. Jonah scanned me up and down. Noticing the bundle of flowers in my hand and the Sand Dollar Bay gift shop bag, he shook his head. "My, my. And gifts too. I'm a'guessin' those posies are for Georgia. Am I right?"

My smile and a slight tip of my head answered his inquiry.

Bea twirled several times, making her way to me. Jonah stood right where he was, a smile spanning from one ear to the other. He looked me up and down. "That's a mighty fine suit you got there, Deon. Yes, sir."

"Didn't know if I'd n-need one. Conference itinerary said smart casual, b-but I brought my suit, just in case."

Truth was, I'd only worn it once. To Mom's funeral. When I had put it on thirty minutes earlier, I'd found her bifold funeral program still tucked in the breast pocket. I'd opened it, then sat on the little metal chair on my balcony with coffee, reading again the words to James Rowe's "Love Lifted Me." Always her favorite, there was no question what hymn my cousin Jenny, Mom's sister's daughter, would sing at the funeral.

Perhaps I'd tell Jonah more about Mom while we rode to church.

"Is it j-just us? Where are the others?"

"Ms. G was still powderin' her nose when Bea Bug and I left. Said we'd swing by and pick her and the boys up on our way. Church isn't more'n five minutes from our place." Jonah clapped his hands. "Shall we?"

Bea slipped her hand in mine and led the way, with Jonah ahead of us, the first to enter the hotel's revolving door. Bea squeezed in with me, and we pushed.

"This door's funny. I want to go round and round." She giggled, her breath against the glass building up condensation, creating a tiny heart-shaped spot of moisture.

"Let's go one more time."

"Really?"

We pushed right on by Jonah, who stood on the sidewalk on the other side of the glass. Though I couldn't hear his laughter, when we made it back around, Jonah was wiping his eyes with a clean, white handkerchief, the last of his bellow muffled behind the cloth.

"I'll be, if that ain't somethin'." He stuffed his handkerchief in the pocket of his gray-and-black pin-striped suit coat. "You two make quite a pair. Wait till I tell G."

Jonah opened the front door of his black Plymouth Satellite. "Here ya go, Mr. Deon. And don't forget to buckle up." He closed the door, then opened the back one for Bea. "And you neither."

"But Daddy, I can't sit on the hump and go bumpety bump if I'm buckled in. Please?"

"I reckon, but only until we get out onto the main road. Then you buckle up, hear?"

"Yes, sir."

After ducking into the front driver's seat, Jonah buckled with a click, then adjusted his rearview mirror. Under his breath, he said, "Yes, sir. Put things in the rearview mirra'. Keep 'em there."

I knew what he meant.

"Thank you for picking me up." I bent to set my leather satchel on the floorboard, along with my bag filled with gifts. After slipping the Bible out, I laid it on my lap. The flower bundle was tucked between me and the car door.

Jonah side-eyed me. "A-ha. The Good Book, eh? Yes, sir."

"Funny. When I went to the gift shop this m-morning, the girl who checked me out told me to keep it. Loraine. Know her?"

He smiled. "Indeed, I do. Wears lots of hats at Sand Dollar. Pretty as a picture."

She was pretty. "We didn't get off on the r-right foot, but I think we're okay now." I snickered. "Lesson learned. You can't j-judge others because of how they speak. I, of all people, should know that."

"What'cha mean?"

"Remember what I asked you when you brought me the hotel

guide? I wondered why southern folks say *y'all*, even if they're only talking to one person."

"I do remember."

"I was referring to a c-conversation I'd had with her, on the phone. Boy, was I irritable. Didn't make a good f-first impression."

"Hear that, Bea Bug? Isn't that what Momma tells you and the boys? You only get one chance to make a good first im—"

"'Pression." Bea hopped up and down in the backseat, still unbuckled. "I'm a bunny, Mr. Deon."

Turning to see her, I grinned. "Cutest bunny ever."

"Bea, buckle up now, hear?"

"Aw, Daddy. Do I have to?"

"Yes, ma'am. Now. We're on the busy road. Gotta keep ya safe."

With a click, Bea obeyed, then leaned her head against her seat, humming a little tune.

"Anyway, I had a chance to m-make it up to her. Loraine, that is. At the diner the next day. She was my waitress. Gave her a good t-tip."

Jonah's head bobbed up and down. "Nice girl. I know her granddad."

"She mentioned he was a Gideon, that he'd replace this Bible in my room."

I reflected on the last couple days. It was Sunday. I'd arrived on Thursday night, had only been in Myrtle Beach for two full days, yet so much had happened in so little time.

"Jonah?"

"Yes."

"I called the n-numbers in the front of the Bible, like you suggested."

"And?"

"One was for the local police d-department."

"And the other?"

How to explain? "It was for someone in Eden. Eden, North C-Carolina."

"You don't say."

"When I called from the lobby pay phone, a young woman answered. Said 'Jackson residence.'"

"Go on."

"I think I fumbled, not sure what to say. Then I mentioned I was staying in Myrtle Beach. That I'd found the n-number, but—"

"She hung up on ya, right?" Jonah clicked his tongue and shook his head. Then, under his breath, "Ava."

"What? Who?"

He side-eyed me again. "Ava. Ava Jackson."

"You know her?"

"Naw. Can't say I know her 'xactly. Know *of* her though. A little, anyways."

"What c-can you tell me? What happened?"

"That there Bible in your hands, that and ..." He stopped, rubbed his freshly shaved jaw. "I got it at home. Will show you when we get back from church. It may fill in some blanks. Answer some of your questions."

What was Jonah talking about? What else was there?

"But how?"

"Miss Ava Jackson, she visited the Sand Dollar Bay too. What's that date she wrote?" He tipped his head to the right. "In that there Bible?"

"March twenty-first, 1969."

"Yes, indeed. That's when it was. Spring breakers for as far as the eye could see."

So, it was Ava. Ava Jackson from Eden who'd written *March 21, 1969, Where were you God? in the margin of Psalm 139.* When she visited Myrtle Beach, for spring break. A couple of puzzle pieces were placed, but there was so much more. Questions swirled.

As if reading my thoughts, Jonah continued, though his eyes

were fixed on the road ahead. "Yes, sir. She stayed in room 212 too, with another girl. What was her name?" Again, he cupped his jaw. Only his index finger moved up and down, rubbing his left cheek. "Elaine. That's it. I member 'cause I kept wantin' to call her Loraine, the girl from the front desk, the diner." He chuckled. "Anyways, I tended their room that weekend, or, should I say, for the day or two they occupied it. Like you, I noticed the Bible by the bed. How could I not? She'd left it open, right there on the bedsheets." Once more, he side-eyed the book I held. Tipping his head toward it again, "Did you find any more markin's? Any more clues?"

Besides the phone numbers and the writing left in the Psalms, I hadn't, but then, I hadn't made much of an effort. After making the call the evening before, I'd forgotten, being so perplexed with the little I'd discovered. The police department. The girl's voice. Jackson residence.

After a moment, like I'd done in room 212, I allowed the Bible to fall open on my lap, right there in Jonah's Plymouth. Again, it fell to Psalm 139. This time, however, I closed its cover and, starting from the beginning, fanned the pages, felt the brush of air as my fingers ran from Genesis to Revelation, eyes glued as they turned. Were there other underlined portions? Any more writing?

"See anythin'?" Once more, Jonah tipped his head toward the Bible.

"Not yet." But on the second run-through, there. Several books past the Psalms, closer toward the back of the Bible, in Lamentations. Ironic.

"There. There's s-something."

Taking advantage of a red light, Jonah glanced my way. "You don't say."

And it was true. Several verses in chapter one had been underlined. Was there more? These pages were water-marked too, though not as wrinkled as those in Psalm 139. I ran my index finger down the page, quickly reading aloud from the beginning, trying to gather the book's context. Someone—Ava?—had certainly read them before me.

> She weepeth sore in the night, and her tears are on her cheeks: among all her lovers she hath none to comfort her: all her friends have dealt treacherously with her, they are become her enemies ... Also when I cry and shout, he shutteth out my prayer ... And I said, My strength and my hope is perished from the LORD: ... This I recall to my mind, therefore I have hope. It is of the LORD's mercies that we are not consumed, because his compassions fail not. They are new every morning: great is thy faithfulness.

I checked the underlined passages' references, then made a mental note. First was Lamentations, chapter 1, verse 2. Then a couple of pages over, chapter 3, verses 8, 18, and 21 through 23. And there, in the margin of page 732, a cross-reference was written, along with two sentences.

Psalm 139:14–18. What are you saying, God? That all life is precious?

My head spun with my many questions. The mystery of it all. My part in it. And I echoed this girl, a young woman whose name I now knew.

What are you saying—

And as if Jonah spoke for him, he interrupted my prayer. "Like I say, Gideon Joseph, seems you've stepped into part of God's purpose. The real question is, what'cha gonna do now?"

CHAPTER 29

GIDEON—JUNE 1969

JONAH PULLED IN THE DRIVEWAY, and I slapped my knee. "So this is the Forney r-residence. And here I am for Sunday d-dinner." I still couldn't believe all that had transpired and in such little time.

Having unfolded from the Plymouth, Jonah came to stand beside me on the passenger side of the car, which had, moments earlier, been crammed full with Forney children. "Well, what'cha think of Sunday worship?"

As soon as the service had ended, Georgia had hitched a ride with a friend. "To get dinner on," she'd explained. "Y'all linger as long as you like."

What did I think of their lively worship service? "Not like church b-back home in Ohio, that's for sure. But I liked it. I really d-did."

I scanned the tidy, cool space of their garage. Stepping inside, I inhaled, breathing in that familiar smell—a little bit automotive oil with some paint thinner mixed in, plus a hint of old, weary things. In a word, it was nostalgic, and I closed my eyes. "Why do I love the smell of a garage?"

Jonah guffawed. "You don't say! Me too. Takes me back to the shed out behind Bibi's, where she'd send us when she needed a ladder or a tool. Smoked more cigarettes in that li'l shed than I dare count." He sighed. "But not no more. No, sir." He paused, then inhaled deeply too, exhaling with a rumble of his lips. "Like'n I said, some things belong in the rearview mirra'."

Our conversation on the pier only the day before echoed. Cast it in the sea of forgetfulness. Remember it no more.

Funny. Since doing so, since our prayer, I'd not thought much about Janet, except once or twice, coupled with a peace I couldn't explain.

"You men comin' in, or are you gonna hang out in that musty garage all day, hmm?" Georgia smiled through the screen door, her hands on her apron-clad hips. "Well?"

"We's comin', G. Gotta unload some things. Be right in."

Jonah took my leather satchel from the front floorboard, and I gathered the flowers and other gifts. The screen door creaked as he opened it, then he motioned for me to enter first. The fragrance of home-cooking wafted through the air, and my mouth watered.

"Welcome to our humble home." Georgia was standing at the stove, stirring something bubbly in a stainless-steel pot. Crackling erupted from something else in a cast-iron skillet on the larger back burner. Skipjack?

Turning around, Georgia's expression spoke her delight. "Why, Mr. Deon, are those for me?"

"Yes, ma'am. And thank you for h-having me."

I extended the bouquet toward her, and she took it, then buried her face deep within and breathed.

"How'd you know? Daisies are my favorite, roses a close second." She stepped aside to pull back a red-and-white gingham curtain hanging below the kitchen sink, then drew out a large green mason jar. "Here. Would ya mind filling this with water, please?"

I took it from her outstretched hand. Georgia returned to the stove to flip what I assumed were tuna fillets, grease popping all around her fork. I ran water at the porcelain basin until the jar was half-full.

"Now, if ya don't mind, please arrange those pretty posies for me. Put them there, on the dining table."

I noticed how, at home, Georgia's manner of speaking was less refined, more at ease. More like the others in the Forney clan. I smiled as I worked.

"If'n you'll excuse me, I'm gonna go change outta my Sunday duds." Jonah stood behind Georgia and kissed her on the nape of her neck. "Be back soon, G."

Alone with Jonah's wife, I fiddled with the handle of a broom, its leather cord hanging from a nail. "Anything I can do to h-help?"

Georgia turned, her gaze moving about the warm, pleasant space that was both kitchen and dining room. "Mind settin' the table?"

"Not at all."

She pointed to a free-standing hutch against the far wall. "Utensils in the drawer there, dishes and glasses behind the doors."

"Yes, ma'am." How odd it was to be nearly a stranger in the Forneys' home and yet feel so kindred, so at ease, like we'd known one another a long time. "I have to t-tell you, Ms. Georgia. You remind me so much of my mother."

Her eyes did all the smiling, and her hands returned to her hips. "You don't say. How so?" She tipped her head to one side.

What was it? "I'm not rightly sure. For one, she loved daisies. And cooking." What else? "And Mom loved my dad and—"

"You. She loved you an awful lot, I reckon." Georgia's lips curled then, like they were trying to meet the tips of her crescent-moon eyes. "I bet you miss her."

"I do. Every day." Had Jonah shared with Georgia all we'd

discussed the day before? "Like you, she l-loved Jesus most of all. That's what helps. When I'm missing her, I mean. To know I'll see her again s-someday. At least, I believe that."

Though she was once again turned away from me, her hands stirring and flipping, she nodded. "Yes. Yes, indeed," and, with that, she began to sing:

His oath, his covenant, his blood, support me in the whelming flood;
When all around my soul gives way, he then is all my hope and stay.
On Christ, the solid Rock, I stand;
All other ground is sinking sand,
All other ground is sinking sand.

Billy. *Build on solid ground. That's most important.* Isn't that what I'd told him, what, only two days ago.

I set the oil-cloth-covered table, like my mom had once taught me, and Georgia continued to sing, her voice indeed that of a song sparrow. Like Jonah had said.

As I laid the last spoon beside the knife, Jonah joined us in the kitchen, clad in black bell-bottomed trousers and a Brooklyn Dodgers T-shirt. "Phew! I tell ya what! This kitchen's hotter than Atlanta in August. But sure does smell better." Standing behind Georgia again, he kissed her neck, then smacked his lips. "And you, Ms. Forney. You're saltier than pork drippin's but tastier, like those strawberry pies I'm guessin' you've got tucked away somewhere. Now, where might'n they be?"

"Hold your horses, Mr. Forney. Dessert comes after this good fish dinner, and it's almost time." Once more, she addressed me. "Would you call the kids, please? They're playin' stickball outside. You can go out through the garage. Can't miss them."

The garage screen door slapped behind me as I stepped out onto the cool concrete. Eying the space, I recognized the same red and green Coleman coolers from the day before, fishing poles lined up neatly against the far wall, beside a waist-high deep freeze. A wagon sat by the exterior door, along with a tricycle. Gardening tools hung in a row beside the screen door, and a pull-down attic cord dangled only feet away. Everything had its place, offering a picture of the life of the Forneys. Why was I struck by how similar their garage was to our own? To Dad's and mine?

Venturing through the door leading to their yard, I felt the heat and humidity hit, and I sucked in my breath. Georgia was right. The three Forney children were playing stickball in the side yard, each still dressed in their Sunday clothes. Further down the dirt road were more houses of similar size and shape, more children playing outside, and some men gathered in a group, thin lines of cigarette and cigar smoke trailing upward, each man with dark skin.

"Kids, your m-momma said to call you for dinner. Gotta eat that good tuna you caught."

"You mean, I caught." Eli reached me first. He was carrying his suit coat, beads of sweat dripping from his forehead. "Joe didn't catch a thing, did ya, Joe?"

Joe kicked the dirt several times as he made his way, never making eye contact. What was it about him? As he passed by me, however, he mumbled something that sounded like "Dang Yankees." So, that was it.

Still holding the door, it was Bea who walked through last, and she hugged my leg before stepping over the threshold. "I love you, Mr. Deon. I'm glad you're our friend."

"I ..." I choked on the words. "I love you too."

Inside the toasty kitchen, each of the Forneys sat at their designated seat. Jonah held out his hand to the one beside him. "This here's the seat of honor. For our guest, Mr. Gideon Joseph."

I sat down, then scooted up close. My gaze ran over each person, each similar but unique. Joe, who resembled Jonah. Eli, with eyes like his father, but whose nose was more like his mother. And Bea she, too, the perfect blend of both these beautiful people.

"Let's give thanks to the Lord for this fine food." Jonah bowed his head, and everyone followed suit. "Father, we thank you for this gift from the sea, for all good gifts, created by your loving hands. Thank you for our family and for our new friend. We ask that you bless him and guide him and us today, as well as in the days to come. Amen."

I lifted my head and caught Joe peering up at me from his folded hands. He quickly shifted his gaze.

"Deon, if you'd please begin. You can start with that there fish. With what I caught, what Eli caught, we had enough for today and some for the freezer." Jonah slapped his knee. "Yes, sir. That's what I call a lucky day!"

I forked out a buttery skipjack fillet, then, after passing it on to Bea, who sat to my left, helped myself to mashed potatoes, fresh sliced tomatoes, and fried okra. Finally, Georgia handed me a basket lined with a gingham cloth matching the kitchen sink curtain. Unfolding it, I saw steam waft up from a pile of golden corn muffins.

My plate heaped with food, I sighed. "I can't th-thank you enough for having me. Ms. Georgia. This is the best meal I've had in a long time. Since Mom p-passed, Dad and I eat pretty simply. Not a lot of homemade, like this."

"Dig in. We're honored you're with us."

With the clinking of forks and knives came the occasional, "There's a bone ... Watch out, there's another." We visited as we ate. Bea told me about dance, and Eli, who loved wrestling, explained moves he'd learned, even asking if I'd allow him to demonstrate after dinner, to which I agreed.

At one point, Georgia rose to run water in the sink. "Bea Bug, you're gonna help me wash dishes in a bit, okay?"

"Sure, Momma." Leaning over, she tugged on my sleeve, and I tilted my head toward her. "Guess what." Bea's voice was only a whisper. "I love to wash dishes. All those bubbles." She smiled.

After Georgia returned to her seat, the conversation turned to favorite subjects, as well as the kids' excitement about the upcoming school year. It was then I learned more about Joe.

"What's your f-favorite subject?"

Without hesitation, he answered. "History, though some of it's hard to hear."

That piqued my attention. "Really? Why's that?"

He set down his fork, then wiped his mouth before looking first at his dad, then at his mom. "You know, the parts about slavery, the Civil War. Those sorts of things."

Likewise, I laid my fork on my almost clean plate, then nodded. "I'm sure."

"Why are you sure? Why would that part of our country's history be hard for you?" For the first time, Joe stared at me, his brow furrowed. "I mean, you don't know what it's like to be a slave. For your ancestors to have been slaves."

He had a point. I shifted in my seat.

Coming to my rescue, Jonah interjected. "Son, mind your manners."

"It's okay, Jonah. I'd l-like to hear how he feels. Really."

It was Joe's turn to shift. "My teacher last year, Ms. Walsh, she told us about the Ku Klux Klan. Told us the Klan still exists in places. We even found out there's Klan up north in Ohio. That right, Mr. Deon? You know anything about the Klan?"

Truth was, I did, though I certainly wasn't part of it, didn't know very many who ever had been. But yes, it existed. I nodded. "Yes, I do, Joe, but that doesn't mean—"

"Got any friends of color back there in Ohio?" Joe's tone

registered anger. His jaw tightened, and his teeth clenched at the end of his sentence. "Do ya?"

"I don't guess I do. Not f-friends anyway. A few acquaintances, from around town and such." I took a sip of sweet tea, my mouth suddenly parched.

Taking advantage of my silence, Joe spoke. "My teacher, Ms. Walsh, she says you can't judge a person until you've walked in their shoes, and I'm guessin' that's truth."

It was Georgia's turn. "Son, that's true on both sides of the aisle. You can't judge Mr. Deon either, just 'cause he has fair skin. Doesn't make him racist. Doesn't mean he'd discriminate. Doesn't mean he agrees with those who do. Isn't that right, Mr. Deon?"

She was right. Still, I sensed a tinge of conviction, several thoughts I'd had over the last twenty-four hours needling me with guilt or maybe sadness. When Bea held my hand, asked me to eat a bite of her ice cream, told me she loved me. And what about being surprised with the Forneys' garage being so similar to my own?

"Joe, I'll make you a d-deal. Because you're right but so is your mom. I can't know what it's like to have dark skin, to endure the hardships that I'm sure c-come with the territory, simply because of your skin color. But what your mom said is true too. It w-works both ways." I took one more swig, then set my glass down. "Let's you and me be pen pals. Share our thoughts and experiences in l-letters from time to time. I mean, after this weekend, with all of you, I sure do have a lot I could write about." I smiled at each member of the Forney family, then rested my gaze on Joe. "How about it?"

Joe let his eyes wander too, seeming to look at each of those around the table. Finally, his gaze landed on me. This time, his brow wasn't furrowed, his eyes softer. "Deal."

With that, Georgia rose again. "Bea, help me, please. Gather the dishes, scrape them, and bring them to the sink. Men, it's almost time for dessert."

"Hallelujah!" Jonah slapped his knee. "Never thought I'd hear it. Thank you, Lord. Thank you for strawberry pie!"

The dishes cleared, Bea placed thick slices in front of her daddy, her brothers, and me. "Want whipped cream?"

"Please." I scooted my dessert plate a bit closer to the bowl near the center of the table, the white cream towering over its brim. "Two d-dollops, if you don't m-mind."

"Sure thing." And she plopped two heaping spoonfuls on my piece of pie, then did the same for the others.

"Mm, mm, mm. G, this is the best you ever made." Jonah smacked his lips, then turned his attention to me and chuckled. "Deon, have I ever told ya how old I am?" He licked his lips, leaning forward in his chair.

"I believe you said you're forty-two. Am I right?" Why this order of conversation?

"That's right. Fo'ty-two in no time 'tall." Jonah snickered. "Today, in fact."

"You don't say? Today?" Why hadn't anyone mentioned it?

"That's right." As if reading my mind, he said, "But we'll be celebratin' later, on Eli's birthday, which is only two days after mine."

So, that was why.

After a beat of silence, he said, "Ya know why I'll love bein' fo'ty-two?"

I shook my head. "No idea."

"What's the number of the best baseball player who ever lived?"

Where was he going? "Are you talking about H-Hank Aaron?"

Jonah threw back his head and roared, then wiped his eyes with his napkin. "No, sir. Though he's a good'n, that's for sure." He leaned back, then pointed to his T-shirt. "This is my team. The Dodgers."

I knew. "Jackie R-Robinson?" It hit me. "Forty-two. I get it."

Jonah bellowed again. "Yes, sir. That's why that's my fav'rite number. Best number there is."

Was Jonah going somewhere with this, perhaps tying together the previous conversation with Joe and this one, about Jackie Robinson?

Once more, as if reading my mind, his words brought clarity, though, this time, Jonah's gaze was fixed on Joe. "You know what he said? Somethin' about knowin' he's a Black man in a White world and that made things right hard sometimes. But he also said he wasn't so much concerned whether folks liked him or not. What mattered most was that he was respected as a human being."

Jonah paused, then took another bite of his pie. As he chewed, he put his hands behind his head. "Yes, sir. I s'pose we can all learn from one another, no matter the color of our skin." He turned his attention to me and concluded. "And Mr. Deon, I reckon we all wanna be liked. Yes, indeed. But sometimes, sometimes what the good Lord calls us to ... well, the most important thing, whether folks like ya or not, is to respect human life. Yes, sir."

What was he saying? Jonah seemed to be weaving something together, like he was preparing me. But for what?

Right then, Bea turned from the sink where she'd been washing dishes. Her arms were covered with white soap suds. Coming to stand beside me, she held out a soapy arm. "Look, Mr. Deon. I'm white. White like you."

Everyone was silent. Then, with a cackle that seemed to erupt from somewhere deep inside, Jonah threw back his head and roared. Georgia, too, laughed as she joined us at the table, standing between her sons, a hand on each shoulder.

My face grew warm. Should I laugh too? When cackling erupted from across the table, coming from Eli and Joe, I let it out, and we all laughed, laughed until we cried.

"Bea Bug, you are something, that's for sure." Jonah swiped his eyes, this time with the hankie he'd pulled from his trousers, then blew his nose.

Sidling even closer, Bea took a finger and ran it through the soap suds, then dotted my nose with it. "And really, you're not white either, not compared to bubbles," and everyone roared again.

Once more, I glanced up and my eyes met Joe's. Only this time, he didn't look away.

CHAPTER 30

GIDEON—1969

"I LOVE MY C-COCKLESHELL, Bea. Thank you." I examined the small, white shell the little girl had fetched from her bedroom after opening my gift to her. In a sing-songy manner, she'd exclaimed, "A treasure from the sea. A gift for you, given by me."

"And I love my Flipper!" Bea twirled around the kitchen, spinning so many times I lost count.

"Boys, what do you say to Mr. Deon? Those are awfully nice car kits." Jonah held the Cobra GT's box, reading its description. "This here'll be right pretty when finished, Joe. Always wanted me one of these."

"Thank you, Mr. Deon." For the first time, Joe smiled at me. He did resemble Jonah.

"Yes, thank you." Eli grinned from ear to ear too. "Never had a die-cast model-car kit before. Can't wait to start buildin' it."

"You can spread things out on the workbench in the garage. That way, you'll have space enough, and it won't take up the kitchen table or the table in the family room. How does that sound?" As she spoke, Georgia untied her apron, then hung it on a nail atop the free-standing hutch. She dusted her hands together and assessed the kitchen. "While you men visit, I believe I'll take me a nice long Sunday nap." She picked up the mason jar with her assorted flowers and breathed deep their fragrance again. "And these here roses. Nothing like that scent."

"Did you know dark-red roses represent unconscious beauty?" I glanced at Georgia Forney. The irony wasn't lost. "Deep burgundy, like a fine red wine." The words out, I regretted saying them, fearing the comparison, given Jonah's past, might be offensive. My worries, however, were quickly laid to rest.

"If that ain't the truth." Georgia inhaled again, and sighed, eyes closed. "Nothin' like it."

She held the flowers in her left hand and ran the backside of her right over Jonah's face. "Now, you and Mr. Deon enjoy a visit in the family room. I turned on the fan, so it should be nice'n cool." Georgia giggled. With a shake of her head, she added, "Cooler anyway. Kids, you go outside and play. Rain's s'posed to set in tomorrow. Might sock us in for a spell."

Without hesitation, the three Forney children scampered out the screen door, and it slapped closed behind Bea.

"Shall we?" Jonah motioned for me to follow, and we walked through a narrow archway and into the Forney's family room.

Georgia was right. Compared to the cramped kitchen, where that miracle of a meal had happened, this room was much cooler. Drapes were pulled over a large picture window, and a box fan's motor whirred from where it stood propped in the far corner.

"I love this here room." Jonah led the way to a weathered green-fabric couch opposite the picture window. "It stays shaded by that palmetto tree outside the winda and stays a might cool most of the day, even in the heat a' summer."

I sat beside him, the Bible on my lap. We stretched out our legs, leaning into the soft cushions, worn with use, over what I guessed were a good many years.

I sighed. "Haven't had a meal like that in a long time. Ms.

Georgia cook like that every day? Or only on Sundays, for company?"

"Naw. G's cooking's always that good, but we eat leftovers when we have a meal that fine. I'm guessin' I'll need a break from fish after the week ahead. Reckon I'll be eatin' skipjack for days, seein' she made 'nough to feed an army." He chuckled. "Speakin' of, any of your folk back home in 'Hio serve our great country?"

"Yes. S-several. One, a distant cousin on my dad's side, didn't m-make it home." I shook my head, recalling the young war hero nicknamed Pits. My age, now he'd never marry. Never have children. After a moment, I added, "And there's another still there. Soldier named Leo, husband to my cousin Kay. Another hero, that one."

"That right?"

"Air force fighter pilot. I admire his c-courage." I shook my head again. After a pause, I said, "Such a s-sad war."

"Any war's sad, that's for sure. How about you? Did you consider enlisting?"

I nodded. "I did, but they wouldn't l-let me, on account of my s-stuttering."

"That right?"

"Yep. But I guess I was thankful. Still, feeling grateful I couldn't go was a mixed bag."

"What'cha mean?"

"I guess I felt guilty. Glad I couldn't go but guilty that I felt that way. Does that make sense?"

Jonah's head bobbed. "Yes'n, it does." He scratched his scalp. "But, oh Lord, you know."

"What's that?"

"It's somewhere in Ezekiel, I do believe. That is, if'n I'm rememberin' rightly. A reminder that, even when we don't understand how or why things turn out the way they do, God does. He knows." Jonah ran the back of his hand over his mouth before continuing. "After all, he doesn't make no mistakes. No, sir. He has a plan, and I'm guessin' it was his plan for you to do great things right at home, right here on American soil." He rubbed his jaw. "There are other ways to demonstrate courage, ya know. Other ways to be heroic."

What was he getting at?

"Jonah, you mentioned there was s-something else you had for me to see. Something that might help place some of these p-puzzle pieces, create a clearer picture of what happened in room 212."

"Yes, indeed. I do. But before that, I wondered. Ever hear of two friends in the Good Book, men named Jonathan and David?"

"David, he wrote a lot of the psalms, but Jonathon—"

"Was King Saul's son. One was royalty. The other, a shepherd who played the harp. Still, they were the best a' friends." He chuckled. "Me? I can't so much as blow a kazoo."

Once again, I wondered where Jonah was going with his line of conversation.

"They were like iron sharpenin' iron, had each other's backs." His head bobbed again. "Yes, sir. Even though they were as diff'rent as baseball and fishin', they were the best of friends. I guess what I'm tryin' to say is, folks can still be friends even though they're diff'rent. All it takes is pullin' up a chair."

"Pulling up a chair, eh? I sure hope Joe will t-take me up on my offer. It's been years, since church c-camp as a boy, that I've had a pen pal. But words, they're powerful, and writing l-letters can bridge a gap. Kind of like pulling up a chair, don't you agree?"

"Indeed." Jonah turned to look at me. "But Joe, he's not like Eli. Carries a chip on his shoulder most of the time, I reckon. Reminds me of ... me. Leastways when I was that age. Speakin' of, remind me. How old are you again?"

"Soon to be twenty-six."

"You don't say." He snickered. "Me, I don't look a day over twenty-six myself, but I tell ya, when you pass forty, you start realizing you have knees and hips." He reached down to massage his left leg.

"I've been told that's true, though I wouldn't know, at l-least not yet." I nudged Jonah in jest.

"I hear it said we Black folk age better than you White folk. If that's true, then I'm guessin' we about the same age." He laughed and returned my nudge, elbowing me in the arm. "Yes, sir. I reckon I'll stay fo'ty-two for a spell. Imagine it'll feel about right."

There was a lull, the box fan's hum filling the space.

"Ya know, folks don't have to be diff'rent colors to treat each other meanly. To hurt each other."

That was true, but again, where was Jonah going? Despite the short time I'd known him, he seemed to see things in a deeper, more profound way.

"That's true."

"Take Ava, for example."

Ava. Ava Jackson.

"She was a nice girl, far as I could tell. Mindin' her own business the best she could, I 'magine. And then she goes and gets mistreated somethin' awful." Jonah cupped his jaw, then rubbed his cheek with his pointer. "I don't' know who it was that hurt her 'xactly. From what I could tell from ..." He paused, then stood and walked to a wooden hutch at the far end of the family room. He opened a drawer and lifted something out.

What was it?

Once again, he sat beside me, then laid the item on his lap. A fabric-covered book. A diary?

"This here, Ava left it behind. I'm sure she didn't mean to. After all, tells much of her secrets and such."

It was a diary. Ava's diary.

"As I was sayin', folks don't have to be diff'rent colors to hurt each other. From the little I know, the one who hurt Miss Ava, he had skin the same color as hers." Jonah lifted one of his arms and held it out. "Not Black, like me."

"Are you s-saying—"

"Yes, sir. I am. Leastways, that's what this here diary says. In her very words."

Was there more evidence, signs perhaps, left in room 212?

"What about in the room? Did anything l-lead you to believe this had happened, like in the actual room?"

Jonah shook his head. "Naw. Not in the room. There were some signs, bloodied towels and such, which I cleaned up. But what happened, it didn't happen in the room."

How did he know?

Jonah patted the fabric book. "As I say, this here diary will answer many of your questions. Yes, sir. I do believe it will." Before continuing, Jonah opened its cover and flipped through one time. "Like the Bible by your bed, this book holds answers, and I've been a ..." He stopped, gave a long sigh. "Gideon, I've been a-prayin' about who might come along, who to give this book to. Yes, sir. Knew in my heart, God would send the right one, the one he had for this ..." Again, he stopped short of saying what seemed to be on his mind.

"What is it?"

"There was more. More than someone stealin' from Miss Ava something she can't never get back." He shook his head. "Then you came along."

Did Jonah think God sent me, sent me for some very specific assignment?

"But, why m-me?"

"That's a question I s'pose you need to take up with God." He handed me Ava's journal. "I've been a-prayin', askin' for a sign, wonderin' who God would provide to help Miss Ava. Even asked him to confirm it, showin' me the one who was right by making him or her a character of ... how's it go?" Jonah paused. "Someone of biblical proportion. I reckon, given a name like Gideon, a stutter like Moses ... you're the one." He chortled and shook his head. "Yes, indeed. And sometimes God answers our prayers in unique ways, his answer comin' in unexpected places. I'm awonderin' if perhaps your answer's here, here in this book and in the Bible."

Taking Ava's diary, I turned it over once, then laid it atop the Gideon Bible.

"But there's more, Gideon. More I reckon will help you understand that it's not just Ava God might be acallin' you to save." Standing, Jonah motioned. "And it's not in those books. Leastways, not anymore."

He led me to a table tucked in the corner of the family room, which held papers and several books strewn about, a lamp, and, beside it, a small, black cast-iron pot.

"Gideon, this is where I talk to God. Kinda messy, 'cause I share this space with the youngins. It's where they do their homework and such. I reckon, if the good Lord meets me here, then he likely meets them here too, and that's fine by me." He ran a dark, weathered hand over the scattered paraphernalia, and chuckled. "Yes, sir. This here's a very fav'rite space. Might near call it holy." He pointed and nudged me with his elbow. "See that there cast-iron pot?"

I nodded. "Yes."

"That's our fam'ly's prayer pot. Georgia and me, the youngins too. It's where we place our petitions before the good Lord. Write 'em down, put 'em in." Jonah tipped his head toward it. "Go 'head. Take a look."

Reaching across the worn oak table, I drew the pot toward me, then put my hand inside, and drew out a piece of folded paper.

Again, he said, "Go 'head. You can read it. I asked 'em earlier, making sure it was okay. Truth is, we all trust you, given you'll promise to pray after you see what you're about to see."

I unfolded the paper, then read out loud, "The mean boy on the bus."

Jonah shook his head. "That there's Eli's, 'bout a bully on his school bus. Picks on him somethin' fierce. We told him, 'Son, we're asked to pray for our enemies,' so that's what Eli wrote."

"And?"

"He ain't moved away yet, but things do seem a might bit better." Jonah grinned.

I picked out another. Like the first, it was neatly folded. "My upcoming school year, the students, and their families."

Georgia.

Once more, I reached in and randomly chose a piece of paper. This one, unlike the others, was wadded up. I opened it, then laid it out on the table's smooth surface and ran a hand over the paper, attempting to iron out the wrinkles. Immediately, I recognized Sand Dollar Bay's stationary. There was writing on both sides, a timeline of sorts on the front, some calculations on the back, ending with a sort of prayer.

"P-please, dear Jesus—No!"

My eyes lifted and met Jonah's. My furrowed brow spoke my confusion, and he clucked sympathetically.

"Gideon, that there's from Miss Ava. It's the only thing I took from the Bible after that weekend. I put it right in there, right with the others, soon as I got home, and that's where it's been ever since. A prayer, I reckon. Soon as I read it, I figured this prayer pot's where it belonged. Guess I've kinda made it a prayer of my own, for her. For Miss Ava."

The words settled, rang in my ears. *Please, dear Jesus—*

No more explanation was needed. I knew, and at that moment, once again, it was Janet's face that flashed before me.

"Gideon, I want for you to see somethin' else." Jonah reached across to the far side of the table and picked up a weathered black leather Bible, its cover cracked with age. He opened it easily, as though it had been opened to a particular passage hundreds of times. "See this?"

My gaze followed where his finger pointed, and I read aloud the passage—Isaiah 42:3. It was underlined in red. "A b-bruised reed shall he not break, and the smoking f-flax shall he not quench: he shall bring forth judgment unto truth."

"Yes, sir. Yes, indeed." After taking his hankie from his back pocket, Jonah dabbed his moist eyes, then blew his nose. "That was one of Bibi's anchor verses. That was what she called it. Any time one of us youngins came to her complainin', tellin' her somebody done us wrong, she'd say, 'Jesus won't crush the weakest reed, child. He takes care of them that's bein' cruel. All you need to do is pray for your enemy. Love 'em who been mistreatin' you.' That's what she'd say. It's like her words still be aringin' in my ears."

Rather than wad it up again, I began to fold the paper, but Jonah laid a hand on mine. "No, sir. That belongs back in the Bible. Your Bible now."

I smoothed it out, then turned it over several times, rereading the timeline on the one side, the calculations on the other.

"These words, what Isaiah wrote, they're true for Miss Ava too. Sure thing. I don't know her, only met her a handful of times as I came and went that weekend. But God put it on my heart to pray for her, and if'n my Bibi was right, and I reckon she was, prayin' makes all the diff'rence. It changes things, yes, sir." Jonah nodded, seemingly lost in thought for a moment. Finally, he said, "Can I see your Bible, the one from the room?"

I'd left it on the couch. I turned to retrieve it, Ava's note in hand, with the intention to tuck it back in the pages. Then, having returned, I handed the Bible to Jonah. "Here."

He took it and flipped to the same Old Testament passage. With a red marker from a mason jar crammed full with pencils, pens, markers, and crayons, he underlined the words I'd, only moments earlier, read. "And Miss Ava's prayer?"

I handed it to him, and Jonah stuck the paper inside, then gently closed the Bible. "That's where it belongs, for now." He laid it on the table, then turned to face me. With one hand on each of my shoulders, his gaze was intense as it met mine. "Gideon Joseph, I don't know 'xactly how, but I believe with all my heart you're here for a purpose. Somehow, even with all the questions you and I have about Miss Ava, about this situation, you're part of the answer."

Once again, I echoed my words from earlier. Had it only been moments ago? "But how? Why me?"

And again, though the intensity of Jonah's expression eased, a slight smile tugging at his lips, he answered. "Miss Ava was broken. You're a builder, but as I said, God made you more than a builder of bridges, of buildings. He created you to be a builder of people. To fix broken folks ... like her." After picking up the Bible, he handed it to me. "Remember how the story of Gideon goes? He didn't think he could do what God was callin' him to do. Felt he was the least of the least of the least. But the good Lord had other plans, yes, sir. And he has other plans for you, Gideon Joseph."

Did names carry so much weight, hold so much meaning?

After a moment, Jonah nodded. "And think a minute 'bout your middle name, what that carpenter did, for a woman who was with child. What that Joseph risked, taking her to be his wife in a time when, given her situation, she could've been stoned. My, oh my. Can you 'magine? My, oh my." He thumped the Bible still hanging between us into my outstretched hand. "This here and Miss Ava's journal, they'll guide you. And don't you forget what the preacher Paul says in that there book to the Romans, chapter eight, verse twenty-eight, I believe. Somethin' about God havin' a plan and workin' everythin' out for good for those who love him and are called accordin' to his purposes. You, Gideon, you love him, of that I'm sure. And there's not a doubt in my mind. You're called accordin' to his purposes. Yes, sir."

I shook my head, the realization that God wanted to use me, despite the mystery of it all, sinking in. Strange as it sounded, I believed it too, believed all Jonah believed. Meeting his gaze, I sighed. "Thank you for everything. T-truly. I'm guessing this weekend was more than you bargained for—unless, s-somehow, you already knew."

"What do ya mean?"

"I don't know. You seem to have a knowing about things. Like you d-discern them, see things more deeply than others."

"Naw. Not at all. Just try to show up where God wants me, then do the best I can. How's it go? Do it all for the glory of God."

"You sure do seem to have a strong c-connection with ..." I pointed upward. "You know, the Man upstairs."

At that, Jonah threw back his head and bellowed. After wiping his eyes with his hankie, he slapped the table with his hand. "What I tell ya? Conversation, with God—others too—just takes pullin' up a chair. We've done a lot of talkin', right here, me and God. Yes, sir."

"I'll keep that in m-mind." I refolded the two petitions that still remained on the table's oak surface and placed them back inside the cast-iron pot. "May I ask, why this c-cast-iron kettle?"

"Belonged to my great-granddaddy. He and his people—my people—were slaves down in South Caroline. Picked cotton by day, kept the animals and such, I reckon. At night, they'd gather 'round for their prayer time." Jonah pointed to the opening of the kettle. "Used to talk right into the pot, quiet like, sometimes only in whispers, I reckon, so the master wouldn't hear 'em. Yes, sir. They'd take turns out in their sleepin' quarters, prayin' their prayers, leavin' 'em there, believin' God would answer. No one ever 'spected the pot to be used for such. To most, it seemed a cookin' pot." Jonah ran a lean finger around its cast-iron brim. "Passed down through gen'rations, made its way to me over time. Yes, sir."

I wondered if Jonah would mind. Picking up a spiral-bound notebook on the table, "May I?"

"Course."

I pulled a pencil from the mason jar, then wrote out my own prayer before folding the paper and placing it in the pot, then mixing it around with the others. Was it possible that, once home, I'd maintain a better prayer life? Read the Bible more?

All it takes is pulling up a chair.

For some reason, at that moment, as I considered Jonah's words, I recalled again the *Time* magazine I'd stolen from the oncologist's office, the day Mom had received her prognosis. Three months. Did I still have it somewhere?

"I hope I can ..." What? What did I hope? "I hope I can grow to be m-more like you."

Once more, Jonah laid a hand on my shoulder and looked me square in the eyes. "Not me, son." With his other hand, he pointed upward. "Spendin' time with him, day by day, we grow to look more like him. Yes, sir. We grow to look more like our Daddy."

I knew who he meant. The notion that, different as we were in some manner of speaking, we were much the same. More, we shared the same heavenly Father.

Still, when Jonah mentioned his daddy, my own dad's face flashed before me, and I couldn't help but wonder. I'd be home tomorrow, home in Lima, Ohio.

How would I ever explain all this to him?

CHAPTER 31
GIDEON—JUNE 1969

"THANKS FOR THE RIDE. FOR EVERYTHING." Why were my eyes burning?

"Safe travels tomorra." Back at Sand Dollar Bay, Jonah stood before me on the curb and extended his hand, which I took. His grasp was firm, and he pulled me into his embrace. "Like brothers, I reckon. Like Jonathan and David."

We pulled back, and our eyes met. His were moist too.

"Do you think the b-bottles God keeps men's tears in are more masculine than, say, those of women's?"

To that, Jonah threw back his head and roared before dabbing eyes, then wiping his brow. "I reckon so. And I'm guessin' they're a might bit smaller too, seein' as we men folk don't cry as much as the ladies." He winked. "Though there are 'ceptions."

I'd cried more on this trip than I had in a long time, something I'd likely not share with Robbins and Ray once home. So much of this conference weekend had been different than I'd imagined.

Once more, as though reading my thoughts, Jonah spoke up. "A few chapters past the one we read earlier, the one in Isaiah, he goes on to say that God's thoughts are much higher than our own, that they're for a particular purpose. Even when we don't understand, God's promises will never come back void." He cupped his jaw, then gazed upward, seemingly deep in thought.

Finally, he said, "Ah yes. It's Isaiah fifty-five. It ends with a proclamation, sayin' we'll go out with joy and be led forth with peace. He even says the mountains and hills will break forth with singin' and a-clappin' of hands." With that, Jonah smacked his together and laughed. "Like that! Isn't that a pretty word picture, if'n I ever heard one?"

It was, and I smiled. "Sure has been nice m-meeting you, getting to know you and your family, Jonah. Can we keep in touch?" I handed Jonah my Robbins and Ray business card, with my home phone number written on the back.

He flipped the card over and nodded. "I reckon we best. After all, I'll wanna hear what you think after readin' about—"

"Hey, you. Move your vehicle. You're in the valet parking area, and we have other cars waiting." The bellman's interruption was abrupt, and he wasn't finished, though what he said next wasn't more than a whisper. "Besides, your kind shouldn't be allowed here."

Heat rose on my face, and I balled my fists. Jonah, however, remained calm. He turned toward the young man and, with a grin, addressed him. "That right? What's your name, son?"

I read his name tag. Steve.

It was then Steve seemed to recognize Jonah as a fellow Sand Dollar Bay employee. His cheeks turned several shades, registering his embarrassment. "I'm ... I'm ... sorry, sir. I didn't ..."

Jonah rested a hand on the bellman's shoulder. "I forgive ya, son. But I offer ya an opportunity to show me you truly are sorry. How about you and me have coffee one day soon, on our break. How's that sound?"

Steve nodded, fumbling for a response. "I ... I suppose we could."

"All right. Soon, it is." He turned back to me. "Like I said, all it takes is pullin' up a chair." He winked. "If'n I can't practice what I preach, then I'm no better than the rest, ain't that right?"

I shook my head before opening my arms, and my friend stepped into my embrace. "Thank you, Jonah. Thank you f-for all of it."

"And I thank you, Gideon Joseph. Can't wait to see what God has in store, yes, sir." With that, Jonah turned and patted Steve on the back. "I'll be goin' now." He flicked me a wave, and his grin was wide. "And I'll be seein' you. 'Member, even when you don't understand ..." He pointed upward, then winked once more before turning back toward his car. Still, I heard him. "Oh Lord, you know." And he guffawed as he folded into his Plymouth.

Back in room 212, I packed my things, making sure I had the notes from Jonah, as well as the Smith's Print Shop business card. I'd call them first thing the next morning, from the airport's pay phone.

My flight was scheduled for ten o'clock, so I planned on catching a cab at eight. I'd grab coffee, perhaps a light breakfast, at the airport.

The thought of another cab ride brought the last one to mind, not to mention the driver with his nub of a cigar. *Walk uphill with pebbles in your mouth.*

I chuckled. The things people believed. There'd been a time I'd have done almost anything to cure my stammering, though I'd grown accustomed to it over the years. The hardest time had been in grade school, when I had to read aloud in class. Kids could be so cruel.

The mean boy on the bus.

And not just kids. The incident that had happened less than

thirty minutes earlier echoed in my mind. *Your kind doesn't belong here.*

Your kind. Jonah's kind. Gentle, loving, forgiving. Always leading by example, it seemed.

I did desire to be more like him. If that meant spending more time with the Daddy we shared, then that was what I'd do.

Are you smiling, Mom?

Still, I wondered how I'd explain the weekend to my dad. I had plenty to take back to work, give William Robbins and Thomas Ray those fresh ideas they'd asked for. But there was more.

You're a builder of people. Wasn't that what Jonah said?

My hotel phone rang.

"Hello?"

"Deon Stallings."

It was Loraine. "Yes. Hi."

"Gettin' ready to leave in the mornin'?"

"Yep. Was p-packing my things."

"Listen, I'm off tomorra. Might'n ya like a ride to the airport? Free of charge. What could be better?"

Did I? "Sure. That's nice of you."

"I have to run a bunch of errands anyway. Figure it'll get me up and out the door early. Besides, I think I'll miss your stammerin'."

"Ha. Yeah, I b-bet."

It was settled. Loraine would swing by and pick me up at eight o'clock sharp. Even offered to bring a cup of coffee. Was this the lady who'd irritated me only several days earlier? The one I'd poked fun at?

I put the finishing touches on my luggage, only leaving out what I'd wear home as well as my toiletry bag. The Smith's Print Shop business card I tucked into my wallet. After opening the coin compartment, I checked to be sure I had change for the pay phone. As my finger rummaged through pennies, nickels, and dimes, there it was. The purple button. Where had it once belonged? *Cute as a button*. Bea's face flashed in my mind, bringing a smile.

Finally, I dialed the Bennetts' room.

"Hello."

"Hey, Patti. D-Deon here."

"Hi, Deon. Mike ..." Her voice muffled, though I could still hear her. "... it's Deon."

"Hello."

"Hi, Mike. I'm l-leaving in the morning, and I wanted to s-say goodbye."

"How nice. Thank you. Sure was nice meeting you. And hey, don't forget. You have an open invitation to visit us in Greensboro. Name the time."

"I will. And p-please tell Billy I said goodbye."

"Sure thing. He's napping at the moment. Too much fun in the sun, I suppose, but I'll be sure to let him know."

After we hung up, I made certain I had Mike's contact info. I located the napkin still in my Bermudas pocket, then placed it in my wallet as well.

Before leaving the room to find some supper, I checked the closet and each drawer. In the third bureau drawer down, there it was. The hotel guide and room-service menu. Why hadn't I checked that one? Why stop after the first two? Still, if I had, perhaps I wouldn't have met Loraine.

Or Jonah. *He works all things together for good, for them who love him and are called according to his purposes.*

Yes. He certainly had. Now I had to trust he'd continue, completing that which he'd begun. But I couldn't help wondering. What exactly was that?

CHAPTER 32
GIDEON—JUNE 1969

PROMPTLY AT EIGHT, Loraine pulled up in her red Alfa Romeo. Only minutes earlier, I'd pushed my way around the revolving door, taking one extra spin. "For Bea," I'd said.

"You ready?" Her eyes smiled as she tipped her horn-rim sunglasses and her blond hair was held back with a scarf knotted under her chin. "Pretty day, ain't it?"

"It is, and yes, yes I am." I tossed my suitcase in the open back seat of her convertible, then folded into the passenger seat, placing my leather satchel at my feet. "Thank you. M-means a lot."

"No trouble. Like I said, I have some errands to run this morning. Pickin' you up early is a good excuse to get up and goin'." She tittered. "I tend to be a bit lazy on my days off."

Assessing the pretty driver beside me, I laughed. "Do you always choose head wraps to match your car?"

Her left hand on the wheel, Loraine lifted her right and patted the scarf. "You talkin' about this ol' thing?" She grinned. "Naw. But I do choose my cars to match my scarves."

"Ha! You don't s-say." A beat of silence wasn't awkward but

comfortable, like we knew one another better than we did. "You live nearby?"

"Not far. Several miles, that's all." She tipped her head toward the bag on her floor board. "You got the Bible, don't ya?"

"Yes. Thank you. Hope it's no t-trouble to replace it."

"Not at all. Like I said, my granddaddy's a Gideon. Already asked him to run one by. Jonah'll put it back in the bedside table when he goes to prepare the room. Gramps'll leave it at the front desk. Maybe already has."

I nodded. "A Gideon, eh?" With all that had happened over the course of the last several days, my name held deeper meaning. I smiled. "What did M-Mom know?"

"What's that?"

"Nothing. Only c-curious about what my mom knew when she and dad chose m-my name."

Sometimes we got to grow into our names. Wasn't that what Jonah had said?

Loraine giggled. "Moms have a special intuition, I suppose. Mine does."

"How so?"

"My name means water, and there's nothing I love more than ..." With her right hand, Loraine swiped it left to right. "All this. The ocean's my groovy space."

"Sure has been good for m-my stuttering." I chortled. "Maybe."

"Guess you'll need to return. And soon."

What was she implying? And why, given all Jonah was expecting of me, some of which—much of which—I still didn't understand, did I feel a tinge of ... guilt? Like, given Loraine's possible intentions, being with her made me somehow disloyal, but to whom? It wasn't Janet.

Ava?

"Hey, I was wondering, though this m-may seem strange." I

paused, considering my words. What was it I wanted to know? "Do you happen to recall anything p-peculiar happening back during spring break, back near the end of March?"

Loraine's head tipped. "Like what?"

"I don't know. Did anyone complain to the front desk about inappropriate activity, you know, between a man and a woman? Between spring breakers? Or request medical supplies, extra towels, or anything?"

At a red light, Loraine turned to me and tipped her glasses again. She lifted an eyebrow. "Yes. But why do you ask?"

She did recall something out of the ordinary.

"What h-happened?"

The light turned. Loraine stared straight ahead and didn't answer right away. Finally, "The police came."

"And?"

"A young woman claimed she'd been assaulted on the beach."

"Ava."

"What? What did you say?"

"I s-said Ava. Apparently, she'd been in room 212."

"But how—"

"She left clues in the Bible by the bed. I found them. That's why I need to keep this copy. And Jonah, he knew something, though not exactly."

"Oh."

What was Loraine thinking? Her one-word response ...

"It's like I'm a d-detective. And Jonah, he thinks I'm somehow supposed to solve this mystery and ..." What? What was it he wanted me to do? "I guess r-rescue this woman?" It was more a question, rather than a statement.

How strange all this must have sounded, but Loraine didn't show signs of surprise. She simply shook her head.

"I s-spent a good amount of time with Jonah and his family yesterday. They'd invited me to their home for Sunday dinner. He shared with me what he knew. Again, it's not m-much. A bunch of jumbled puzzle pieces." Should I share about Ava's journal? "He also g-gave me something Ava left in the room. Most likely an accident." Pulling it from my leather satchel, I said, "This."

Loraine glanced at the fabric-covered book. "A diary? Ava's diary?"

"Yes."

After a lull, Loraine removed her sunglasses, then placed them on her lap. "And have you read it yet? Does it explain things?"

"No. I'm waiting until I get h-home. Don't know why exactly. Just feel I should, so I c-can piece together the things she likely wrote with the clues she left in the Bible."

"The Bible by your bed." Loraine's head bobbed. "Ya know, I was raised to believe that God guides those of us who seek him. His Word, a lamp to our feet, a light to our path."

Mom's face flashed before me. "You b-believe that too?"

"I do." Her two-word response, simple though it was, settled the tinge of whatever I had felt. She understood. That was what mattered. "Jonah. He's a good man. Someone you can trust."

"Yes. S-strange as it may seem, it's as if I've known him my whole life."

There was one more thing, a question perhaps Loraine could answer.

"Jonah marked a page in the Bible, in the book of Judges. He wanted me to read about Gideon." Had that only been four days earlier? "He m-marked the spot with a business card. Smith's Print Shop. Do you—"

"No kidding!" Loraine turned on her signal, then transitioned into the far-right turn lane preparing to veer off. We'd reached the airport.

"What? What d-do you know?"

"You're not going to believe this, but that's one of my errands. Gotta pick up new letterhead stationery for the hotel. Sand

Dollar's contracted with them." She shook her head. "That almost seems too coincidental."

I agreed. What were the chances? "You do wear a lot of h-hats in your job." I chuckled. "But why do you think Jonah would use their b-business card as a bookmark?" Hadn't he said he didn't know anything about Smith's? That he'd found the card after Ava had checked out? "Jonah told me I should call the print shop. That he discovered the card in room 212 but didn't know why it was there."

"I don't guess I know either. Jonah doesn't deal with Smith's, not as room attendant, anyway." She replaced the sunglasses, adjusting them on the bridge of her perky nose. "Tell you what, I can ask when I get there. Ask them to check their calendar, see if they have any info on .... Wait, what were the exact dates she stayed in that room? Do you even know?"

March 21, 1969. Where were you, God?

"She was there on March twenty-first. That m-much I'm sure of."

"How?"

"That was one of the c-clues she left, in the Bible. She'd written that particular d-date in the margin."

Again, Loraine's head turned side to side as her mouth fell open. "Well, I'll be. This truly is a mystery. Guess'n if you're a Hardy boy, then I'm Nancy Drew."

"I liken you more to Trixie B-Belden. But yeah, any help you can offer, I'll take."

She thrust the gear into Park, having pulled up to the airport's curb. "Here ya are." After digging in her purse, she pulled out a receipt, then wrote her number. "Call me later, if you like. Maybe I'll know something." Tipping her sunglasses one last time, she smiled at me. "Nice to meet you, Mr. Stallings. Y'all come back now, hear?" She winked.

~

Right on time, Dad pulled to the curb at James M. Cox-Dayton Municipal Airport. After exiting his Mercury Cougar, he enveloped me in a hug before tossing my suitcase in the trunk.

As we traveled northbound on I-75, I inquired about things at home, being particularly curious about my aging golden retriever.

"How's Ginger?"

"Fair to middling, I reckon. She'll be happy to see you, I know."

After a few minutes, I said, "Dad, I wondered if we m-might talk a bit."

"We've got nearly two hours to kill, so shoot. What's on your mind?"

How to explain all that had happened? "The weekend was different than I'd expected."

"Yeah? Explain."

"It was full of things that, perhaps a m-month ago ... no, a week ago I'd have considered coincidence. But I guess I kinda sensed Mom was with me. Like she was on m-my shoulder, reminding me of things I'd sort of forgotten."

"Like?"

"In a nutshell, that God guides us. That he has a plan. Calls us to be part of that plan. That sort of thing."

Dad's head bobbed up and down. "Yes, I believe that too. And you're right. Sure does sound like something Mom would say." He chuckled. "Good ol' Jocelyn."

"I was thinking of the t-time I went with her to an oncologist appointment. The one where Dr. Green gave her three months."

"Yeah. I was sick and couldn't go. Was thankful you could, especially with that devastating blow."

"Funny. I stole a *Time* magazine from the waiting room. Slipped it in my jacket and walked out with it. Not sure why."

"That so? Still have it?"

"I wondered m-myself. I'll check in my cedar chest when we get home. If I do, that's where it will be." What more to tell him so he'd better understand. "There was this B-bible in my bedside drawer in my hotel room."

"A Gideon Bible, no doubt."

"Yeah. But this one was different." I inhaled, then exhaled slowly.

"How so, son?"

"It was marked up. Someone had underlined passages, written in the margins."

"Hmm. A mystery."

"Yes, but then I met my room attendant. A man named Jonah Forney. He knew who'd written in the Bible. She'd been there, in that same hotel room, back in March, for spring break." Another deep breath. "She left her diary, which Jonah found while cleaning her room. Dad—"

It was his turn to sigh. "Why do I have a hunch this is why you sensed Mom was with you? That God was guiding you?" With a chuckle, "Sounds like the two of them might be up to something, don't you think?"

Perhaps explaining all this to Dad wouldn't be as difficult as I'd thought. "And one more thing. I went fishing with Jonah. I can't put into words all that happened because none of it's out of the ordinary, and yet ..." Extraordinary from the commonplace, like the man. Like Jonah.

Like ... me.

"Jonah experienced something similar to what Janet and I went through with—"

"Yes, son. I understand."

"He prayed with me, right there on that weathered pier. It was as though my heart was healed, a weight was lifted after I ..." A smile erupted, interrupting my explanation. "Cast it into the sea of forgetfulness."

Yes, sir.

"Yes, sir. That's what happened, like an inner healing. And I'm changed. Not only that, I have a purpose. Strange as it may sound, no matter where it may take me or how many think I've lost my mind."

Dad side-eyed me, a smile spanning the width of his face. "Son, I believe you. Know why?"

"Why?"

"You didn't stutter. Not once. That's proof enough."

Home. No sooner had my feet crossed the threshold than a furry beast nearly knocked me back out the door.

"Whoa there, Ginger. Glad to see you too." I scratched her ears as she stood against me, front paws pressed against my chest. "Good girl!"

"Son, do burgers sound good for supper? I can get the grill fired up in no time. Fresh sweet corn from Clark's farm."

"Yes, thank you. And after dinner, I'll probably turn in. I'm tired and have a lot to process."

"Perfect. We'll be eating in no time. Mind shucking half a dozen ears?"

I sat on our back patio, Dad manning the burgers while I tore husks off corn the color of butter. Though I'd lived away throughout college, after Mom had passed, I'd moved back to my childhood home on Elm Street. There, I'd made memories as numerous as the fireflies lighting up the field behind our house, most of them pleasant.

I finished the final ear, then brushed my hands together, sending several silks falling. They landed on Ginger's golden head as she slept at my feet, and I laughed. "They're the same color as your fur, girl." I picked them off and rubbed where they'd been. "Hey, Dad, can I ask you something?"

"Sure, but one minute. Let's get those ears in the pot. Got the water boiling. Be back in a jiffy." In no time, he returned. "Eight minutes and we'll eat. Now, what was it you wanted to talk about?" He removed the burgers and placed them on an avocado-green platter before returning the lid to the grill.

"I was wondering. Have you spoken with Janet's dad recently?"

"As a matter of fact, I did. The other day. Ran into Geoffrey at the supermarket. Called across the produce aisle, 'Hey there, George Stallings.' Suppose we talked for five minutes, give or take a few."

"And? Any word on how Janet's doing?"

Dad sat down at the patio table and sighed. "Said she's moving to Pittsburgh, end of the month, I believe. Accepted a teaching job in an inner-city school, if I'm remembering correctly. Fourth grade."

An image of Eli Forney's face flashed. "That right?" I unfolded my napkin. "She'll love it. Janet was made for teaching."

Dad excused himself and, moments later, returned with the corn. After blessing the meal, we dug in.

Shaking ketchup on my burger, I continued. "Regarding Janet, I think I need to ask her to forgive me. Maybe that will bring healing, for us both." I sank my teeth into an ear of buttery sweet corn and chewed. "What do you think?"

"I agree, son. Saying you're sorry is never wrong and can only bring about good. That's my opinion, anyway."

And right then, I knew. Before my head hit the pillow, I'd make that call. And the thought, even though a tinge of anxiety stirred, brought a peace I'd not experienced for a long time.

~

After dinner clean up, I stretched and yawned, then pounded a soft fist on the patio table. "Man, I'm beat. Mind if I turn in? It's early, but I work tomorrow and need to unwind a bit before bed. Not to mention, make a phone call."

Dad gave my back a hearty pat. "Not at all. Glad you're home, son. And I'm thankful your trip was ... productive." He winked at me. "And on Robbins and Ray's dime too."

"If you only knew how many times in the last few days I've thought the same thing. If I had a ..." But a button flashed in my mind. "Button." I chuckled. "Anyway, if only Robbins and Ray knew." I hugged Dad. "Goodnight. Ginger, you coming?"

The golden pooch, a smidgen of white dotting her muzzle, leapt from where she'd been lounging under the table. She stretched, then followed me to the kitchen. I opened the refrigerator and removed a Pabst, then considered. Was beer what I craved? I returned it to the fridge and chose a Pepsi instead.

In my bedroom, Ginger walked to her favorite spot under the east-facing window and turned a few times before flumping on the carpet. She smacked her lips and closed her eyes.

"Good ol' girl." I laid my suitcase on the bed and unpacked, taking care to remove Mom's funeral program, which was still tucked in the breast pocket of my suit coat.

Love lifted me ...

"Yes, Mom. I know. Even from heaven."

Hearing my voice, the golden's tail thumped, though her eyes never opened.

Having unpacked, I finally sat on the edge of my bed and laid the Gideon Bible and Ava's journal on the bed beside me. Why was my heart pounding?

The phone call. After picking up the handset on my nightstand, I dialed the number I knew by heart. As if reaching for courage, I placed my left hand on the Bible.

On the third ring, Janet said, "Hello."

I cleared my throat. "Janet? This is Deon."

A beat of silence hung on the line.

"Hi."

What to say? "I … I mean, Dad said he ran into your father the other day. Told me you were moving. To Pittsburgh. That right?"

It was Janet's turn to clear her throat. "Yeah. I'm finally gonna teach."

"Fourth grade, Dad said."

"Yes. I'm excited." Her voice registered a hint of a smile.

"I'm happy for you, Janet. You were made for this."

"Thank you." She cleared her throat again. "And what about you? You all right?"

"Yeah. Got home from a conference for work." Jonah's face flashed this time. How to relay what was on my heart? "Something happened while I was away, and I …" I swiped a bead of sweat from above my lip. "Janet, it may sound strange, but God's convicted me of … I want to apologize for how I hurt you. For—"

Janet was crying, her whimper coming through the phone line, and she sniffed. "Excuse me a moment."

"Of course."

After several seconds, a tissue rustled, and Janet blew her nose. "There. That's better."

"You okay?"

"Yes. Yes, I'm fine."

"I hope you'll forgive me, for everything."

"I do. Already had, though it's good to hear from you. Good to hear this acknowledgment; that's what I'm trying to say."

"I'm happy for you, Janet. And there are good things in store, for us both. I truly believe that."

"Me too. Thank you again."

After she hung up, I held the receiver in my hand for a moment. My heart was lighter, and I smiled.

Perhaps it was the air-conditioning or my emotions, but a chill ran over my arms and legs. I rubbed my hands together before lifting the corner of my bedspread. As I did, something brushed my hand. The manufacturer's tag, Sears, Roebuck & Co. stitched in black. Mom had purchased the spread for my college dorm room when I was a freshman at Ohio State. Fingering the tag, I recalled her coming to help me set up, how she'd delighted in giving the drab room a touch of feminine pizzazz. That was what she'd called it.

As I ran my finger over the tag, something caught my eye, and I sucked in my breath. Right there, below Sears, Roebuck, Made in Eden, NC.

I never slept that night.

CHAPTER 33
CASSIE—AUGUST 2016

"What do you mean, 'That's that?'" Cassie threw her hands into the air, her mouth a gaping O.

"That's my story." Gideon closed Ava's journal with a snap.

Cassie shifted on the couch, then realized she was sitting at the cushion's edge. "Don't tell me you're gonna leave me hanging out on a cliff like Ava did."

Gideon snickered. "Is that what I'm doing?" He slapped both knees with his hands. "I figured you have a lot to process after all that." He lifted his hand to read his wristwatch. "I've been yapping on for, what's it been? More than two hours now."

Had it been that long? The time had flown.

"But what did you discover when you read Ava's journal? What pieces of the puzzle were you able to place?"

Gideon's gaze shifted from Cassie to his wife, his eyes tender. "Let's just say I knew. I knew Jonah was right. God was calling me to do great things after all." With a chortle, he added, "Me, Gideon Joseph. Who'da thunk?"

"And the stammering, what about that?" Cassie's fingers lingered over her computer keyboard, longing to race again.

"Gone. After more than two decades of stuttering my way through words ..." Gideon snapped his fingers. "Disappeared."

Cassie shook her head. Unbelievable. Yet, after all he'd shared, not unbelievable. Miraculous.

"The bedspread, it served as confirmation enough. Gideon was to be my covering." Ava sighed. "His banner over me is love, like Solomon said in his song."

"And how I love that song." Gideon winked at his wife.

Cassie stretched her memory, trying to recall something Ava had told her at their last meeting. "Didn't you consider a job at the textile mill after graduation? As a secretary?"

"I did. Fieldcrest Mills always seemed to be hiring, and many graduates from Rockingham took jobs with them, either as secretaries or to work the assembly line. Many a towel, blanket, and bedsheet's been made in Eden. It's not that coincidental that my Gideon's bedspread was from Fieldcrest, yet it is." She smiled at her husband. "And ... here we are." Turning her attention to Fiona, she said, "Here you are, right, love?"

Fiona smiled. "Now, Momma. Daddy. You two lovebirds never stop."

Though her face warmed with this intimate line of conversation, Cassie shook her head, so many questions making her dizzy. "This is where you're leaving me? I'd almost say that's plain mean."

Gideon chuckled again. "I don't mean to be." He winked at her. "No pun intended."

Cassie was uncertain how long she'd have to wait for the rest of the story. For its conclusion.

"I know you're on pins and needles, dear. But we won't wait long this time." Ava came to the rescue, putting Cassie's mix of emotions to rest. "In fact, prior to getting here today, Gideon and I talked. We'd like to present an offer, an invitation to our home, the one my Gideon designed and helped build. A wedding gift, you might say, though we lived with my parents for a year while it was being finished." Her gaze, too, shifted from Cassie to her husband. "'Wij hebben een huis!' Isn't that how you say it?"

What was this secret they shared, concealed in Dutch, its meaning known only to them?

Ava turned again to Cassie. "It's not far from here, on Glovenia, tucked in among the most fragrant gardenias, with a hint of pine from a towering evergreen out back. At least when the wind blows just so." Ava closed her eyes, inhaling deeply, as though she were taking in its scent from right there where she sat.

"Refinement." Eyes pinched tight, Ava almost whispered *that's what this life's been about.*

"Refinement." Without missing a beat, Gideon echoed Ava, his voice, too, soft. "Coming forth as pure gold."

Once more, Cassie sensed an almost holy aura in Fiona's living room, as though she were in the company of angels who smiled at this couple who'd endured—

What all had they endured? What hardships had brought them to this day, other than—

"So, it's settled!" A clap of Ava's hands brought Cassie back to the present.

"When were you thinking we could meet on Glov ... Glov ... how do you say it?"

"Glovenia, dear. And yes, one week from today. Will Thursday, August twenty-fifth work for you?"

Cassie ran a finger over the screen of her smartphone, then pulled up her calendar. "Yep. Suits me fine. But do I have to wait an entire week?"

In unison, the couple laughed, Gideon's deep and rich, while Ava's was soft, almost childlike.

"You're telling me I don't have an invitation to this grand finale?" Fiona stood up. "And I even served snacks." She giggled.

"But I admit. I'm already privy to much of how their story goes, so I'll allow it."

Taking her lead, Cassie and Gideon stood. Only Ava remained seated on the couch, her gaze fixed upward, seemingly deep in thought. "Oh Lord, you know."

"What's that, Momma?" Fiona sat back down, and Gideon and Cassie followed.

"'Oh Lord, you know.' I'd forgotten about those words of Jonah's, quoted from the prophet Ezekiel." Ava shook her head, then sighed. "He certainly does, doesn't he?"

Cassie glanced from Ava to Gideon, then back to Ava. What memory was stirred by those words? What deeper meaning did they perhaps hold?

One thing Cassie knew. She'd have to wait another week to find out.

"How was your day, Cass? You look exhausted." Grant embraced Cassie as soon as she stepped over the threshold into the foyer. "Ready to write that book?"

Cassie sighed into her husband's broad chest before answering. "They've left me hanging again." Her chuckle was muffled in Grant's polyester golf shirt. "But at least they're not gonna torture me for long this time. We're meeting next Thursday in Gideon and Ava's home."

Grant pulled away. "How do you feel about that? This switch of scenery, I might call it."

"It'll be nice. A change of pace. Perhaps the new setting will birth the conclusion of their story. I hope so anyway."

"Now Cassie, there's no real completion to any story, not until—"

"I know. I know. But you get what I'm saying." She tipped her face to gaze up at her husband, her arms wrapped around his waist. "Even though I've known some of their story over the years, there's much, so many details I didn't. Boy, I have a lot to process."

"Did you take good notes?" Grant stepped back and took Cassie's hands in his, then held them up for inspection. "I'll bet your fingers are tired. Need a massage?" With his hands he squeezed Cassie's, warming them in his own.

"Maybe after dinner. I'm starved." She peered around her husband and scanned the room. "Where are the kids? It's awfully quiet in here. Too quiet."

"Your parents invited them for the evening. Overnight, in fact. Which means ..." Grant smiled down at Cassie. His blue eyes held a tinge of mischief. "If you're up for it, I've booked a reservation for two at Frankie's. Seven o'clock. Then after—"

"I love you, ya know that?" Cassie stretched to stand on tiptoe, then kissed Grant. His lips, like his hands, were warm, and her insides fluttered. "I'll go shower and change. Sounds like we have a date."

Grant stepped aside. With a swoop of his right hand, he smiled. "After you, my lady."

Behind the couple's closed door, prior to any shower or change of clothes, Cassie and Grant enjoyed the blessing of marriage, under bedsheets and a spread not manufactured in Eden, though their love was paradise, as God intended.

And in those moments, a song echoed in Cassie's mind, its lyrics as ancient as Solomon's itself.

His banner over me is love.

CHAPTER 34
CASSIE—AUGUST 2016

"Someone wanna say grace?" Cassie nudged Grant, who sat beside her on the wooden bench. Sunlight peeking through a canopy of green created dancing shadows on the picnic table.

"I'd be happy to." Grant bowed his head, and the others followed.

With *Amen*, the trio echoed the same, just as Grant's hand slapped the table like an exclamation point. "So, Pete, what's this I hear?"

Pete and Jenn Gentry, each with their favorite Mexican street food in front of them, forks suspended midair, sat across from the Billingses.

"Yep. I'm leaving. Had enough." Pete poked at seasoned, shredded chicken in a paper bowl. "I guess, like you, my thinking's changed. My worldview."

Grant nodded. "Any pushback? Anyone giving you grief?"

Memories of her husband's exodus from Orchard View more than a year earlier ran through Cassie's mind. She recalled the threats, though Grant never seemed too concerned. Yes, he'd signed a noncompete clause, but he'd moved to a new practice, one not even in the same particular section of Greensboro. Could any of those threats still carry weight?

"Greg Sommers says you're the reason I'm considering leaving," Peter said, as if reading Cassie's mind. "Says that's a breach of your noncompete." Peter chewed, then belched.

"Pete. Gross." Jenn elbowed her husband.

"Excuse me. Mexican gets me every time." He wiped his mouth. "Anyway, Sommers even threatened to sue. Said he's already spoken with an attorney."

"That right?" Grant leaned forward, resting an elbow on the picnic table.

The late-night conversation between Cassie and her husband months prior echoed. So that was what Jane Freemont had been getting at when she'd asked if Grant kept up with any of his Orchard View colleagues.

"Anyway, I'm leaving, and that's that." Pete wadded his napkin and threw it down.

Jenn nodded sympathetically. "It's been a long time coming."

"And how are you ... you know, with all this?" Cassie recalled how her husband's news of leaving had stirred anxiety. Fear even.

"At peace. Strange, but it's true." Jenn smiled. "Nice to know we have others who've walked this path."

"We're here for you. We understand how difficult this is." Grant took a sip of his sweet tea. "We remember. But hey, we believe you're making the right decision. Once one concludes that life begins at conception, something I believe science proves, is there any other choice?"

Choice. How ironic.

Pete tipped his drink, an orange-flavored Topo Sabores, then set it down. "I still wonder about the three exceptions. You know, in the rare cases when a woman's life is at stake or when she conceives from rape or incest."

Grant's head bobbed. Cassie knew he understood, more than Pete knew.

"Yes, and those are that. Exceptions. And they can't be discounted, but, comparatively, they're fewer, farther between. I wish women ..." Grant cleared his throat. Was he treading on dangerous ground? But this was Pete he was talking to. "I wish women would see themselves as ..." He paused again. "Even in the case—"

"I think what Grant's asking us to consider is, if one believes life begins at conception, and if the baby's and mother's health aren't at risk, might a woman choose to carry, then place with a loving family? Even ..."

Would Pete and Jenn consider their line of thinking—their story—too extreme?

"Take our family." Grant squeezed Cassie's hand. "Three of our kids are here because a birth mom made the better choice, each having gone through a difficult circumstance, leading to pregnancy."

Cassie searched Pete's face, then his wife's. Were they offended? Pete didn't make eye contact as he ran his index finger along the rim of his empty Topo Sabores bottle. Jenn, however, smiled Cassie's way, though her attention appeared to be directed beyond, to something behind her.

Grant broke the silence. "Does that make sense? I mean, with the morning-after pill and so many other means to quick abortions, babies too many to count die every day. But maybe if she knew her options, that she doesn't have to go it alone."

An image of Millie Kate's birth mom flashed before Cassie. She and Grant had done all they knew to do to show their support, including offering her a place to live for a season, which she'd declined.

Pete shook his head. "Man, you know how many women would hate you for what you two are implying." He pointed at

Grant. "Especially you. And Cassie, you're a woman yes, but until you've walked in another's shoes—"

"You can't understand. Is that what you were going to say?" Cassie's voice shook a bit. As she lifted her tea, hoping to quench her suddenly dry mouth, her hand, too, was shaking.

Pete stared at her, eyes wide. "I mean, I guess it's softer when a woman suggests it, but a dude?"

"I know. Who am I? But if only people knew ..." Grant squeezed Cassie's hand again. "This woman, right here—battling health issues, taking on the daunting task of writing another's story, and not any story, her—"

"Now, Grant, you make me blush." She squeezed back, and Grant kissed the top of her head.

Pete gathered his trash, then stuffed his and Jenn's in the brown paper to-go bag. "I do appreciate you taking time to help me process all this, Grant. Cassie, you too. To show us a different perspective. Not one that belittles women but ..." Pete's gaze met Cassie's. "One that calls women to rise up and see themselves as something more beautiful and amazing than what the world says. To see themselves as ... as life-givers. When you stop and think about it that way, what an honor!"

Grant also gathered his and Cassie's trash. "It's been my pleasure to walk this with you. Helpful too, since I'm still learning and growing, figuring out my part in the story."

What had Grant said to Cassie only days earlier? Something like, *There's no real completion to any story, not until—*

"It's just my two cents, for what that's worth. I mean, what do I know? I'm merely a scientist." Grant snickered, nudging his wife. "Now, my Cassie? She's—"

"The smarter one." Pete's eyes flitting back and forth between Cassie and Grant. He turned to Jenn and guffawed. "Isn't that what he was gonna say?"

Jenn giggled. "You know it, babe."

"Yep, took the words right out of my mouth. Always the smarter one." Grant leaned his head against Cassie's. "I'm sure your wife agrees."

Jenn snickered. "You bet."

Right then, another woman, who once had auburn hair, flashed across Cassie's mind.

"Heroes. That's what they are." Grant pecked Cassie's cheek.

And Psalm 139 echoed. *You formed my inward parts, covering me in my mother's womb.*

Cassie's lips curled into a soft smile. "And that includes birth moms."

CHAPTER 35

CASSIE—AUGUST 2016

CASSIE TAPPED HER FOOT, waiting for Grant to answer his phone.

On the fourth ring, there was an answer. "Hey, Cass."

"Got a sec?"

"For you, always. Everything okay?"

"Yeah. Guess what! I got something in the mail today, from Ann."

"Don't tell me—a puppy?"

"Not funny. It's a figurine. You know, one of those Willow Trees?"

"Like our faceless Mary and Joseph? Aren't they Willow Trees too?"

Cassie giggled. "Yep." It was their family joke. Cassie loved displaying their Willow Tree nativity each Christmas, the holy family along with shepherds and wisemen, not to mention several barn animals and the wise men's camels. "Faceless. You're funny. Anyway, when she brought Hunter for that weekend before school started, we talked. I told her about my commission to write Gideon and Ava's story."

"Go on."

"She sent me a Willow Tree woman holding a book and included a note. 'A book captures a reader's attention. Each word on the page possesses power to make a difference. Your words, Cassie, make a difference. Write to change the world. Write to change a life.' Isn't that thoughtful?"

"And true."

After they hung up, Cassie knew who she needed to call next. Maybe change a life.

"Come in. Good to see you." Cassie stepped back to allow Jane Freemont to pass. "Yucky weather. You're welcome to take off your shoes. Phew, it's a monsoon out there."

Jane removed wet Toms, then laid them under the coat rack, where she'd already hung her slicker and umbrella. "Good thing I'm not made of sugar."

Cassie led the way to the kitchen. "Speaking of which, coffee?"

"You know it." Jane plopped down in a chair, then rubbed her hands together. "Chilly too." She blew on her fingers before folding them on the oak table. "How ya been?"

Cassie set a mug of steaming coffee in front of her friend. "Sugar and cream are there, if you like." She sat down across the table and sighed, then echoed Jane's question. "How have I been? That's a loaded question."

How was she? Something niggled, but what was it? Her husband's suspicions regarding Patrick Freemont? Was his curiosity concerning Grant's ongoing Orchard View relationships because he was an attorney? But how to broach the topic?

"I've been worse, that's for sure." She chuckled. "Got word I'll be doing some follow-up radiation, now that my chemo's over. Thought I was out of the woods, but not quite yet."

Jane's gaze went from Cassie's face to the top of her head, to the colorful bandana holding back her auburn bangs. "Your hair looks nice. That's a plus." A quizzical expression crinkled her eyes, then furrowed her brow. "Did you lose much?"

"Nope. Very little. That cold cap I tried worked its magic. Expensive but, at least to me, worth every penny. Sure wish insurance would cover it though, so others could do it too."

Instinctively, Cassie's hand went to her head. "The psychological difference keeping my hair made, for me and my family." She lifted her left arm, then punched the air. "And when fighting the beast, a woman needs all the mental and emotional stamina she can muster." Cassie blew on her coffee, then took a swallow, hoping the beverage would cure her sudden cottonmouth. Should she dive right in? "Can I ask you something?"

"Shoot."

"Last time you were here, you posed a question, but the clock chimed, and you never got an answer."

Jane's eyes tipped upward as she thought.

"You wondered if Grant still keeps up with any of his former colleagues at Orchard View."

"Ah, yes."

"Why?"

Jane blew across the rim of her mug before taking a sip. "It was something Patrick was curious about when he found out we were having coffee. Asked me to ask you."

"And?"

"I never got an answer. When I got home and he inquired, I said we'd run out of time."

Cassie nodded. "Which is true." She paused. "Did Patrick want you to ask me again, by chance?"

"He did." Jane squinted. "What are you getting at?"

"Aren't you going to?"

After a beat of silence, "Does he?"

Cassie shifted in her chair, then pulled her shoulders back. "He does." If Jane wanted to play this game, why waste time? After all, this was likely the reason Jane had accepted her invitation to come for coffee.

"Peter Gentry?"

"Yes."

Jane bobbed her head. "That's what Patrick thought."

Was this conversation a breach of confidence? On Jane's part? On Cassie's?

"It's no secret that Grant and Pete were friends prior to Grant's leaving, Jane. Everyone knew that."

"Listen, I don't want to get in the middle of things. Honestly, I don't even know why Patrick is suspicious, except—"

"Pete's considering leaving the practice. Isn't that what you were going to say?"

"Is he?"

Cassie and Grant had discussed this possible line of conversation after Sunday's sermon about speaking truth in love while staying true to one's convictions. Grant had told Cassie to do exactly that.

"Jane, I'm not sure what your husband has to do with Grant and Pete's relationship. Maybe it's because some at Orchard View, namely Greg Sommers, think their friendship is related to Pete's discontentment at work. His possible resignation." Cassie shook her head. "Sommers has threatened to sue, stating it somehow violates a noncompete clause. But ..." How to explain? "How does one continue working in an environment where he or she no longer agrees with the practices, with how things are handled?"

"Like what?"

"Take Grant, for example. When he signed his contract with Orchard View more than a decade ago, he didn't have strong opinions regarding women's reproductive health. He simply wanted to help women and deliver babies. That was what he thought anyway." What changed? "But then, his worldview shifted as he ..." What had he done? "Grew in his faith, read the Bible, learned more about what it means to think biblically rather than humanistically."

"Humanistically?"

"Meaning, to see the world through a lens that places human thought above what the Bible says, which is, in my opinion, what God says." Cassie's insides flip-flopped. Was she having this conversation? "When one comes to believe, for example, life begins at conception, then he or she has to evaluate how that affects other choices."

"Like abortion. That's what you're getting at, right? Like allowing a woman to choose what's best for her own body. With her own future." Jane set her mug down with a thud. "And this from you, Cassie. A woman."

What could she say? "I am a woman, and I care about women. But that includes unborn women. Men too. When Grant and I began to see the world through a biblical lens, it changed the way we viewed things. How we voted. Who and what we supported."

"Like so many crazy conservatives." Jane rolled her eyes. "Guess you're like all the rest."

"I'd like to think not, but I can't convince you merely with words. It has to be lived out in my actions. In Grant's actions. In Peter's actions. Otherwise, we're hypocrites."

If only Jane knew, knew why she was, why Grant was, so passionate about this topic in particular. "Look at my family, Jane. More than half of my children came to us because a birth mother chose to carry to term, even when it would have been easier, more convenient, to terminate her pregnancy." But there was more. "From the beginning of time, regardless of legislation, women have chosen whether or not to have a child. Even when laws made it more difficult, terminations happened. Always have. Likely always will." What was she trying to say? "I guess I'd love for more to make the better choice, because I believe, when we do things God's way, there's blessing. And I believe all life is precious to the Creator."

Jane didn't blink as she stared at Cassie. Her mouth was tight, jaw clenched. "I suppose we simply see things differently, probably because we've lived different experiences." She traced the grain of wood on the table. "And don't think for one second I'm not a Christian. I am. Have been since I was a teenager. But then ..." Her eyes shifted, meeting Cassie's, then down again, fixed on the table. "I was molested by an uncle. Got pregnant and ..." A tear fell, then another. "How can I say the very thing I did, the very thing that enabled me to go on with my life, is wrong for another? For another girl ... like me?"

Cassie reached behind her, then took a tissue from a box atop a yellow kitchen cart situated under the window. "Here."

Jane blew, then dabbed her eyes. "Now, that wasn't what I expected from this coffee date."

Cassie laid her hand on her friend's arm and squeezed. "Sometimes things happen we don't expect, but that doesn't mean they shouldn't have happened." She gave her a pat. "And Jane, please don't underestimate what I know. My experiences." She released Jane's arm. "Surely we can have discussions, even with differing worldviews, sharing what we think and why. And at the end of the day, remain friends." Cassie smiled. "Right?"

Jane met Cassie's gaze. "Yes, I ... I think we can."

"All it takes is pulling up a chair. Someone said that once, not long ago. Guess that's true for us." Cassie sighed. "And now, I feel better." There was one more thing. "But Jane, I'm sorry about what happened to you. Truly. And I'm thankful you shared. I'm sure that's not easy to talk about."

Jane's head turned side to side. "Haven't talked about it in ..." She glanced up, a slight smile tugging at the corners of her lips. "I'm not quite sure, but I feel better too. Thank you for listening."

"Of course. And can I offer you a challenge? First, if there's something you'd like me to read, an article, even a book, for example, that you value, something that will help me better understand your way of thinking, I will. But will you do me a favor?"

Though it took a moment, Jane nodded. "Yes."

"Will you read Psalm 139? Take it verse by verse. Read it slowly. Then, let's have coffee again. Soon."

Later, Cassie sat at her desk. She flipped open her laptop, her family's smiles erupting as the screensaver came to life. How long had it been since she'd written a column for the newspaper? The morning conversation with Jane had inspired her.

Heartbeat.

That rhythmic pulse of my evidence, like a song. And no matter one's stance on my sanctity, science doesn't lie. Rather, it points students to truth, if they pay attention.

I wake, stir in the form of the unformed. At least, for now—until the choice is made for me to flourish. Or to die.

Because it is a choice. Despite legislation. Laws.

Even love.

After all, love isn't always enough to sustain me, not the imperfect love that exists in this hour. Some might argue love's passion is the catalyst that both births me and sometimes snuffs me out, like a flicker extinguished—ironically, again, by my evidence, as breath blown pulls the curtain on flame.

Indeed, I'm often extinguished by human hands, and with my death comes a million shattered dreams—shards scattered far and wide, most unknown. Except to my Author, the one who has a plan, who breathed me into being, spoke me into manuscript.

With a word, I was. And with The Word, I am.

And with words, an intended tale for each individual is written in his Book, even before that which was unformed takes shape, is pushed forth and gasps. Again, evidence of my presence. Essential to my existence. Each breath a word on a page, comprising sentences, paragraphs, and chapters to complete a story.

Mine is but one of those, in the vast library of volumes. And though merely one, its beauty—its significance—is equal to all others, despite any tragic beginning.

Because even when love seems absent, when I have my beginning in one whose start is the result of hatred fueled by selfishness, he's there.

And the Word breathes out, and I begin again, my song manifested in the tempo of a quiet heartbeat.

There. She hit Save, then attached the document she'd titled "Life" to an email addressed to Frank Cooper, the editor of the *Greensboro News and Record*.

Perhaps she'd include it in Ava and Gideon's memoir.

She and Jane would have coffee again soon. But before that, she'd meet with Ava and Gideon, on Glovenia. Their home. The home Gideon had built for his bride. To be a covering.

Maybe this meeting would wrap up their story. Cassie could begin writing it, then meet with Jane, tell her more, more about why this issue was so important to her. Why it fueled her, helped see her through surgery, chemo, and soon, radiation.

And her own words, ones she'd typed minutes earlier, echoed. *With a word, I was. And with the Word, I am.*

"Yes, I am." Cassie smiled, then closed her laptop.

Millie Kate's giggles came from her room, and a muffled whine from Merle, who always slept with her, told Cassie: Chapters of her story were yet to be written.

She was alive.

CASSIE BENNETT-BILLINGS'S STORY

O Cross that liftest up my head,
I dare not ask to fly from Thee;
I lay in dust life's glory dead,
And from the ground there blossoms red
Life that shall endless be.

—George Matheson's
"O Love That Wilt Not Let Me Go"

CHAPTER 36

CASSIE—AUGUST 2016

HAVING KNOCKED, I stepped back from the Stallingses's front door, then tightened my ponytail with a quick yank.

The door opened. "Come in, Cassandra. Welcome to our home." Ava stood in the doorway of their white-painted brick cottage, her arms extended. "Let me hug you."

Stepping through the wisteria-covered archway, I leaned in to the embrace of the woman before me, inhaling Avon's Spring Song.

"Welcome. I see you found us." Gideon's deep voice resonated from behind his wife as he, too, entered the foyer. "No trouble, I hope."

Pulling away from Ava, I shook my head. "Not at all. The directions were perfect." Scanning the space, I smiled. "Last week, you said something in Dutch, I believe, about your home. What was that?"

Ava giggled. "Wij hebben een huis! We have a house!" Stepping aside, she said, "Yes, do come in, dear." She patted my arm as I passed. "Of course, your sister-in-law, Ann, is half Dutch. When my friend Elaine married Daan, who'd only been in the

States a short time when they met, she taught me some of the Dutch she'd been learning." Ava tittered. "I'll never forget how your brother was taken with Ann right from the start, even as kids. Too bad they didn't meet again until much later, after Ann's divorce." She paused, and her eyes lifted, as though in thought. "I believe the very first time we were all together, Elaine and Daan, your parents, and us was for your father's baptism." Ava turned from me to face her husband. "Is that right, Gideon? For Mike's baptism?"

He scratched his cheek. "I believe that's right. But perhaps we're getting ahead of ourselves. Let's get coffee and settle in. How's that sound?" He led the way to a cozy living room awash with morning sunlight. "How's this? Make yourself at home, and I'll help Ava with the coffee."

Alone, I stepped into the warm space. A walnut curio cabinet against a wall the color of a robin's egg caught my eye. Leaning toward its glass front, I analyzed the contents. Filled as it was with what seemed a lifetime of memories, one object in particular piqued my attention. Propped up against the cabinet's back was a framed cover of a *Time* magazine dated March 13, 1964. A black man's face filled the cover. "Tanganyika's President Nyerere" was written in white letters in the lower left-hand corner. "From Africa to Vietnam: New Policies in a Changing World" was in the upper left.

"Jonah," I whispered. "Exactly how I pic—"

"So many memories tucked in there." Ava's voice startled me, and I flinched. "I'm sorry, dear. Didn't mean to frighten you." She carried a butter-yellow Fiesta tray with a trio of matching cups and saucers, creamer, and sugar bowl. Gideon rounded the corner carrying the set's matching coffee pot.

"I ... I was looking at all these things, thinking how many years they must span." Why was my hand trembling, my heart pounding?

"Yes, many years indeed. And please, continue looking, dear. Do you take cream and sugar?"

"Cream, please. Thank you."

Perusing the shelves of the wooden cabinet, I tried to absorb it all, connect the dots of four decades. More even. A framed tapestry with "Love Lifted Me" stitched in red, green, and blue threads. A single purple button, a remaining lavender thread hanging from its single hole, nestled in a speckled half-cockle shell. A framed black-and-white wedding photo, a much younger Ava and Gideon smiling at one another, seemingly oblivious to everyone around them. Several more seashells, in a variety of shapes and sizes. And a red-and-white gingham ribbon wound around the gifts from the sea.

"You sit here, dear." Ava pointed to a floral upholstered wingback chair. "This belonged to my parents, who lived not far from here."

Momma. Daddy. You've already said no, but I wanted to ask if you might reconsider the spring break trip. And please, hear me out. I could almost hear Ava asking, see her parents sitting before her, Elaine—my brother William's mother-in-law—to her left, holding her hand.

I sat. Though my hands had ceased their shaking, my heart still pounded. Why?

"Today's the day." Gideon's mouth turned upward, his eyes sparkling. "Let's finish this story, put you out of your misery." He chuckled. "Did the week tick by?"

I nodded. "Slower than the internet in rural Indiana. The only thing that helped make it go even that fast was Lannie's spelling bee, a sleepover Ben hosted with several friends, Millie Kate's potty training, and the twins' dental appointments." I laughed. "Life of a mother of five."

Little crinkles formed at the corners of Ava's eyes. "I haven't forgotten those days, dear. Even though it was only Fi, she kept us busy, busy, busy." Ava sat beside her husband on the dusty blue sofa adjacent to me, then patted his knee. "Gideon, I believe you left Cassandra hanging." She giggled. "How was it, with the snap of my journal."

"Something about not sleeping a wink. After all, I had a fabric-covered book to read. A Bible to explore." Gideon held an invisible magnifying glass to his eye and smiled. "A mystery to solve."

What had he discovered?

"Rather than type this time, so I can fully engage, I thought I'd record you in voice memo, on my phone. Would that be okay?"

"Of course." To Ava, Gideon said, "Are you ready, my love?" His gaze met his wife's.

"Yes, dear."

He took a deep breath, then exhaled slowly, as though preparing himself, and I hit Record.

"The journal confirmed what Jonah had implied, what I already knew. From Ava's first entry in January, having received the diary from her mom for her nineteenth birthday, until ..." He paused. "Perhaps reading her words is best. Is that okay, my love?"

"Of course."

Gideon opened the book, not at the beginning but nearer the middle. He ran a finger over a page, then stopped. "Here. March eighteenth, 1969. It was the last entry prior to Ava's leaving for Myrtle Beach." With his deep, calm voice, he read—

"For I know the thoughts that I think toward you, saith the Lord, thoughts of peace, and not of evil, to give you an expected end." Here, it seems God's thoughts are about us, so does that mean the thoughts he thinks about me are precious? That his thoughts of me outnumber the grains of sand? I sort of feel I've gone

full circle. I wish the Bible was easier to understand. Rereading my first entry back on January 13, I wrote, "... [if] there's already a plan that God already knows—well, that bothers me. Confuses me. Makes me wonder why God can't keep me from sin." And concerning my questioning—wondering why he allows bad things to happen when he clearly could stop them—I guess that's where my mistrust comes in. Do I believe: First, God has a plan? Second, his plans are good? And third, does he think of me more times than the number of grains of sand on the shore?

Gideon gazed up from the journal to fix his attention on Ava. "And do you know the answers to these questions now, my love?" His eyes were tender.

"I do."

Gideon turned to me. "Sometimes we find answers in difficult places, Cassandra. Hard, even painful places."

I nodded. I knew this to be true.

"Ava made it to Myrtle Beach. Unpacked her things in room 212. She and Elaine got all dolled up for an evening of dancing, the tide beyond, moving in and out, waves crashing. The moon was just a sliver in the night sky, a million stars overheard."

Ava began to hum, though I couldn't decipher the tune. Gideon, however, obviously knew.

"'Crimson and Clover.' That was the song, wasn't it, my love? The one you and Bobby danced to, your purple dress swaying, your buttons touching his." His gaze met mine. "I'll read what Ava wrote."

Friday, March 21, 1969. Last night, I was raped.

Gideon paused and cleared his throat. Was his face turning red? He continued reading—

How much did I drink? Too much to allow me to remember, not enough to knock me unconscious. Enough to leave me vulnerable, unguarded. And I knew better. God, I knew better. But I kept thinking, telling myself, I could go back and ask you for forgiveness.

Gideon patted Ava's leg.

I heard Momma, heard what she'd said too many times to count, that which sometimes irritated me. "It's because of love." I tried to drown her out. It wasn't her voice I wanted to hear at that moment. It was Bobby. I wanted him to tell me he loved me. I'd been waiting so long. Hadn't I predicted he'd one day be my—

Once more, Gideon cleared his throat. Laying the journal on his lap, he rubbed his eyes before continuing.

He'd be my husband? So, I'd show him. I'd make him love me. And I let down my guard, with one beer and another and another. Then our dance, his hands on my hips, running up and down my sides.

Gideon let out a long, slow exhale.

"This is difficult, reliving this, rereading my words." Ava dropped her gaze, staring at her hands folded in her lap.

As though the pause had given him the courage to continue, Gideon read more.

Bobby stepped back, then took my hands in his and mouthed, "Let's walk." There was a stirring inside. Like I was about to step toward something from which there'd be no turning back. And I had a choice. And I chose. I walked, allowing Bobby to lead me. Far from others, only the faint melody of some song carried on a breeze, he stopped, and we sat. His kiss, what I'd waited so long to experience, was soft at first, but then it grew in intensity, his movements sporadic. I was scared, and I wanted Bobby to know what I wanted, but he had to slow down. To make the moment last. To love me. But that wasn't what he did, and when I resisted, he grew angry, angry with a force that seemed to come from someone...something...

"Furious." Ava stared straight ahead, her face stripped of its rosiness, her eyes glazed. Was she once again on a beach, not with her beloved but with a beast? With Bobby. "Furious with the world. Furious with the war in Vietnam. Furious with his broken body, which he—"

"Wanted to test. See what he was capable of." Gideon shook his head, and I noticed his left fist clench. His voice quivered. "And it worked, didn't it. In his rage, b-buttons flew, and he took from you something that could never b-be replaced."

My head spun. Had Gideon stuttered on his words, after all this time?

"Yes." Ava looked at her husband, and her voice softened. "But still, he was not my husband. You are, as God intended." Her eyes pooled, but the tips of her mouth turned up. "And in his goodness, God confirmed it when you—"

"Finished reading your journal and knew. Jonah's words echoed his belief that I was the one to find you and—"

"You did. You certainly did, dear." Ava smiled at me. "Yes, God called him to rise up, be courageous, and live out his name." Gazing at her husband again, she patted his knee. "My Gideon Joseph. When I returned home from Myrtle Beach, I realized I'd forgotten my journal. At first, I panicked. But with everything else, my belief soon confirmed with my missed cycle, I let it go. How was I to get it back? Or so I thought." She paused. "But I should've known. Jonah had been my room attendant too. Elaine's and mine. Bobby's too, until ..."

Until what?

"How kind Jonah had been. I think he suspected something. Offered medical supplies when he came to remove several bloodied towels from our room the following morning. I wore sunglasses to hide a blackened right eye, but I think he knew."

But what happened to Bobby? "May I ask, did you call the police?"

"They came. Questioned me, right there in room 212. Took my dress and undergarments as evidence. They questioned Elaine too, but Bobby ..." Again, Ava's voice faded at the mention of his name. "He up and disappeared. For years, in fact." Ava shook her head. "Poor Elaine was beside herself with worry, for me and ..."

"Of course. It was only natural," I said.

"For several years, they'd hear from him now and again. He'd call from some pay phone, from some city or town. Never told them where he was."

"Did you press charges?"

Ava's head turned side to side. "No. Perhaps I should have. Perhaps I should have made more of an effort to bring him to justice, but—"

"Elaine. Her family."

"They'd been through so much. And honestly, for some time, I blamed myself too. After all, I'd—"

"Been drinking?" As soon as the words were out, I regretted saying them.

"Yes. It doesn't justify Bobby's actions, but I did ... I did want to be with him then, and ..." Ava sniffed. "There have been times I've looked back, wished I'd done things differently, but—"

"God sent me." Gideon nodded. "Ava, you mentioned Bobby making calls from pay phones. Tell Cassie about the pay phone in Eden, the day you made the call that would change everything."

Ava giggled. "Ah yes, but first things first, dear. You arrived at the library where I worked. Bouquet of bright daffodils in your hand, though you were as white as a sheet. Walked right up and asked if I knew an Ava. 'Ava Jackson from Eden.' I think you may have even stuttered once or twice."

Gideon chortled. "I was a nervous wreck."

"When I told you I was her, I swear you blushed. Even with everything going on in my life, with my upcoming appointment to ..." She turned her attention to me. "I didn't know what else to do. Had convinced myself it was the only way, the only way to get my future back." She turned to her husband. "You held out the bouquet of the prettiest, happiest daffodils I'd ever seen, wrapped in parchment, tied with a red-and-white-checked ribbon." She pointed behind her. "The one in the curio cabinet. I've kept it all this time."

"And you whispered, 'New beginnings.' Isn't that right, my love?" Gideon swiped a tear.

"Yes, and then you asked, 'What did you say?' and I repeated it. 'New beginnings.'" Ava smiled. "After all, that's what the daffodil means."

"And here, I had no idea when I chose them. That was the first thing I did when I pulled into Eden that Wednesday. I wasted no time, driving through the night even. After reading the journal when I returned home from the conference on Monday, I went to work the next day. Told Robbins and Ray I had some unfinished business to attend to, related to the conference, of course, which was true." Gideon sighed. "Cassie, imagine your parents' surprise when I called them up after having said goodbye only a couple of days earlier. 'Still up for a visit in Greensboro?' I asked, and Mike laughed. I'll never forget his laugh."

"He does have a great laugh." My dad's cheerful face flashed across my mind. "Always has."

"He said, 'Sure, come on.' And I arrived at the Bennetts' on Wednesday morning, June twenty-fifth. Before leaving, I knew I wanted to give a gift to Billy. A sort of peace offering, seeing as I almost crushed his dreams, so to speak." Gideon chuckled.

"Which you didn't." The corners of my mouth curled into a smile. "My brother is one of the finest, most generous architects ever."

"Since we both loved baseball, I decided to give him my brand-spankin' new collection of baseball cards, which, I hear, he only recently parted with."

At that moment, Ben's face flashed in my mind. My Bennett Jonah, the ten-year-old with a wish he eventually shared—*make Momma well.* I believed, I prayed it would come true, after radiation.

"Anyway," Gideon continued, "it was as if Jonah's words were coming to fruition. I was a builder-up of people. Coming to Eden to ... let's say, my excuse to take a few extra days off work was truer than Robbins and Ray could have ever known, at least until—"

"Until you gave your resignation only a short time later. Moved to Eden permanently. I'll never forget my parents, after all those years, clearing out John Paul's room. Replacing his crib, where he'd passed away, with a full bed, which, after our wedding, became ours." Ava's face turned a shade of pink, all earlier pallor gone.

"Weren't they skeptical? I mean, everything happened so fast, it seems." My mind raced, trying to calculate the days, figure out the timetable.

"Perhaps. But not for long. Momma and Daddy loved Gideon from the start," Ava said. "I mean, look at him. Kindest man in the world."

Gideon's smile was tender. "You made, have always made, it easy, my love."

"But what were you going to say about the pay phone? The call?" I asked.

"My, yes." Ava snickered. "After Gideon's unannounced visit to the library, when he sat me down and showed me not only the Bible by room 212's bed, the one I'd written in, but my journal too ..." Again, she shook her head, and her green eyes widened. "Can you imagine my surprise? My journal!"

"It's so amazing." I could hardly believe everything they were telling me.

"I was scheduled to ..." Ava's gaze met mine. "On Friday. But after meeting Gideon, hearing everything he had to say, rereading my own words, the places in the Bible I'd marked ..." She glanced from me to Gideon, then back to me. "I thought, *Maybe I'll wake up and this will all be a dream*. Went to sleep on Wednesday night, thinking that very thing. But when I awoke on Thursday morning to my phone ringing, and when I answered I heard Gideon's voice, I knew. It was true. And I had a choice to make. A choice."

A choice. Ava had a choice.

Words I'd just typed, then emailed to the editor of the *Greensboro News and Record* only days before—*Even when love seems absent, when I have my beginning in one whose start is the result of hatred fueled by selfishness, He's there.*

Yes, God's there, no matter the choice.

CHAPTER 37

CASSIE—AUGUST 2016

"YOUR GARDENS ARE BEAUTIFUL, Ava. You must spend a lot of time out here." I plucked a pink Knock Out Rose from a bush lining the walkway, then lifted it to my nose. "And it doesn't smell shabby either."

"And can you smell the fragrance of our gardenia?" Ava closed her eyes and inhaled.

I breathed deeply, took in the sweet scent. Refinement. Purity.

As we strolled from the backyard and onto the couple's screened-in patio, Ava ran her fingers along a trellis, alive with green and purple. "And of course, we can't forget clematis, though I've never known why it stands for poverty. It's rich in abundance, coming back every year, as sure as the rising sun." She picked up a long tendril of honeysuckle intertwined with the lavender blossoms. "Wish people could live together so peacefully." Ava sighed before adding, "And sweetly. Breathe this in."

It was a favorite, and I obeyed. "I love honeysuckle. Momma taught me long ago how you can break the blossom away right where it meets the stem, then lick up all that sweet nectar."

Ava giggled. "Yes. I love that too. Years ago, when Gideon and I were younger, Mike and Patti too, we loved getting together for cookouts. We gals talked for hours, meandering about her gardens or my own." With a sigh, she said, "We taught each other a lot over the years." Her gaze met mine. "You, my dear, toddled around. As you got older, you skipped across the paving stones like a gazelle. Such a fond memory."

She remembers that?

"Anyway, honeysuckle. Know what it represents?" Ava plucked a butter-yellow blossom at its base, then pulled the stem near the bottom, revealing a tiny bead of nectar. She held it out.

Before touching the flower's gift to my tongue, I shook my head. "Can't say that I do."

"Devotion." Ava's eyes lit up. "Yes, devotion. Something many these days simply don't know enough about. But you, Cassandra—"

It was my turn to smile. "Imperfect devotion anyway."

Gideon approached, two tall glasses of sweet tea in hand. "Some refreshment, ladies?" He handed me my glass. "And now, shall we continue?"

Back in the Stallingses's living room, nestled again in the wingback chair, I took a long drink of my tea before setting the glass on a coaster on the cherry coffee table separating me from Ava and Gideon.

"Now, where were we?" Ava shifted on the couch, looking as eager as a little girl awaiting Christmas, her eyes wide.

"The pay phone, my love." Unlike his wife's, Gideon's eyes expressed a tenderness.

"Ah, yes. But before we explain that, tell her about Jonah."

Gideon smiled at Ava. "That is an important piece of the puzzle, isn't it? Let me see here." He pinched the tip of his jaw, his gaze fixed upward for a moment. Finally, he said, "Right after I returned home from Myrtle Beach, on Tuesday, I believe. Or was it Monday?"

"Tuesday, dear. It was after you'd met with Robbins and Ray, to tell them you were leaving to tend to some unfinished business." She winked.

"Yes, that's right." Gideon patted his wife's hand, which rested on his knee. "I was packing to leave, throwing things in my suitcase, putting the journal and Bible back in my leather satchel, when the phone rang. Dad answered and hollered up to tell me the call was for me. 'A man named Jonah.'" Gideon smiled. "Of course, I was excited to hear my friend's voice. After all, it had only been a couple of days." He chuckled. "Anyway, when I picked up the call in my room and said hello, it was as though Jonah was right there with me."

I fidgeted in my chair. "And?"

"First, he asked me about my trip home, how it went, and such. After a spell, he jumped right in, asking if I'd finished reading the journal, if I'd decided what to do." Gideon opened the worn Bible beside him on the couch, turned to a page, then slipped out a brittle, yellowed piece of paper. "Here." Gideon rose, then stretched across the coffee table between us, handing me the paper.

It was Sand Dollar Bay Resort stationery. I scanned the page and recognized what it was. It was what Jonah had removed from the Bible, then placed in his family's prayer pot. On one side, a sort of timeline. On the back, calculations ending in a plea.

"Go ahead. Read it." Gideon returned to the couch. Once again, he patted his wife's hand before enveloping it in his.

I read:

March 20, 1969—Description and Timeline. 7 PM
Elaine and I met Bobby on the dance floor. Danced with each other and lots of other spring breakers. Had a few drinks. (How many? Three?) Bobby and I began to slow

dance to "Crimson and Clover." Before the song ended, he asked me to take a walk. We strolled on the beach, stopping at a wooden pier. He began to kiss me, then tore my dress, forced himself on me. His elbow caught my right eye, which bled and is bruised. After, he disappeared somewhere on the beach, leaving me alone. Somehow made my way back to the hotel, to room 212.

I stopped. Ava's hand covered her mouth, her complexion pale again. The words I'd read had upset her.

"Should I go on?"

"Yes." Though Ava's voice was muffled behind her fingers, she was clear.

I turned the paper over.

Last period—March sixth. Counting fourteen days—March nineteenth or twentieth. Oh, please, dear Jesus, no.

Ava leaned toward Gideon and, for the first time, wept. He took a hankie from his trousers and handed it to his wife. "There, there."

"I'm so sorry." What more could I say? Still, as difficult as it was to hear those facts again, wasn't it redemptive too, knowing how God had used that piece of paper to guide Gideon to save a girl he'd never met? To save—

"Jonah went on to quote Scripture," Gideon interrupted me. "A passage from the book of Esther. I've never forgotten." Gideon turned in the Bible. "Esther four fourteen. I can hear his voice, even now, all these years later. 'Now, you listen here. "And who knoweth whether thou art come to this place for such a time as this?" Yes, sir. Yes indeed, Gideon Joseph.' That's what he said."

Gideon kissed Ava's head, and she sat up, dabbing her eyes.

"That was that," he said. "I left less than an hour later with Jonah's words ringing in my ears. 'For such a time as this.'"

"And you arrived at the Bennetts' in the middle of the night."

"More like the wee hours of morning. I only slept a little, then showered and drove over to Eden with dawn's early light. Purchased those daffodils and headed to the library, then—"

"Showed up, my architect in shining armor." Ava's gaze met mine. "Though I must admit, at first I thought he was a tad crazy." She twirled her index finger, making circles in the air close to her ear. "I soon learned better."

"And the pay phone?" I was busting to know this mysterious part of their story.

"On Thursday, I took Gideon to visit John Paul's grave under the oak in Eden's First Church cemetery right there at the corner of Reeves and Greenwood. It was a lovely day. I said, 'JP, meet Gideon.' His gravestone's etched with a lamb, The Lord is my Shepherd above his date of birth, his date of—"

"Home-going." Gideon smiled. "The day he went to be with Jesus, his Good Shepherd."

"Yes, dear. What a comfort. And I'll never forget, Gideon quoted the twenty-third Psalm in its entirety. Said his momma taught it to him prior to her—"

"Home-going." It was my turn to interrupt. "And she's with JP and my Grant's mom, and so many who've gone before." Jonah's and Gideon's babies, the ones whose lives were snuffed out before—

"Yes, how true." Ava shook her head. "Imagine the day we'll get to be there too. What a reunion." She wiped her nose once more, then handed Gideon his damp hankie. "It was there, right there in that cemetery, right by JP's grave, I knew. And I knew what I had to do. Gideon drove me to the nearest filling station." She giggled.

"One of the only filling stations in Eden with a pay phone. And what did you do, dear?"

"I opened the ashtray where I kept loose change," Gideon said. "When I reached in to get a dime, it fell out."

Ava smiled. "And what was *it*?"

"The button?" I couldn't help interrupting. Gideon had said he'd tucked it in his wallet's change compartment while in Myrtle Beach. "When you got home, you kept it safe in your ashtray?"

Ava giggled, nodding. "Yep, and if everything else hadn't been confirmation enough, if I had even one smidge of doubt, it was laid to rest, right then and there. In the vast expanse of that beach, among all those grains of sand, my Gideon found a button. My button. Now, if that isn't the most redemptive thing ever!"

Gideon's head bobbed. "I handed her a dime, and she made that call, didn't you, dear?"

"Indeed, I did. Told the receptionist on the line, 'I have an appointment tomorrow morning, but I ...'" Ava's gaze lifted to meet mine once more. "'I've made a choice, and I need ... no, I want to cancel it.' I chose my words carefully. Because I did have a choice. I chose life."

My eyes welled, then tears fell. How close she'd come. But Gideon.

But God.

"The rest is history. It was a blur. Of course, I took Gideon home to meet my parents. We sat in the same places Elaine and I'd sat, where they'd sat ..." Ava pointed to the chair I was sitting on. "Daddy sat in that very same chair on the day I offered my proposition, explaining how I had the money and an opportunity for work—"

"Which I've wondered about." I couldn't help interrupting. "You never made it to Smith's Print Shop for your interview, did you? That's what Loraine found out when she ran her errand that day, after she dropped Gideon off at the airport."

"That's right. I was a no-show. Mr. Smith called the hotel, having learned where I was staying from Professor Barnes, who was his wife's cousin. As a matter of confidentiality, nothing was said about what had happened. Only that I must have been detained." Ava's focus shifted, and she glanced upward. "I've wondered about whether they were the ones who ..." She stopped, shook her head. "No. Certainly not."

Something inside held me back from pushing the issue, though I was curious what Ava meant.

"And what about the Bible? When you investigated further, Gideon, did you find other passages marked? Underlined? Other places Ava had written?" My eyes went from Gideon to the Bible on his lap.

"There were several others. One in particular stands out."

"Hosea, chapter two, verse fifteen. That's one of them, isn't it, dear?" Ava patted the Bible.

"Yes, my love. Says something like, 'And I will give her back her vineyards, and the valley of Achor will be a door of hope, and she shall sing there, as in the days of her youth.' Not exactly, but close. And why did you underline that particular passage, dear?"

"After ... you know ... I felt like a whore. So dirty. Like it was my fault, at least in part." Ava's head turned side to side. "I was reading in Hosea, having opened quite randomly, desperate for a word of comfort. As I continued reading, verse fifteen struck me, offered a glimmer."

"And don't forget about Deuteronomy, chapter thirty-three. I believe it's verse nineteen." Gideon lifted Ava's hand and kissed it.

She quoted from memory. "They will feast on the abundance of the seas, on the treasures hidden in the sand." She sighed. "Another passage I came across in my desperate search. This one spoke of treasures in the sand, a treasure like—"

"The button." I simply couldn't believe it. How specific God had been in guiding Ava in his Word, then to guide Gideon to find the button.

"Yes, love. A treasure indeed, as are you." Gideon held his beloved's hand to his cheek and closed his eyes.

"And Jonah?" I was curious about this man who was so familiar from the description Gideon had given, from the love he had for this man he'd only spent a little time with, prior to rescuing Ava. "Is he still living? Have you visited over the years?"

Gideon's expression changed, his eyes narrowed, and his brow furrowed. "Now, that's—"

"Go on, tell her, dear." Ava's countenance, too, had changed.

"That's a difficult part of the story. When I returned home late that Friday from my visit to Eden, I knew I'd only be there long enough to gather more things. Ava and I had already made a promise, and I couldn't get back quickly enough. My first night home, the phone rang. What was the date, dear?"

Ava took her journal and opened it to the middle. "I wrote it here." She flipped several pages. "Here it is. June twenty-eighth, 1969." She read:

Last night, right after returning home, Deon received a call from his friend Jonah's wife, Georgia. Through tears, she explained that Jonah had passed suddenly, in his sleep. He'd had a headache and retired early. He never woke up, having suffered a heart attack.

She paused and clucked sympathetically before continuing

Deon is beside himself with grief, and I'm sad to know I'll never meet this man who was instrumental in all that's happened. Momma's words ring true yet again. Grief—

just another word for love unending. I'll share that with Gideon when we return together for Jonah's funeral. I wonder how being back in Myrtle Beach will feel. Somehow, it will be okay. With Gideon, everything will be okay.

Ava's face tipped up. "And now Jonah's with Jesus."

I shook my head. "It's like he said. Didn't he say he'd stay forty-two? And he did."

"Yes, indeed. As I told you, Jonah had a way of knowing things. Maybe he knew this also, discerned it somehow. Maybe God called him home after he used him to help—"

"Lift you, lift me, lift us up out of the pit of despair." Ava's eyes welled again, though she smiled. "May I have that hankie once more, dear?" She dabbed her eyes. "I never quite thought about it that way. Jonah, Jonah, Jonah." Shaking her head, "Dear, do tell Cassandra about the significance of that *Time* magazine."

The *Time* magazine, the one in the curio cabinet.

"Funny. It stayed in my cedar chest for years. It's the one I swiped from the oncologist's office the day my mom received her three-month prognosis. No real reason for me to take it. An act of rebellion, I suppose. But I must admit. When I returned home from that Myrtle Beach conference, after Jonah's funeral and all, I searched for it. Found it there, underneath other memorabilia. When I lifted it out, I could hardly believe my eyes. I understood why Jonah was familiar, right from the start. He looks so much like that man. President Nyerere."

"Simply amazing. Almost too much to take in." There was a lull in the conversation, and I pushed Stop on my iPhone's voice memo, then stretched. "So much to process." Through a yawn, I said, "And I'm sure you're weary, both of you, but ..." A question still lingered, something pressing, but it was met with a sense of dread, as if the future—my future—hinged on the answer.

"But what, dear? Perhaps there's still a question you'd like to ask us." Ava's smile was tender. "And about being weary? In a pleasant sort of way, like being on a long journey. After all, it's good to remember. To consider our stones of remembrance, so to speak. God is, always has been, faithful."

Gideon nodded. "Always." He paused. "But there is one more thing, isn't there. Something you need an answer to, am I right?"

I did. "Yes. And I believe you know what it is." I pushed Record again. "It would bring closure … for me."

Gideon's gaze met mine, and his eyes smiled as his head bobbed. "Ava and I returned to Myrtle Beach for Jonah's funeral. Seeing Georgia and the children was … how to say? Painful, yes, but hope-filled. After all, they knew where Jonah was. I can almost hear him. 'Right with my Jesus. Yes, sir. Best place there is, I reckon.' Anyway, Joe and I reaffirmed that we'd write, which we did, for years, until—"

"That's for another time, dear." Ava patted her husband's hand.

"Yes. Another day, another story, my love." Gideon took his wife's hand in his. "Ava and I were married on a hot September Saturday. September twentieth, to be exact. My bride was, by then, six months pregnant, though she showed very little. Still her best friend, Elaine was her maid of honor, and my cousin Jenny, the one who sang at Mom's funeral, sang George Matheson's 'O Love that Wilt Not Let Me Go,' her angelic voice filling First Church's sanctuary. By the time Ava was to walk down the aisle, arm in arm with her daddy, my cousin was singing verse three.

"O Joy that seekest me through pain,
I cannot close my heart to Thee;
I trace the rainbow through the rain,

And feel the promise is not in vain
That morn shall tearless be."

"Even though very few would understand the meaning of this hymn's lyrics, their symbolism, we'd chosen it specifically."

Ava picked up from there. "As Pastor Wyatt pronounced us man and wife, right before our lips met, I whispered to the one I'd known for such a short time but loved more than words could express. 'It's our love, Gideon—only and always our love.' And it was. It's always been."

"Later, in our simple room in the quaint bed-and-breakfast in Roanoke, I took Ava in my arms and held her to myself. On the bedside table, the innkeeper had left us a note, including an embroidered tapestry." Gideon paused, then pointed. "It's in the curio cabinet too. Did you see it?"

"I did."

"It was a gift. That hymn had been a favorite of Mom's, and though she wasn't with us on our wedding day, it was a beautiful confirmation that she was there.

"Love lifted me!
Love lifted me!
When nothing else could help,
Love lifted me!"

"How she loved to sing those words." Gideon closed his eyes for a few seconds.

Ava took her husband's hand. "In the ardor of this, our first night, Gideon held me to himself. Despite all that had happened, I felt no shame. Only love for this man." She glanced up at him. Though the couple was reliving an intimate moment of their past, the beginning of their union, their oneness, there wasn't a hint of self-consciousness. "Softly he hummed this tune, his mother's favorite, in my ear, and he only stopped when he began kissing me. He ran his fingers through my hair and caressed my cheeks, my neck, continuing downward until his lips rested on my ribs, below my heart. There, he stopped." A beat of silence followed, Ava breathless, it seemed, with the memory.

"Leaning over my wife's swollen belly, I pressed my lips to her navel."

Ava inhaled slowly, deeply, then, in the exhale, said, "The warmth, warmth from his breath birthed heat, beginning at my toes, enveloping all of me." Ava's face flushed, though less from embarrassment it seemed. More from the passion she was reliving.

Gideon's eyes were closed as he, too, recalled. "I lifted my head, then whispered to the life within her, below her skin. 'I was sinking deep in sin, far from peaceful shore, very deeply stained within, sinking to rise no more; But the Master of the sea heard my despairing cry, from the waters lifted me—Now safe am I.'" Gideon's eyes remained closed.

Ava whispered, "He rose up on his elbows, hovering above me. Though naked, we were unashamed as we gazed deeply into one another's eyes. I was unable to hold back emotion, and I cried, as did he, whispering through tears, 'Every scar holds a story, but love lifted us, and—'"

Gideon opened his eyes, which glistened. "'Now, my darling, we become one flesh, a most holy moment.' That was what I said."

With the word *holy*, Gideon's gaze met mine, and I gasped, my heart pounding.

"With lips only a breath from her stomach, my Ava's womb, I spoke to someone else." The corners of his mouth tipped up. "Yes, I said to you, Cassandra, 'You are loved, and you are safe.' And you were."

And I was.

I am.

CHAPTER 38

CASSIE—AUGUST 2016

EXHAUSTED BUT HAPPY AFTER hours with the Stallingses, I stepped through the front door.

"Surprise!" A chorus of voices rang out as my feet met the hardwood foyer.

"Welcome home, dear." Mom was the first to reach me. Leaning in to her embrace, I wept as she rubbed my back. "I know, sweets. I know." She stepped back and met my gaze. "Though you've known for much of your life that Ava was your birth mom, I pray today sealed the promise in your heart that ..." She seemed to consider her words. "That you were, and have always been, loved—by her. By Gideon."

I nodded, swiping tears. "Yes. And thank you, Mom. Daddy too. For ..." For what? "For choosing me. For loving me."

Grant whispered in my ear, wrapping me up from behind. "You did it, Cass. I'm so proud of you."

Someone tugged at the hem of my ankle-length broomstick skirt. "Momma, Momma."

Wriggling free, I glanced down. "Hello, love." I scooped Millie Kate into my arms. She wore a bright-pink shirt with a black typewriter on the front, the image of a single sheet of paper popping up from its carriage, *She believed she could and so she did* ... across the top. Scanning the room, I could hardly believe it. Everyone was wearing the same T-shirt, in a rainbow of colors.

"And here's yours." Dad handed me the same one in heather gray. "And guess where we had them made."

"I still can't believe you pulled that off, Dad. That they're even still in business." Grant grinned ear to ear as he patted his father-in-law on the back.

What was he saying? Where had the shirts been made?

"Smith's Printing. Seems they've expanded their product line." Dad's smile was broad.

"You've got to be kidding." I couldn't wrap my mind around this detail.

"Nope. Called them up about a month ago, when we began planning this celebratory occasion, though we didn't know the exact day. Asked them to please have the shirts ready mid-August." Dad nodded, his eyes glistening. "Still a family-owned business. The young woman I spoke with—Emily, I believe—is the great-granddaughter of Mr. and Mrs. Smith, the original owners, the ones Ava's professor from Rockingham .... What was his name?"

"Barnes. Mr. Barnes." I brushed another tear.

"That's right. Mr. Barnes's cousin, Barbara Smith—it's her great-granddaughter. Sweetest, most helpful young woman." Dad peered down at his own shirt as he continued. "Told her about your book, the reason for our party. She said, 'If you need a printer—that is, if she's self-publishing—we'd love to help you. We've won awards in Myrtle Beach for our quality service.'" He chortled. "Directed me to their website to see for myself, and it's true. They're quite accomplished."

"I'm speechless." I scanned the room, seeing the smiles of all those I loved. All those who'd walked with me, encouraging me, through the last several months. Months that included an unfavorable diagnosis, surgery, and chemo. Months of sickness and fatigue. Months of meetings to gather information for the book I couldn't get out of my mind—eating, sleeping, and breathing Ava and Gideon's story.

My birth mom's story.

Grant hugged me again. "Shall we get this party started?"

He led me by the hand to the dining room, the bright space decorated with streamers and balloons, a beautiful, flower-adorned cake in the table's center, atop a yellow-and-white-checkered tablecloth.

"I helped set the table." Charlotte pulled out a chair, then directed me. "Sit here, Momma."

"You didn't do it by yourself, Char." Chester plopped in the chair to my left. "I helped too."

"Thank you. Everything looks wonderful." I leaned over to kiss my son's curly head, then, "Come here, you," and Charlotte leaned in to my hug. "Love you both."

Ben sidled up. "I went with Grandma Patti to pick up the cake and balloons." He smiled under the bill of his Yankees cap, and I squeezed him around his middle.

Finally, Lannie stepped up before sitting in the chair to my right. She leaned over, allowing her auburn head to rest against my own. "I'm so proud of you, Mom." She pecked my cheek, then giggled. "And for the record, I cleaned."

"Thank you, dear. Thank you for everything." I swiped one more tear. "I love you all so much."

After everything was cleaned up and my parents left, Grant and I sat on our porch, Merle curled at my feet.

I inhaled. "Geranium." It was no more than a whisper.

"What?" Grant's eyes were closed, his head leaning against the rocker.

"Do you smell that?"

He breathed in, then exhaled slowly. "Smells like ... dog."

I snickered. "That too." I reached and took my husband's hand, intertwining my fingers with his. I said, "'Geranium.' Can you smell it?"

Once more, Grant breathed, and smiled. "Yes, I do."

"It means true friendship." I squeezed his hand. "That's us. My forever best friend."

Grant turned, and his gaze met mine. "Yes, Cass. For more than twenty-five beautiful years, even through hard places." He paused. "No, let me rephrase. The hard places, the painful places, have made us more beautiful."

I nodded. "I agree. Thank you, thank you for being there. For everything."

"Thank *you*." Grant's emphasis on *you* spoke volumes. I, too, had helped carry us through. "And thank God."

My lips curled upward. "Yes, thank God."

A cord of three strands.

"May I ask you something about today? About your time with Ava and Gideon?"

"Of course."

"You knew much of their story, though many details were perhaps new." Grant paused. "Right?"

"Yes."

"You've always known you were adopted, that from birth Mike and Patti were, will forever be, your parents. Ava and Gideon chose them, but ..." Grant paused. "Was anything more ..." His voice broke. "I don't know. I guess I'm wondering if anything new was ... revealed?" With his free hand, he wiped his cheek. "Cass."

"What? What are you asking?"

Grant turned to me, his brow furrowed. "Were they able to bring any healing, any closure to a part of your story that—"

"I'd wondered about?" I nodded. "Yes."

Crickets chirped, and a tree frog sang from somewhere close by.

After a moment, I said, "Even though I've known for years how my life tragically began—at least ... what? Seven? Eight?"

"Yes, you've known about that long, I think."

"It wasn't long after you joined Orchard View, in fact, when I found out Ava was—"

"Yes."

"That painful detail, that my life began from rape, must have been difficult for Mom and Dad to tell me, and finding out had ..." What had it done? "I guess, like many adopted children, I'd struggled for a long time, questioning my worth. Like the enemy wanted to keep me in a place of insecurity. Then, to find out I was conceived in that manner? I thought I'd come so far, but that piece of information ... well, it kind of threw me for a loop. Made me question all over again. But today ... today, with all they shared, I know beyond doubt, without question, I was, I've always been ..." I choked on the words.

"Chosen." Grant spoke for me. "You were chosen."

I nodded. "Yes, they had a choice. They chose ... they chose to give me life."

"Yes, Cass. They chose. And this fact feeds our passion now, doesn't it? Our desire for others to understand that, while there's a choice, and there will always be a choice, there's a *best* choice. If each woman, even if pregnant through a difficult circumstance, could see herself as—"

"A life-giver, just like you told Pete and Jenn." I squeezed Grant's hand. "When one comes to believe life begins at conception, the unborn life must be considered too." I leaned toward my husband, and our heads met with a small thump. Where does he begin and I end?

The two shall be one flesh.

"If she'd see herself this way, then maybe, just maybe she'd choose—"

"Life."

"Yes, life." I breathed in the evening, its fragrant air, closing my eyes. "And I guess today affirmed that ..." What? What had it affirmed? "That I'm ... I'm loved, and not only by Mom and Dad, but—"

"By Ava. By Gideon."

"Yes. And it brought closure, even though I'm still processing."

"That will take time." Grant lifted my hand and kissed my fingers.

"Yes. Time, like grains of sand too numerous to count, slipping through an hourglass."

"Like God's thoughts toward us, right, Cass?"

"Yes. Too numerous to count." I giggled. "Like the details of Ava and Gideon's life. They sure did pack a lot into their almost fifty years."

"How so?"

"You know. Travels. Friends. Raising Fi, not to mention Deon's work with Gideons International. Ava's volunteering." My gaze met Grant's. "Details they promised to continue sharing in emails and texts in the coming days. Tidbits that, though they may seem minor, are part of the mosaic of their beautiful lives. Snippets that also belong in their love story, details I'll weave in, no doubt. I'll start—"

A whine interrupted me.

"Merle's singing." Grant chuckled.

"What Merle tune do you suppose it is?"

Grant considered. After a moment, he said, "'Sing Me Back Home,'" and he hummed Haggard's melody.

"Yes. Back home." The irony struck, and I sighed once more. "One day, we'll be home, but for now, this home's pretty fine by me."

"Speaking of." Grant reached into his shirt pocket, then pulled out a small brown box. "I almost forgot."

I took it. Though it wasn't wrapped, it was tied with a red-and-white-checked ribbon. Ava. Daffodils. New beginnings. "What's this?"

"Your silver-anniversary gift. Finally."

I slipped the ribbon from the box, then lifted the lid. Folding back blue tissue, I uncovered a piece of folded paper. "Whatever could this be?"

"Go on."

I unfolded the paper. A single sheet of Sand Dollar Bay stationery. "But ... how?"

Grant winked. "I have my ways."

I read aloud what he'd written. "For our twenty-fifth anniversary. A trip. To where it all began."

"Wait, what?"

"Yep. Already booked. Weekend of September sixteenth, during a full moon." He leaned against me again, and our heads bumped. "We'll walk the beach, maybe find a weather-beaten pier."

"Like ..." I choked on my words. "Grant, thank you."

"I love you, Cass. I love you so much."

And with his words—the words of my husband, my true friend—another man, a hero, flashed across my mind, and his voice echoed.

"But the Master of the sea heard my despairing cry, from the waters lifted me—Now safe am I."

To be saved twice in a lifetime?

Yes. Love lifted me.

THE CONCLUSION

2019–2020

CHAPTER 39

CASSIE—DECEMBER 2019

CASSIE AND HER CHILDREN loaded into their Honda Odyssey, then pulled out onto James Street. Leaning over to look at the floorboard on the passenger side, she checked to be certain she'd gathered everything. Although the trip to Eden's Graceland Manor—the Continuing Care Retirement Community where Ava resided—was less than thirty minutes from their home, she didn't want to have to run back to retrieve anything. It was Cassie's birthday, after all, and the Billingses were going to celebrate with Bibi Ava, along with Cassie's half sister, Fiona, and her family. Grant would meet them there, arriving after work.

Ava had made the move from her and Gideon's longtime residence on Glovenia after his passing the year before. Only days shy of their forty-ninth wedding anniversary, he'd slipped peacefully away in his sleep on September 17, having enjoyed a pre-anniversary meal at their favorite restaurant the evening before.

By early November 2018, Ava had settled in her apartment at Graceland. Though it had taken time, she was learning to enjoy the plethora of activities the facility offered, not to mention the camaraderie with other women, and the health club where she walked a mile almost daily.

Mostly, she enjoyed her weekly Bible study, which met every Tuesday morning. Although not a large gathering of women, there were usually half a dozen or so. Continuing the work her husband had been so passionate about—his faithful service as a member of Gideons International—Ava distributed small pocket New Testaments every chance she had.

"How can I stop doing what my Gideon did for more than thirty-five years?" she'd explained. "No, I'll carry on his work until the good Lord brings me home to him."

Having pulled into Graceland's parking lot, Cassie found a visitor's space near the front door. With her foot on the brake, she peered in her rearview mirror at her children, all buckled behind her, with the exception of Lannie, who sat in the passenger seat.

Turning to face her almost fifteen-year-old, she smiled. "Landry Hazel, this is driving lesson one thousand two hundred and fifty-six. Prior to turning your vehicle off, keeping your foot on the brake, make sure you've moved your gear to Park."

"Thanks, Cassandra Lynn. But I think that's actually one thousand two hundred and fifty-*seven*." Lannie winked at her mom. "Besides, I'll start driver's ed in January, and I'm sure they'll review all these rules then too."

"What would I do without you, dear?" Cassie patted her daughter's knee. "I love you, but I'm just not ready to think of you behind the wheel of a car. Where has time gone?"

Ben, Charlotte, and Chester unbuckled, and Charlotte helped Millie Kate unstrap from her booster.

"Don't forget your backpacks, please. You'll likely have some time to entertain yourselves. Momma wants to talk to Ava privately before the party begins."

"What about?" Always the inquiring mind, Charlotte furrowed her brow. "Pops?"

During the writing of Ava and Gideon's story, the Billings children had come to know the couple better too. They even began referring to Cassie's biological mother and Gideon as Bibi Ava and Pops, much to their delight. Cassie's mom and dad weren't offended. Rather, they, too, rejoiced in their family, which had, with Cassie's commissioned memoir, grown them in beautiful ways.

"Maybe a little. Mostly about Ava. About her life. Their lives." Cassie kissed the top of Charlotte's head. Her hair was neatly braided in cornrows, colorful beads embellishing each chin-length strand. "I guess I still have some questions, that's all. And hey, it's my birthday."

"Will we ever get to know our birth mothers?" Chester kicked a pebble in the parking lot, then chased it around a green VW Bug until it disappeared underneath. "Like you know Bibi?"

Cassie considered her answer. Would they? Definitely not Millie Kate's. A year and a half earlier, Cassie and Grant had received a letter from their adoption attorney telling them of their youngest's birth mom's passing. Drugs. The very thing that, up until adding Merle to their family, had seemed to haunt Millie Kate's dreams. Cassie wasn't sure how or if drugs were part of her daughter's nightmares. She simply knew, once Merle was permitted to sleep in Millie's bedroom, he never wanted to sleep anywhere else, and her night terrors had ceased. At first, he'd slept under her crib and then, once she matured to her big-girl bed, he'd slept at the foot of it, every night.

And to think, Cassie had been against getting the mongrel pup.

The memory of her and Grant's walk the night Merle arrived, how she'd argued at first, came back, and she recalled again the echoes of that summer evening in their neighborhood.

Chester had stopped his rock-kicking and stood before her, hands on his hips. "Well ... will we?"

"Maybe, one day." She stared at her son, the boy whose eyes

held a bit of worry, not dancing eyes like Charlotte's. Who did he resemble? She almost whispered those two words again.

One day—

The troop reached Graceland's entrance. The automatic sliding doors opened, and they entered the warm space of the senior citizens' residential home.

"I don't like the way it smells." Chester's nose crinkled. "Like a stinky basement."

"Shh!" Charlotte nudged her twin. "Not so loud, Ches. You may hurt someone's feelings." The twins linked arms, then led the way past the front desk and into a parlor decorated for the holidays.

The notes of "Jingle Bells" filled the room, the tune coming from an old upright, played by a dapper gentleman wearing a Santa hat. Men and women of varying ages, some much too young to be in what Lannie often called the "old folks' home," were gathered around tables. Several sat hunched in wheelchairs, some with their arms bound to chairs with soft but sturdy ties. Others peered on, many with empty eyes, rheumy with age. One man in particular sat slouched in his wheelchair, a Vietnam USS *Enterprise* cap perched on his head.

He reminded Cassie of someone.

Most smiled and waved at the entourage as Cassie and her children filed in. Only several grumbled under their breath or offered silent stares. The lights from an artificial Christmas tree captured Millie Kate's attention, and she lagged behind for a moment, mesmerized.

"Come on, slowpoke." Ben took his sister's hand. "Bibi's waiting."

Suite A-11 was located down a long corridor, its double-door entrance adorned with colorful twinkle lights, tinsel, and shiny ornaments. On either side were several motion-sensitive, battery-operated decorations. As the family passed, one began playing "We

Wish You a Merry Christmas," with an elf hammering a shiny toy truck. Once more, Millie Kate stopped, her mouth ajar.

"That's Th-anta's helper, Mommy." Like her siblings, it was her turn to lisp, her two front teeth missing as theirs once had been.

As they passed, another elf came to life, this one sawing a piece of artificial wood for a rocking horse. Mille Kate jumped.

"It's pretend, silly." This time, it was Chester who took her by the hand. "We're almost there."

Lannie reached Ava's door first. "Should I go ahead and knock?"

Cassie nodded. "Yes. She's expecting us. We're only a few minutes early."

A plastic wreath of red and white poinsettias hung on Ava's door, with a "Jesus is the Reason for the Season" door hanger dangling from the knob.

Lannie knocked once. Twice. Looking over her shoulder at her mother, Lannie shrugged. "Is she home?"

Cassie had confirmed that afternoon. Surely she was.

Before Lannie could knock a third time, the door opened. Ava, her face aglow, met the crowd with open arms. "Come in. Come in, dear ones." She stepped aside, allowing each of the Billings children to file into her cozy apartment, the space Ava had made her own.

Last was Cassie. Stepping forward, her gaze met her birth mother's. "Hello."

Ava reached out, and Cassie leaned in to her embrace, inhaling again the fragrance of Avon's Spring Song.

Flowers, even in winter. Cassie smiled as she stepped back.

"Welcome, dear. Happy birthday. Fifty already? Your year of jubilee." Ava eyed Cassie up and down, shaking her head. "My, oh my. You are beautiful, dear."

Cassie's cheeks warmed. "Thank you." The poignant irony of all *happy birthday* meant—so much more than simply Ava's celebratory expression—brought tears, and she brushed them away.

"Do come in. Let me get a good look at all these lovely children." Ava turned her attention to the brood behind her. "So nice of you to come. I've got hot chocolate on the stove, and there's popcorn ready on the kitchen table. Lannie dear, do you mind serving your brothers and sisters? Char, perhaps you could help." She turned and pointed to a round oak table nestled in the corner of her living room. Upon it were a women's study Bible, a notebook, a mason jar of pens and pencils, and a small stack of orange pocket New Testaments. "And children, please don't forget. If anyone has a prayer request, write it down and put it in the prayer pot. I'll be sure to pray."

The two girls disappeared around the corner, though their voices rang from the kitchen—Lannie giving directions, the clinking of mugs, the occasional complaint from Charlotte.

Cassie hung her coat on an oak hall tree. "Children, don't throw your things on the floor. Please hang everything up. More company will be here in an hour, so let's keep Bibi's house tidy."

"Yes indeed. This house will soon be filled to the rafters." Ava's joy was apparent, spilling out in her smile. "How I love great big family gatherings. Kids, would you like any Christmas music?"

Before they could respond, Cassie answered. "That's okay. They each brought a backpack with their tablets and books to read. I knew they might need to entertain themselves for a bit. Is it still okay if we talk for a few minutes, Ava?"

"Of course, dear."

"Children, mind Lannie." Cassie raised an eyebrow as her oldest rounded the corner from the kitchen. "And Lannie, be patient. Remember, everyone. Others live in the apartments above Bibi's, as well as on either side. Let's keep a good reputation and not get kicked out for too much yelling and roughhousing. Got it?"

Five Billingses shook their heads, some barely glancing up from their tablets.

"Yes, ma'am." Lannie held a tray with mugs of steaming-hot chocolate topped with whipped cream. "Don't worry. I've got this."

Cassie knew she did. Lannie always did.

And on this particular evening, she needed her eldest's help more than ever. After all, before the others arrived, remaining questions lingered. And only Ava could offer their answers.

CHAPTER 40
CASSIE—DECEMBER 2019

Ava led the way down the narrow, carpeted passage to her bedroom, a room she'd never shared with the love of her life. How must that feel?

The room was sparsely furnished. A small table with a lamp, alarm clock, and framed photograph atop a cream-colored doily was situated by a twin bed. An oak dresser against the far wall stood between two small windows, each with a yellow valance. Finally, a cedar chest sat at the foot of the bed, and a glider rocker was tucked in the corner, a navy-blue afghan draped over its spindled back.

Cassie approached Ava's bed. A colorful quilt in a sparrows' pattern was drawn tight from one side to the other, and two pillows with light-blue shams were propped against the headboard. Cassie smiled as she read "Always kiss me goodnight" across the length of a decorative throw pillow.

"May I?" Cassie sat on its edge, and the springs creaked under the added weight. "I'm not sure why, but I love that sound."

"Me too, dear." She tittered. "Now its creak reminds me of ... me." She laughed again. "This was my bed as a girl. For years, it was in our guest room. But now ... it's all I need."

Cassie reached out to take Ava's cool, thin hand. "How are you?"

"You know. I have my good days and my bad. Mostly good. I miss him, that's all. But one day."

Cassie's use of those words when answering Chester's question earlier came to mind.

One day.

And right then, a memory. Those had been Grant's words—those same two—after Ben had shared his tenth birthday wish with him. Had that been more than three years ago? And his wish had come true. After surgery, chemo, and a season of radiology, she'd been in remission for more than two years, praise the Lord. She'd beat ca—

The clank of metal hardware pulled Cassie from her thoughts as Ava opened her side-table drawer, then lifted out a well-worn Gideon Bible and a tattered fabric book. "Here they are." She laid them on the bed beside Cassie. "I imagine you might like to look at these again, it being your fiftieth birthday and all. This, your year of jubilee."

Cassie fingered the Bible's weathered cover, tracing the outline of a golden lamp embossed in its corner. Opening it, she turned to a page, much of it marked with black underlining, a feather tucked in its crease. Psalm 139.

She closed the Bible, then turned her attention to Ava's journal. Running her index finger down the frayed edges of the fabric book, she smiled. "May I?"

"Of course."

Cassie knew right where to turn. Near the back. Ava's last entry, with the few remaining pages left blank. She opened it and read.

December 20, 1969

Dear One,

Today, we welcome you—a gift the world almost didn't meet, would forever have missed. You're here because of love, dear—only and always because of love.

Cassie brushed tears, then fanned again, her thumb running over more pages of the journal. She felt the stirring of air, like breath. Ava's breath on every page.

Her thumb stopped, and she opened to read its date and entry. March 20, 1969. Exactly nine months prior to the last entry Ava had written. Though she'd read it before, she read it again.

I fumbled with the tiny buttons remaining on my cotton dress, the poor lighting in the hotel bathroom making it difficult to see, not to mention the swelling of my right eye. I'd thought those buttons so dainty, so charming, when I'd purchased the dress only a few weeks ago, anticipating this upcoming trip to the coast. I'd even twirled like a little girl ...

Ava. The slightly stooped woman before her had been a girl once, like Millie Kate, Charlotte, and Lannie. Only several years older than Lannie when—

"Remind me. Do you still have the dress?" As soon as the words were out, Cassie regretted her inquiry, wishing she could take the question back. What a terrible thing to ask. "I'm sorry. I should—"

"Yes, dear. I do." Ava walked to the end of the bed, then opened the chest and pressed its lid against the footboard.

"Sellman's Furniture" was stamped in the upper-right corner of the cedar lid.

Leaning over, Ava inhaled. "I love that smell. Never changes, never diminishes." She paused, seemingly savoring a memory. "This was a wedding gift from Gideon. My hope chest, he called it. After returning home to Ohio, prior to his final move to Eden, he purchased it at the same store where his parents had bought their bedroom suite years earlier." Ava hummed, then scratched her head. "Now, where was that?" After a moment, "Ah, yes. A town not far from Lima. Covington, I believe. Said the nicest salesmen helped him pick it out. I've never forgotten because, coincidentally, they had the same names as my two granddads. Dennis and Fred. Isn't that funny?" She giggled, then stopped and sighed.

Cassie recalled how, years earlier, Ava had described her childhood bedroom, with the oak desk and the watercolor painting, each from grandparents. "Which grandpa gave you the desk? Was it Fred or Dennis?"

"Ah, good memory." Ava clicked her tongue. "You certainly are one for detail, aren't you, dear? The desk was from Grandpa Fred. Had it special made—not from Sellman's though." She shook her head. "Gideon told me he'd take me there, when we visited Ohio. Had a cousin in Covington." Ava rubbed her temple. "Kay, that was her name. Said we'd be the best of friends. Her husband, man named Leo, was killed in action over in Laos. It wasn't long after we'd married. Buried in Arlington National Cemetery, I believe." Ava brushed her fingers over the black "Sellman's" on the inner lid of the chest, seemingly deep in thought. "A Vietnam fighter pilot, a hero. Someone he admired." Ava shook her head. "Never got to Ohio though, never met his cousin Kay. My Deon struggled for years, feeling inadequate for not being allowed to serve. Imagine, only because he stuttered." She clicked her tongue again.

The irony struck Cassie. "But he was your hero." She rested her hand on Ava's.

"Yes, dear. He was."

With that, Ava rummaged through several layers of memorabilia—photo albums, yellowed newspaper clippings, and articles of clothing. Finally, she lifted a zippered plastic bag, lavender faintly showing through the semitransparent cover.

Without thinking, Cassie gasped. To her, the space already held a sort of holy aura, and with the addition of the dress, the room seemed—

Sacred.

"Go on." Ava nodded, encouraging Cassie to unzip and remove the dress.

With trembling hands, she obeyed, first moving the Bible and journal aside. The dress was folded, and Cassie carefully unfolded it, then spread it out on the bed. Small stains could still be seen in places.

Blood?

The long row of pearl-shaped, purple buttons running from the neck down the front, all the way to the bottom, were as she'd imagined. Only several were missing.

"But why? How?" Tears ran down Cassie's face, but she had no concern about smearing her makeup. "I mean, it seems keeping it would be too—"

"Hard?" Ava nodded. "Yes. I suppose it might, but ..." Her voice trailed off. Was a memory overtaking her words? "All things can be redeemed, my dear. Even a dress."

Cassie's brow furrowed. "How so?"

"Even though it was the dress I wore that night on the beach, the night that ..." Again, Ava appeared to ponder. She shook her head. "But it was also the dress I wore when Deon and I left for our honeymoon. Just seemed right. Redemptive somehow. He loved it too, and he was, after all, the one. My husband. Even though someone else tried to take that place by taking my ..." Another pause. "That wasn't what God intended. And with a good cleaning, even with a missing button or two and a couple minor, much-faded stains, it served the purpose well." Ava's gaze met Cassie's. "And to think, you were there that day too."

The emotion was almost too much, and Cassie leaned over the bed and wept. Ava stood beside her and rubbed her back.

"So much. So much. And these details don't necessarily belong in a book. That's why some of this is new information, and I'm sure it's a bit overwhelming."

After a few moments, Cassie sat up. "May I have a tissue, please?"

Ava opened the side-table drawer again and pulled one out. "There, there. Give a good blow."

Once more, Cassie obeyed. She blew, then wiped her eyes. "Honestly, I didn't expect all that, but a good cry's healthy for the soul, isn't that right?"

"Indeed, dear."

One fact was still unclear to Cassie.

"Remind me. Didn't you say you'd given your dress to the police for evidence? How was it returned to you?"

"Now that's a funny story." Ava's eyes were sympathetic. "Perhaps some humor's exactly what we need." She sat down, then patted the bed. "Sit here, and I'll tell you."

For the third time in only minutes, Cassie obeyed the woman who, had she raised her, would have asked her obedience in much more serious ways. Now, doing what Ava instructed, even though they were only simple commands, felt right.

Ava's dress was between them. "Do you recall hearing how Gideon arrived at Rockingham's library that day, the day he came to rescue me? Or should I say, us?" A smile tugged at the corners of her mouth. "Anyway, I was preparing to leave work. I had a few errands to run, one being a trip to the post office. I'd received a notice the day before telling me there was a package waiting for me.

When Deon arrived, however, I completely forgot. You can imagine why."

Cassie loved the way Ava's eyes danced as she told the story. "Yes, I'm sure a stranger, a man, coming to visit you at work was a bit surprising."

"To say the least. And then, all that he shared with me ... I completely forgot about the post office until the next week. Everything happened so fast, you see. Even now, I can hardly believe all that took place in so little time." Ava closed her eyes.

What was she recalling? "If this is difficult—"

"No, no. It's not. Not at all, in fact. It's good to visit our stones of remembrance, reflect upon the goodness, the faithfulness of God." She sighed. "Now then, where was I?"

"You forgot about the post office."

"Yes. Deon showed up at the library with a bouquet of daffodils. Looked like he'd seen a ghost, that's what I recall." Ava giggled. "Imagine, coming to meet a girl you'd never met, only having read her words in her journal." She patted the book at the foot of her bed. "This and the Bible, his only guides. And Jonah."

"Jonah." Cassie spoke his name in a long exhale.

"When Deon left Eden that Friday to return to his home in Ohio, we'd already made a promise to one another, as ludicrous as that may seem compared to today's standards. Or,perhaps I should say, the lack thereof." Ava wrinkled her nose. "Couples these days. Moving in and out of relationships like the changing of socks." She shook her head.

"Sad but true." How many times had she and Grant considered, even threatened, separation? Marriage was difficult. The fact that Ava and Gideon didn't know each other well yet were able to stay true to their commitment, and for almost fifty years, struck Cassie as—

Simply God.

"After my momma and daddy learned the story, about the journal and the Bible by the bed and, of course, Jonah's part in all of it, I think it solidified their love for him right from the start. Momma even told me after he left, having only met him, 'Gideon, he's like Joseph who took Mary to be his wife when she, too, was facing an unplanned pregnancy.' Like you said, he was my hero."

"And mine." Cassie patted Ava's hand. "And in some manner of speaking, you were his."

"Yes, dear. At least, that's what Deon said. 'We saved each other, raised each other up from the pit of despair.'" Ava's eyes pooled with tears, though none fell, merely gathered on the edges of green.

Like dew on grass.

It was Cassie's turn to reach for a tissue. "Here. You may need this."

"Thank you, dear." Ava ran her fingers along the buttons of her dress. "As you know, we returned to Myrtle Beach, together this time. Deon had just gotten home, having left Eden, but he flew to Greensboro again the very next day. Saturday, June twenty-eighth. He was heartbroken over the news of Jonah's passing and wanted to offer his support to the Forney family, say goodbye to his friend. We met at the airport and drove to Myrtle Beach, arriving Saturday evening. I'll never forget ..." A beat of silence. "I'll never forget how returning to Sand Dollar Bay felt. Not what I expected. Instead, it was redemptive. Covered in grace. Washed over with mercy, like waves of the crashing tide. That's the only way I can explain it. None of the pain or fear I thought I'd have."

The ticking of the clock on the bedside table was the only sound for a moment. Cassie counted each one, reaching ten before—

"Deon and I walked down the beach barefoot, the sand cool on our feet. The sun was setting, like a finger-painting before our eyes. Finally, we stopped at a weather-beaten pier." Ava's face was quizzical, as if recalling a piece of the story long forgotten. "I'm remembering now. I ... I glanced down, and there, right before my eyes, half buried in the sand, was a sand dollar. Almost too much to believe, given—"

"The legend of the sand dollar?" Cassie's excitement spilled out. She'd only recently read the story to her children, part of their Advent devotion. But this was a snippet of Gideon and Ava's story she'd never heard.

"That, but also being back, staying at the hotel bearing that name. It was almost too much to conceive." Ava's gaze met Cassie's. "The sand dollar, it's long gone now, fragile as they are. It was a beautiful night, though windy, cooler than was typical for late June. Maybe it was the excitement, but I was chilled. Either way, I'd worn my plaid jacket."

Ava reached across Cassie and picked up the framed photo on the bedside table. "Here. A sweet couple passing by took this photo of us."

Cassie took the frame. The black-and-white photograph depicted a happy, though much younger, couple. Ava's head was thrown back in laughter, while Gideon's gaze was fixed on her. She wore a plaid jacket, the ocean spread out behind her.

"You were with me—with us—then, Cassandra. The morning prior, I was supposed to— was scheduled to—"

"Yes. But love stepped in and—"

"Lifted me." Her tears finally spilled over, though Ava smiled through them. "Lifted us."

Cassie took her hand, felt her rhythmic pulse, a sign of life still beating in her veins—Ava's story not yet finished.

The older woman began humming a tune, which Cassie sang, and then, a duet—

Love lifted me! Love lifted me!
When nothing else could help, Love lifted me.

Love lifted me! Love lifted me!
When nothing else could help,
Love ... lifted ... me.

The harmony was imperfect, like their lives, but still beautiful. Their eyes met.

"And what about your dreams? Did God fulfill the desires of your heart, even though ..." Cassie's voice broke.

Ava took her birth daughter's face in her hands. "Yes. Despite it all, even with all the pain, with some remaining scars reminding me, he did, more than I could have ever imagined. Knowing you were safe, the gift of you making another family happy ... what more could a woman—a mother—want?" Ava brushed her hands over Cassie's cheek, then lowered them, placing one over her own heart, the other over Cassie's, where their left breasts had been. "And don't forget. Every scar holds a story, reminding us that even pain has a purpose, for those who love the Lord."

They were both crying. Cassie chuckled. "Imagine how my fiftieth birthday pictures are going to look. I'll have to remind Lannie not to post any on social media, at least not without showing—"

A knock interrupted her, then a muffled voice. "Momma?" It was Charlotte.

"Yes?" Cassie stood from the bed and walked to open the door. "Everything okay?"

"Chester made me spill my cocoa."

"Heavens. Let's go clean it up." She turned to Ava. "Will you excuse me a moment?"

"Of course, but please don't worry too much. Spray a little carpet cleaner. You'll find it behind the louvered pantry door, dear. Paper towel on the counter. I'll spruce up a bit, if you don't mind. We've a party to attend."

But as Cassie closed the door behind her, the lingering

question remained. How had the dress been returned? Was it what the post office had notified her about?

No matter what, Cassie still had questions needing answers, and with guests arriving soon, her time alone with Ava was running out.

CHAPTER 41

CASSIE—DECEMBER 2019

"WHAT A MESS." It was worse than Cassie had imagined, with dark puddles of cocoa still standing in several spots, melted whipped cream dotting Ava's coffee table. "All this, and from only one mug of hot chocolate?"

"Maybe two." Charlotte hung her head, trying to conceal a sheepish grin. "Mine and—"

"Mine." Chester slugged his twin in the arm.

"Heavens to Betsy. Charlotte Beatrix, you said Chester made you spill your cocoa. You didn't say anything about you spilling his." Cassie's sigh sounded like a deflated balloon. "Ben, will you please go and get carpet cleaner from Bibi's pantry? Should be easy to find. And then grab the paper towels off the kitchen counter too, please. Lannie, get a dishcloth from the sink. Can you wipe up the whipped cream there? There … and there too. Heavens, clean up any whipped cream you find." Turning to face her twins, she scowled. "You two, sit. Now."

Chester and Charlotte plopped on the couch. Sulking, they kept several inches between them as each mumbled under their breath that the mess was the other's fault.

"Quiet. Not another word." Cassie's attention turned from them to her Apple Watch. Less than thirty minutes remained. Soon the others would arrive.

"Momma, are you mad?" Millie Kate tugged at the corner of Cassie's cardigan.

"Frustrated. You go sit over on the rocker, please. Watch your tablet."

Moments later, with Ben and Lannie's help, the chaos was under control, with only a few remaining dark patches on the carpet, mostly from the spot-treatment.

Standing back, hands on her hips, Cassie nodded. "Okay. That's good for now. We can do another round of cleaner if necessary. At least the carpet's not white." Shaking her head, she then faced her couch-confined children. "Ches, Char, say you're sorry."

Slowly, seemingly pained, they turned to look at one another. Then, almost in unison, they apologized.

"You'll need to tell Bibi you're sorry too."

They nodded. "Yes, ma'am."

"And tell Ben and Lannie thank you. It should've been you two cleaning it up, but I was mad, and I was afraid you'd make it worse." She scowled once more at her twins. "Now, behave. I need to wrap up a few things with Bibi. May I do that without you burning the place down?"

Again, "Yes, ma'am."

Cassie knocked before opening the door, which was still ajar. "Hello."

"Come in, dear." Ava's voice floated from the little half-bath off the bedroom. A bit of light peeked through the partially closed door. "I'll be right there."

The clock on the sidetable told Cassie they only had twenty minutes more. Fiona would be arriving with her gang. Grant too.

While Ava finished up in the bathroom, Cassie walked to the other side of the room to look at the framed photographs sitting atop Ava's dresser. A black-and-white one depicted a baby in a christening gown. Another was a much younger Ava. In a white, two-piece bathing suit, she stood thigh-deep in water, waves crashing behind her. With eyes closed, arms outstretched, she wore an expression of wonder.

"That photo was taken some years after our wedding, on one of Gideon's trips to teach. Never got tired of accompanying him to Myrtle Beach."

"It's lovely. And this one?"

"John Paul, probably only a week or so before he passed. Such a precious little baby." Ava smiled. "And to think, he and Gideon can visit now. I sure hope Deon's not telling all my secrets." She giggled, her laughter so much like a little girl's.

The last photograph was of Gideon and Ava on their wedding day. Though six months pregnant at the time, Ava's figure surprisingly didn't give anything away.

"Do you see how Gideon's hand is resting on my tummy?"

Cassie nodded. She'd noticed, and the reason birthed a smile.

"Very few knew I was expecting. My parents, of course, and Deon's dad. A few others, I suppose. We'd talked about it, right before that picture was taken. Gideon had whispered in my ear, 'This one. He or she is with us.' Truly, Cassandra, he relished such pride—the good kind, that is—in knowing God used him to rescue me. To rescue you."

Tears welled again in Cassie's eyes, though no words came.

As if reading her mind, Ava continued. "Now, back to the dress." She motioned for Cassie to sit, though she remained standing. "See those few mismatched buttons?"

Cassie scanned the length of its bodice. She hadn't noticed

earlier, but now several down the line were different, though only slightly.

"When Deon and I returned from our whirlwind weekend to Myrtle Beach, once he'd left again for Ohio, I remembered the notice from the post office. That Monday, first thing, I went to get the package. It was my dress, along with a note and several other articles of my clothing, undergarments and such. Though the note stated that the dress had been cleaned, mended in a couple places, too—buttons replaced—it didn't say who'd taken the time to do it, nor who'd sent it back to me. There was simply no return address."

Cassie shook her head. "Amazing. You didn't even know who to thank."

"No. Though I suspected someone at Smith's Print Shop. When I didn't show up for my interview, they called the hotel to check on me. I was told they weren't given any information about what had happened but ... Anyway, it remains a mystery." Ava closed her eyes. "As I mentioned, Deon loved the dress. Maybe because he'd found one of its buttons on the beach, like a sign." She opened her eyes again and met Cassie's gaze. "Do you recall how he kept it in the ashtray of his Pontiac? When it fell out, I knew. I wasn't yet sure I wanted to know—to go forward with something so unplanned, so unexpected—but with the button ..." Ava shook her head.

Unplanned. Irony struck, though Cassie knew what Ava meant. The story, all the confirmations, the symbolism—they all pointed to a redemptive plan that had brought them to this day, to celebrate her fiftieth birthday.

Cassie's year of jubilee.

"Anyway, with my momma's help, we were able to let it out in several places. After all, it was a bit snug." Ava patted her abdomen. "Right here." She sat down beside Cassie. "And that button, the one he kept in his ashtray—" Ava sighed. "It's with him now. That and his wedding ring—both tucked in the pocket of the suit he wore when ..."

Cassie nodded. "I understand."

The ticking of the clock told her only minutes remained before they'd hear a knock on the door. "One last question."

"Of course."

Cassie reached over Ava to retrieve the Bible. Opening it near the front, she read once more. Under the "What the Bible Says About" portion, under the words *Christ—His Work* with Isaiah 53:5–6, were two telephone numbers written in pencil.

Cassie pointed. "Here. This is the number for the Myrtle Beach police department, but this one." She tapped the paper. "Why on earth would you have chosen to write phone numbers here, on this page, and also, why'd you write your own number at all? It's strange, given you knew your own home number by heart."

Ava shook her head. "No one, not even Gideon, ever asked me. And the only answer is, I simply don't know."

That was her answer? Its anticlimactic nature struck Cassie. Surely there was some deeper explanation, some other, more specific reason she'd have written those telephone numbers, especially her own, in the Bible.

"You mean to say, you have no idea?"

Ava shook her head. "I've never known, nor do I recall ever writing them. Not even certain it was me who did. I must have looked up the police department's number when I decided to file a report, but why it was—they were—written there, I don't recollect."

Cassie glanced again at that page in the Bible. It was, no doubt, a miracle of sorts. Had they not been there, Ava's number in particular, Gideon might never have known how to contact a girl named Ava.

Ava Jackson from Eden.

And if he hadn't contacted her, she might have followed

through with her plans, because it likely did seem to her the only way.

"It's amazing. Simply amazing." Cassie's gaze met Ava's. "And, here I am."

Ava reached to stroke her birth child's hair, hair like hers had been. Leaning over, she kissed Cassie's forehead. "It's because of love, dear—only and always love."

There was a knock, and children's voices wafted from the living room.

"I guess it's time." Cassie, the Bible on her lap, reached for the journal too, then walked around the bed to place the fabric book back inside the nightstand drawer. The Bible, however, she laid on top, beside Ava's clock.

Cassie followed her from the bedroom, then turned off the light before closing the door.

The remainder of the evening would be spent celebrating, filling suite A-11 with joyous laughter and Christmas carols to commemorate a life that almost wasn't, but God ...

A Love that never let go.

CHAPTER 42

CASSIE—SEPTEMBER 2020

GIDEON AND AVA'S MEMOIR, *More than Grains of Sand* by Cassandra Billings, was self-published the following autumn, as leaves were turning and beginning to fall. And Cassie followed through, having it printed at Smith's Print Shop in Myrtle Beach.

When Cassie and Grant had visited there four years earlier, for their belated silver anniversary, they'd stopped in and introduced themselves. A young woman named Emily greeted them.

Emily asked about Cassie's manuscript. When she gave her a synopsis, the girl's eyes welled, though Cassie wasn't sure of the reason.

When the books arrived, three cardboard boxes full, a handwritten note was on the top of one of the containers.

September 12, 2020
Dear Mrs. Billings,
I want you to know that it was my—our—pleasure to print your beautiful story. I've never forgotten what you said to me, four years ago now, when you and your husband visited our print shop.

When you told me about your book, gave me the summary, your story stirred something inside me. You see, I was pregnant, though very early in my pregnancy. I honestly didn't know what to do or who to talk to. I even considered having an abortion.

I'd prayed and asked God for a sign, begging him to please show me. And then ... you.

Little Alicen Mary started preschool a week ago. She has eyes like mine and a nose and mouth like her daddy, who's no longer in the picture. Still, she is. Allie's in the picture. And in part (I believe, a BIG part), we have you to thank.

So, thank you, Mrs. Billings. I pray your book touches many more lives, like mine. Oh, and don't forget our deal. (Wink! Wink!)

Your friend,
Emily Catterson

Their deal? Cassie had promised, should they choose to use Smith's, to send Emily an autographed copy, along with a dozen more, as long as she would pass them out to area crisis-pregnancy centers and leave a couple of copies in local OBGYN offices. Signing and sending off those books was the first thing Cassie did after opening the long-awaited boxes. Knowing how her book had touched a life—saved a life—made its fulfillment that much more special.

As a prologue, Cassie had chosen to open *More Than Grains of Sand* with a mystery narrator. Her idea derived from a favorite book, *The Book Thief*, in which Death is the storyteller. Only, for Gideon and Ava's, it was death's antithesis.

My existence is measured in time—those seconds, minutes, and hours which accumulate into days, months, years.

And my worth? It's often determined by accomplishments and failures. Wins. Losses. But who sets the standard, says this or that adds or detracts from my value?

And who's to say the person who reached a hundred, held down a successful job, earned a smart living but failed to love in earnest, is more accomplished than the one who, though only living half a dozen years, brought happiness and laughter to the world? Though she passed from this place having never earned a paycheck, doesn't the gift of her laughter amount to something, despite her brief stay where my duration in months and years is concerned?

I awaken, then give up all my rights from the beginning. Indeed, I'm at the mercy of the broken world, this often cruel place —with its joys and sorrows. Sometimes I linger. Other times, I'm cut short.

After all, isn't it a contradiction to say there's one who ultimately holds me, who determines my length, but then causes me to be wiped out of a thousand fleshly frames in one fell swoop—say, by a tragedy of faulty, perhaps even insidious, human hands?

There is one who has a perfect plan. Not a puppet master, he has allowed those originally created in his image, though now stained by selfishness, free rein to hold the reins. And thus, the length of my days is often determined elsewhere, by others. For now.

Honestly, I know there is one who weeps much more than he laughs, though one day, true Love will win, and I will kiss eternity. Until then, there will be many unfinished stories, despite the words —that dream of me which was best—filling volumes too numerous to count.

Does the Author place a bookmark where I ceased, all those other should-have-been words left unread? I wonder.

This is but one such story, and it, too, is contained in a book.

It grieved Cassie that those for whom she'd been commissioned to write would never read her words, but she trusted God's bigger plan. Their passing prior to their story's publication was, after all, no surprise to him.

Only weeks shy of her seventieth birthday, less than a week after hosting Cassie's birthday party, Ava passed away on Christmas Day. Seemed she couldn't bear to be separated from the love of her life.

When Cassie and Fiona mustered enough fortitude to go through Ava's things, they discovered a poem tucked in Ava and Gideon's Bible, something Cassie included in their memoir. Penned by Gideon less than a week after Jonah Forney's funeral on June 29, 1969, it depicted his own lifelong pursuit, influenced by a most humble, wise man, though their time together was brief.

The poem was folded, pressed between two pages, one with a date in the margin—June 30, 1969—and the words *O Lord, you know* written in black next to Isaiah 42:3, which was underlined in red. "A bruised reed shall he not break, and the smoking flax shall he not quench: he shall bring forth judgment unto truth."

The poem was a beautiful testimony honoring a life lived in service to Christ.

"On Wings of a Dove"
Gideon J. Stallings

A humble man of honor,
Jonah was his name;
He lived his life to please the Lord,
For God's glory and his fame.

Born into a cruel world
That did not treat him fair,
Jonah learned the hard way
Of Jesus's tender care.

Like a sheep which wandered far,
He knew the Shepherd's rod;
Knew a thing of rough roads too,
For on them he had trod.

By God's grace they brought him
Full-circle to the fold,
And though some things had shamed him,
His story should be told.

Holiness is not a thing
One's born in from the first;
Rather it's what Jonah strived to attain
With a hunger and a thirst ...

That brought him to his Savior's feet,
And there he bended low,
Poured out, like nard, his gratitude
On the one who loved him so.

For even though his sin was great
His love for God was greater;
Jonah knew that to offer grace
One must know his Maker.

Spending time with Jesus
Enabled him to love,
Then spread his wings and fly
With the wings of a gracious dove.

For that is what his name means—
"Dove"—God's symbol of his Spirit,
And Jonah only wanted to carry

His message to all who'd hear it.

He'd offer Jesus to anyone
With love and tender care
"It's not hard," he'd often say,
"Just takes pullin' up a chair."

I was one whose life was touched
By this gentle man of color;
Even tho' diff'rent in manner and speech
He called me his friend and his brother.

He was used by God to guide me
And lift me up out of despair;
Our friendship—tho' brief—was like a pearl,
So treasured and so rare.

"For such a time as this,"
That's what Jonah often said.
"It's right here in God's Good Book—
In the Bible by the bed."

And because he told me to take a look
I discovered on my own
His good and precious promises
Which are now forever sown ...

Into my very heart and soul,
Hidden there they are,
To be carried with me wherever I go,
Whether near or far.

Jonah's now with Jesus

In his eternal Home,
And tho' I'll often ask God why,
I know, "O LORD, you know."

God wanted his faithful servant Home.
Yes, O LORD, you know.

As Cassie read and reread the poem, she welled with pride for the man who'd rescued her, much like Jonah had, in some ways, rescued him.

Gideon. One who hadn't believed in himself, questioning how God could or would use him to make a difference.

Gideon. The one who had missed his mother, but because of what she'd taught him, knew where to turn in times of need.

Gideon. A man God wanted to use much more than merely in the designing and building of objects made of wood and steel. He had been called by God's design to build up others. Change others. Fight for others.

Rescue others.

As half sisters poured through the items in Ava's cedar chest, discovering hundreds of entries kept in journals spanning many years, Cassie couldn't help but think, despite her birth mother's love for words, it was Gideon who'd perhaps, somehow, instilled in her a passion for writing.

The part of her book she had completed last—the dedication—she pondered for some time. Finally, she knew. The page that would come at the very beginning of Gideon and Ava's love story summed it up. Though they'd never read her words, Cassie wrote:

To Jonah—Who knew the one who sees.
To Gideon—Who knew Abba, the one who adopts.
To Ava—Who knew the Good Shepherd, the one who
bends low.

To my Savior—
How precious to me are your thoughts, God!
How vast is the sum of them!
Were I to count them, they would outnumber the grains of sand—
When I awake, I am still with You.
(Psalm 139:17–18 NKJV)

O Love That Wilt Not Let Me Go!

Most of Gideon and Ava's things were divided among Fi's family. The rest were sold at auction. There wasn't much. After all, they'd lived simply.

Their prayer pot, always on a desk or table in their home on Glovenia and later in Ava's apartment was, according to Fi, one of the only coveted possessions. After all, it was special, having been given to Gideon and Ava as a wedding gift, sent with a handwritten note from Georgia:

Jonah would want you to have it. Even said as much. Possibly the last words he spoke, in fact. Told me before retiring that night, "G, I reckon this here prayer pot belongs with ol' Gideon, seeing God used Ava's plea—her prayer—to show him the way. Yes, indeed." I'm sure you can almost hear him. Am I right? Well, after his passing, I simply couldn't part with it, until now.

Through the years, like the Forneys, Gideon and Ava had encouraged family and friends to place prayer requests inside, over which they faithfully prayed, believing God would answer.

One day, several weeks into the new year, Cassie received a package and a letter.

January 24, 2021

Dear Sis,
I hope this finds you doing well. I just finished More Than Grains of Sand. Oh, Cassie, I can't tell you what this means—what Momma and Daddy's story means, especially now. Thank you. It's beautiful, and your voice comes through perfectly, which, I must say, is ironic. Poignant.

As a thank you, we would love for you to have their prayer pot. As you know, everyone here would fight over it. Hahaha! Besides, it belongs with you. You were here and were able to write their story because of prayers from long ago, prayers that changed the course of history—enabling his-story—God's perfect plan—to play out.

Again, thank you. Thank you. Thank you.

All my love,
Fi

Under several layers of newspaper, wrapped tightly in bubble wrap, was the cast-iron kettle—the one that had, over many years, held petitions and praises too numerous to count. Cassie lifted it out, then set it on their kitchen table. Standing back to admire it, she heard a whisper.

Send it to Beatrix.

And she knew. Though she might keep it for a couple of days, the kettle belonged with Jonah's youngest, the girl—now a woman, a teacher—whose name was also Charlotte's middle name.

After a week, Cassie once again wrapped the cast-iron pot, but not before placing a copy of Gideon's poem about the man he loved, whom Bea no doubt missed, inside.

Then, opening the front-facing drawer of her desk, the piece of furniture where she'd spent countless hours writing *More than Grains of Sand*, she fumbled around until she found it—a small, hideaway compartment in the far-left corner, near the back. She removed its lid and blindly searched its smooth interior until her fingers landed on one, then two objects. First, a small, white cockleshell. Next, something cool and round, like a pearl. Though Cassie hadn't understood their significance when she had received this present for her college graduation, they'd been with the weathered oak desk when it had arrived, a gift from her birth mother.

Pulling back, she closed the drawer with her left hand, then opened her right, palm up. The purple button, an extra from the manufacturer, that Ava had kept.

Just in case.

Cassie took a ziplock baggie from the kitchen pantry and dropped the button inside, then zipped it closed. This, too, she placed in the kettle. The seashell, however, she'd keep.

Seated again at her desk, she opened its drawer once more and slid out a single sheet of stationery. She knew. The button needed some explanation. And writing? That was something she could do.

The only other items of Ava's that Cassie had received, the only things she desired, were a hand-stitched tapestry with *Love Lifted Me* in faded red, green, and blue threads. And of course, Fiona had been kind enough, generous enough, to give her both Ava's journal and the Bible.

Like her birth mother and the man who'd rescued them, Cassie had kept these books, either inside the drawer or beside the clock on the nightstand.

Because she knew. Even after the lights were out, the door closed behind her, the Bible by the bed shined a light all its own—a lamp to her feet, a light to her path.

As long as Cassie kept it wound, the clock ticked, rhythmically counting seconds, minutes, hours that, added up, accumulated like sand in an hourglass the passing of days, months and years. The Bible, however, wasn't constrained to the dimension of time. Nor was it dependent upon any human involvement.

Faithfully, it whispers thoughts that are more than grains of sand on the seashore, comprising words that pierce any darkness, used to rescue. To save. And they were, are, and always will be, first and foremost, his.

It's because of love—only and always love.

ACKNOWLEDGMENTS

Birthing this book—which is, in part, my own story—has been "a long obedience in the same direction." (Thank you, Friedrich Nietzsche and Eugene Peterson, for these wise words.)

An idea that began in early 2007 from what I call a holy whisper, *Gideon's Book* was affirmed when a woman I didn't know —Jocelyn Gordon—handed me a Gideon pocket New Testament while I was visiting Eden, North Carolina, for a speaking engagement. This story finally began taking shape in 2018 when, with several thousand words on a page, I met with Redemption Press founder Athena Dean Holtz at Write to Publish 2019. I pitched the idea with a one-page and a smile, and she believed in its redemptive message. I signed a contract that same year.

This story wouldn't be if not for three selfless women—each with a unique history of choosing life through pain. *Gideon's Book* is a tapestry of Cindy's, Michelle's, and Jenna's testimonies. Their individual circumstances are colorful threads which, woven together, create beauty. Their masterpieces? Three precious born-in-our-hearts children. And each came to us because of the efforts and passion of Carri Uram, our "special link" adoption advocate.

Dorian, Jacob, and Allie, I've had the precious privilege of loving you because of these birth moms. Thank you for giving me the most beautiful name—Momma!

I am so grateful for the Redemption Press team—for their love, support, and prayers. Thank you, Athena Holtz, Carol Tetzlaff, Sara Cormany, Liz Tolsma, Christina Custodio, Teresa Crumpton,

Tracy Wren, Shelly Brown, Heather Rider, Lesley McDaniel, Joleen Graumann, Micah Juntunen, and Ray Dittmeier. Your passion for Christian publication helps writers' work shine, for God's glory and the good of readers.

Dori Harrell, Denise Loock, Cindy Sproles, Edwina Perkins, Lori Roeleveld, Lori Hatcher, and Lin Forney, as well as Linda Summerford and our Maggie Valley Word Weaver group and my Christian Writers Fellowship friends—you've helped with edits, offered suggestions, and given encouragement in this journey.

To my "*Gideon's Book* Prayer Team" as well as my "Sabbath Writer Sisters"—your prayers carried, encouraged, and pulled me across the finish line. I don't know if I'd have done it without you. Love you all!

Beth Brown, Dakota Meissner, and Carol Tetzlaff—thank you for using your talents to help create a cover that, in and of itself, tells a "symbolic" story. I am grateful.

Robin Matthews and Kristine Shallenberger—thank you for taking the time to help me better understand chemotherapy, radiation, and the use of the cold cap. Your expertise and personal experience made this story a better, more accurate one.

Thanks to Gideons International and Pastor Jimmy Haynes. Your passion to spread the gospel through Bible distribution has changed this world, and I can't wait to hear all the stories in heaven! (To learn more about the work of Gideons International, go to www.gideons.org.)

Author Vanessa Diffenbaugh—though we've never met, your words, including your flower glossary in *The Language of Flowers*, not only inspired me but moved me deeply.

Alice Hundley—thank you for helping me see Eden through your eyes. Listening to you share about growing up on Glovenia was like stepping back in time.

To my dear angel momma Lucy Adams—you instilled in me a love for writing through your love for Jesus and hymns. Your friendship means so much.

Stacey Thompson and family—you've taught me more about the gift of grief. Your lives are a testimony, proclaiming truth from Matthew 5:4—"Blessed are those who mourn, for they will be comforted."

Kay McKinney, no sorrow is wasted. Bless you for allowing me to weave part of your and Captain Leo T. Thomas's story into Gideon's. (I believe you and Ava would have been the best of friends!) Don't you think your sweet momma and daddy are smiling? Who knows? They just might find their way into a future *Bible by the Bed* novel. After all, I can't resist a good hardware store.

Precious Beth—your story of healing after abortion and miscarriage is a testimony of God's mercy and grace. I know three little ones are waiting to give you great big hugs in heaven.

Katie, Lisa, and Amy, your encouragement along the way has helped me believe that, with God's help, I could! Your friendship is a treasure.

To my parents, Joseph and Mary—thank you for always believing in me. I'm here because of you, and no words could ever adequately express the depth of my love. Your example of a godly marriage and commitment points our family and others to the One who created the union of husband and wife, calling it good.

And to my husband, Bill, my forever friend—walking with you through all of life's seasons has offered me the comfort and encouragement I've needed to be brave. Your support through the years, your faithfulness and love, know no bounds. Thank you, thank you, my Resolute Protector. I love you more!

Finally, Jesus—thank you for being my sweet Savior, for redeeming my life and giving me purpose. You've never wasted a suffering, and you've always brought beauty from my brokenness. Yours is my greatest story!

To learn more about Maureen and how to order books, scan the QR code or visit www.maureenmillerauthor.com

DISCUSSION QUESTIONS

1. What lie(s) does Cassie hear? Perhaps you or someone you know is adopted. What is a common insecurity with which many adopted children struggle? What Scriptures speak truth to these lies?
2. Who/what are the antagonists (enemies/villains) in *Gideon's Book*?
3. Read Psalm 139. What does this song of David confirm regarding the sanctity of human life? Why do these words matter when considering a woman's reproductive health?
4. Symbolism in story is a literary device that adds depth by comparing something concrete with something more abstract. What is your favorite symbolic element in Gideon's Book (i.e., the purple button, flowers, etc.)? Why did you like that particular symbolic element(s)?
5. How did Jonah encourage racial reconciliation? How might those lessons enable us to work toward the same in our lives and in our communities? With whom

might you consider "pulling up a chair"—creating an opportunity to speak truth in love?

6. Cassie and Grant are pro-life, and their worldview drives their passion to share with others from their personal/professional experience. How might one who shares their biblical worldview be the voice for the "voiceless," while maintaining a spirit of love in a world fueled with hate?
7. How does the Bible by the hotel bed serve to figuratively and literally guide Gideon Stallings? How does the Bible guide you?
8. Do a study of the character Gideon in Judges 6:11–8:35. What parallels do you discover between the biblical Gideon and Gideon Stallings?
9. Is there a character in *Gideon's Book* with whom you most identify? What about their story resonates with you?
10. What is meant by "every scar has a story?" Do you have a scar story? How might it point others to a redemptive, Romans 8:28 God?

FOR DEEPER STUDY

1. Names hold meaning. Do a name study of the characters in *Gideon's Book*. How do your findings make for a deeper, richer story? Did each character live up to his/her name? If so, how?
2. There is power in the lyrics of timeless hymns. Often these songs were written by people going through difficulties. Do a hymn study of those woven into this story. Is there one that specifically speaks to you?

3. Abortion wasn't legal in all fifty states in 1969, though it was (in cases of rape, for example) in North Carolina. With the Roe vs. Wade decision in 1973, things changed drastically. Study further to understand the slippery slope such decisions have created from then until now with regard to women's reproductive rights.

HELPFUL RESOURCES

If you find yourself in crisis and/or are facing an unplanned pregnancy, please don't journey alone. There are many who want to help you, many who've walked the path you're on. There are helpful resources at www.optionline.org (1-800-712-4357) and Prolife Across America—1-800-366-7773.

If you're a birth mom (or are considering placing your baby) and want loving support, check out www.bravelove.org.

If you've placed for adoption or had an abortion and desire loving, compassionate support, check out the following: www.pregnancyresourcecenter.org.

The National Adoption Hotline is 1-800-923-6602.

ORDER INFORMATION

To order individual copies go to
redemption-press.com/bookstore

For discounts on bulk orders
send an email to
bookorders@redemption-press.com.
subject: bulk orders

www.ingramcontent.com/pod-product-compliance
Lightning Source LLC
Chambersburg PA
CBHW030822160525
26644CB00004B/12

* 9 7 8 1 6 4 6 4 5 9 0 4 9 *